Coming to God

Coming to God

A Psychospiritual Approach

William F. Kraft

WIPF & STOCK · Eugene, Oregon

COMING TO GOD
A Psychospiritual Approach

Wipf & Stock
An Imprint of Wipf and Stock Publishers
199 W. 8th Ave., Suite 3
Eugene, OR 97401

www.wipfandstock.com

ISBN 13: 978-1-4982-0442-2

Manufactured in the U.S.A.

For Heather
Who Manifests
God

CONTENTS

PREFACE

MOST OF US EVENTUALLY wonder about our source, destiny, and reason for being. In our efforts to make more and ultimate sense of our lives, we religious, theists, atheists, agnostics, and nonreligious reflect on the relevance of God in living a healthy and happy life. A life without God is atypical.

If most people deem God or a similar reality significant, one might reason that psychologists would include God in their approaches toward health. Indeed, William James, who is arguably the father of American psychology, wrote more than a hundred years ago an enduring classic on the varieties of religious experiences. Since then, however, most psychologists have virtually avoided God and/or religious experiences as essential components of mental health.

In spite of some psychological studies on the relevance of spiritual experiences, academics and practitioners in the helping professions are still prone to ignore or devalue God. Even though most students and clients consider God to be important, academic and clinical mental health programs rarely include God as integral to their curriculums or treatment programs. God is usually off limits, given minor recognition, or forgotten.

Indeed, for various and debatable reasons, there has been little room for God in the house of psychology. Based on my research and practice, such professional sterility hinders rather than helps people to live good and healthy lives. My goal is to give God a principal place in the theoretical and therapeutic domains of psychology. To that end, I analyze what people call experiences of God, and explain their relevance to health.

Indeed, religious resources and conceptions of God are important to many people, and we respect them. However, my sources do not rely on religion or theology, divine revelation, sacred scripture, or magisterial teaching, for I am a psychologist and not a theologian. My approach is to integrate relevant data of psychology and spirituality primarily from phenomenological and existential perspectives.

Most people believe in or subscribe to God or a Higher Power (of their understanding). However, the majority more or less practice a spiritual life, but for various reasons, they take little time and energy to practice a formal religion. Indeed, some go to religious services when they celebrate a holy day or a wedding, or when they suffer from severe fear or stress. Their religion is not a consistent part of their lives, but seems to depend more on environmental circumstances.

Moreover, agnostics and atheists are increasing in number, and they seriously question or refute the relevance of God to health. They may see God as unnecessary, a benevolent illusion, or a malevolent ruse. We will listen and respond to all of these people.

I attend to the following and related questions. Should psychology include God experiences? What are healthy and unhealthy experiences of God? How would a personality theory account for them? In short, the book is about how and why we come or do not come to God, and what difference it makes to health.

We begin our journey with people who share their stories about seeking God. These God seekers give their thoughts and feelings about God and religion in their efforts to make sense of life. After this experiential introduction, we present how psychology can relate to religion and God. We then proceed to explore ways we can come to experience God, avoid, forget, dismiss, or displace God, and the consequences of such approaches. Finally, we describe healthy and holy persons.

I thank Bill, Doug, Fred, Heather Jack, Jim, Joan, and Marlene for their editorial feedback, and Pat for her secretarial support. I thank my family and friends as well as clients, students, and teachers who have challenged and helped me to be honest in my quest for God. I thank God.

GOD SEEKERS

THE FOLLOWING VIGNETTES BRIEFLY describe and discuss people's experiences of God and religion. Indeed, they help us to understand that there are many varieties of religious experience. Some of these people may initially sound negative or jaded, but actually, they give courageous words to many of our silent thoughts and feelings. Let us begin with Matthew, a senior citizen.

"Some people say that I ask too many questions and that my faith is weak. Others tolerate me, or change the subject. A few say that it is about time I think out of the box, and encourage me. So, what am I, an 82-year-old man, doing?

"Well, after a life-time of reflection on sacred scripture and religious books as well as church participation, I find myself questioning the relevance of religion, the competence of its leaders, and even the existence of God. Who is God, or is God a what? Does God really exist? Is there a life after death? Is this all there is? Has religion really helped me? Especially lately, I have pursued such issues relentlessly—and, they have pursued me.

"Look, it's not easy to question who and what you based your life on. The fact is that I am entering the homestretch of my life, or perhaps near its finish line. I could die tonight, or twenty years from now. Whenever death takes me, I want to be ready. Until then, I will confront death with life.

"It is not easy to question the validity of what you were taught by parents who loved you and by teachers who supposedly knew the truth.

In my circles, it was and is not popular to partake in religion while challenging its teachings. It was more common to follow obediently and silently, or to drop out. I wish I could do this because it seems simpler and easier. Perhaps unfortunately, I cannot stop my mind, nor keep my mouth shut. Neither am I going to drop out. I am going to hang in there with my questions.

"Is God an illusion to allay our anxiety about death, or a desperate theory to make sense of life? Is heaven a false promise for good behavior, or a way to make sense of senseless suffering? Is religion simply a means to maintain order, to foster solidarity, and to empower its leaders? Is faith an excuse to circumvent reason and a tranquilizer for our restless hearts? Is the whole thing a well-intentioned sham because it seems better than nothing?

"Look, it is a sociological fact that increasingly fewer people regularly attend religious services. Many are Christians, those who attend only on Christmas and Easter, and perhaps at weddings. Even then, it often seems more like a secular event than a sacred experience. Where is God?

"It seems to me that people are simply disenchanted or perhaps disillusioned with what religion and its leaders have to offer. Moreover, they see increasingly more people who have little or nothing to do with religion or even God, and they seem to do just as well as religious people.

"Think about it. If you take God stuff seriously, you will invest considerable time and energy in prayer, religious services, and living a life that is often contrary to conventional living. Conversely, if you avoid religion, you will save considerable time and energy. What difference does it really make if you follow the so-called ways of God, or not? Surely, a person can be good and spiritual without partaking in religion or even believing in a God.

"For myself, I wished I got more out of religion and its services. Church services give me some communal support and guidance, but they too often frustrate my mind, fail to comfort my heart, and seldom inspire me. Inane or terribly abstract homilies drive me nuts, or simply leave me empty or bored. Charismatic preachers are entertaining and emotional, but a secular motivational speaker could do much the same without mentioning a God.

"Nevertheless, when I join a motley group of people who gathers to thank and worship God, it is somehow consoling and inspiring. Something beyond my criticisms, questions, and restlessness is going on.

Could they and I all be wrong? Could we be following an illusion, or chasing something that does not exist? Perhaps we are, and perhaps not.

"Most likely, I will continue to pursue God because I feel and think that someone or something, more than I, is pursuing me. Maybe my atheist friends are right, that this is all there is. Nevertheless, the words of Augustine relentlessly move and resonate in me—my heart is restless until it rests in Thee. But who is this Thee, and how can I be more intimate with Thee?"

This spirited elder questions and challenges his religion, its leaders, and God. Contrary to common assumptions, his age does not guarantee religious certainty and contentment. Indeed, like many in his or other age cohorts, he is uncertain and restless. Perhaps this courageous and wise man echoes the heartfelt murmurings that challenge our religion and wrestle with our God.

I, as a nonprofessional and as a psychologist, would encourage him to continue to engage God and confront his religion and its leaders. I would urge him to listen to his atheist, agnostic, and nonreligious theist friends as well as to his religious companions. I would support his probing mind and resonate with his restless heart. I would celebrate and suffer his search for ultimate meaning. We will show how Matthew's feisty mind can lead to a serene spirit, doubt to faith, absence to presence, lonely restlessness to resting in Love.

Listen to Shelly who is more than three decades younger than Matthew. "I guess I am sad and glad that our three children are out of the house and learning to live on their own. Although I miss them, I am happy to have more time for me. Moreover, my marriage is better than most, and Jeff and I have more opportunity to enjoy each other. In many respects, I have entered a new era of my life. So, why am I discontent?

"I know that with the grace of God, luck, or whatever, I could live forty or more years. Actually, I may not have yet reached the halfway point of my adult life. I also know that I could die today or within a year. Not to be morbid, but death questions my life. For instance, how and why should I live the remaining years of my life? Is this it, or is there life after death? If so, what is it? Is there really a God in this mix?

"I guess I believe there is a God, and that God gave us his only begotten Son, Jesus Christ. My religion, Roman Catholicism, its community and leaders, and the Bible guide me so I guess I know how and why to live. The Pope is supposedly infallible in certain matters of faith, and we believe that the church is one, catholic, holy, and apostolic, and therefore true and trustworthy. So why am I so restless?

"Questions, criticisms, struggles, and a general thirst for more have been around since my college days. However, now I am more seasoned and assertive as well as have more time to read and study. I can give more experience and thought to my questioning mind. The fact is that questions about religion and its God will not let me alone.

"I truly respect my priests; most of them are dedicated men who try to live good lives. However, they seldom really listen to and personally engage me. It is as if they, not we, are the source of truth. Too many look down on me, and do not work with me. Their homilies are similar—too much theoretical explanation that does little to help me live a better life.

"Rarely do they interact with you, or say that they don't know. God forbid that they learn from you. Sometimes they seem so distant or patronizing. When stymied, they always have the standbys—it's a mystery, have faith, check the catechism, pray . . . I wished that one would say: I wonder about that myself. What do you think? Tell me more.

"When I try to discuss God issues with my priests, they automatically quote the catechism or some theological theory. I can see them withdraw into their mental warehouses for answers. I realize that my thinking is a bit simplistic, but take me seriously. Instead of rushing to set me straight, humor me, and affirm the truth in my view.

"On another level, how can I respect and trust priests—the leaders of my religion? So many priests have permanently wounded so many minors as well as adults. In many respects, I am more distrustful of the bishops and cardinals who enabled the priestly perpetrators—and, they still do not get it. Moreover, their present draconian approach of zero tolerance seems to apply to everyone, except themselves, the church hierarchy.

"For me, it is difficult to respect and trust these men in personal matters, especially intimacy. They live so out of their minds, and are so out of touch with the real world. Their theology of the body is so much abstract gobbledygook. Do they really walk their talk? How can they teach and guide me about intimacy and sex when they seem so out of touch with these matters. To paraphrase Pope Francis, do these pastors smell like their sheep?

"Look, I am no flaming feminist, though I do respect them. Moreover, I am not a victim of sexual abuse; however, I do know victims of priest sexual abuse. When these suffering souls tell me that it is rare that a priest really understands and feels for them, I sadly have to agree. Well, I have ranted enough, but you wanted to know what I think.

"Nevertheless, in spite of and maybe because of my restlessness, I participate in Mass on Sundays and often during the week. Sacraments help me to seek and connect with God. Moreover, I try to pray throughout the day, do spiritual and reflective reading, am active in parish activities, and do volunteer work. I think my saving grace is that my heart desires and knows far more than my mind can grasp."

Clearly, Shelly is not a silly, arrogant fool, but quite serious and smart. Like Matthew, she is courageous to question and seek answers, for she loves her church, albeit with ambivalence. She has more trouble with religion and its leaders than with God. More importantly, Shelly worships her God, and she tries to walk her religious talk.

More than angry, Shelly is frustrated and insulted. Priests rebuff her lay theology instead of encouraging her efforts. She feels that they put her into ready-made theological boxes where she feels suffocated. Our response to Shelly will not be theological or catechetical, but rather psychological and spiritual. We will engage Shelly and others like her with respect and openness. We will see how her religious and spiritual discontent is significant to her health, for indeed, her heart desires and knows more than her mind.

Listen to Shelly's elderly Aunt Hilda. "I have always been fond of Shelly. I get a kick out of her feisty self. She was like that when she was a little girl. In college, she almost drove her parents nuts. Most importantly, Shelly is a fine woman, mother, and wife. She always has been fresh air to my soul.

"In religious matters, I can appreciate to some degree what Shelly is talking about. I have felt some of her concerns, but unlike her, I am not so involved with them. I put them aside, for I can't do anything about them anyhow. Furthermore, I don't question so much, especially the religious and theological. I give that task to the experts.

"I do admire her passion and doggedness. Although her criticisms of the priests and bishops are usually valid, she can miss seeing the whole picture. Although she admits that there are many decent priests, she can sure get in their faces, which to me is admirable and irritating. Why does she question so much? Sometimes I wish she would shut up and just leave matters be. What is wrong with keeping things simple, to go along to get along. Still, I love her to death.

"What about me? I shy away from stirring the religious stew. I accept what religion gives to me, and make the best of it. Sure, I have some questions and frustrations, but I put them aside. I don't get very far when I think too much. I simply go to church, and give and get what I can. I try not to get in the way of God.

"I try to be still and be open to what may happen in the liturgy. Usually, I feel better when I leave. I don't think that it's a mortal sin to miss Sunday Mass, but I do think that I miss something. Thus, I rarely miss Mass, and I often go during the week. Somehow, I am a better person for that.

"I can tell you something of what the catechism and priests say about the sacraments, but really their explanations do not make much of a difference. On Sunday, I probably couldn't tell you much of what the priest said in his homily. Maybe it's my fault. Nevertheless, I hasten to add, my experience in church does make a difference, one that is difficult to explain. I know that church services give me what nothing else gives.

"I guess the bottom line for me is that despite the limits, scandals, and irritations of my church, I get a sense of God, see some light, and have some consolation. Religion and its people help me to have hope and security. I know God loves and waits for me. That God moves me to worship.

"Without God, my life would be very different. To jump on Shelly's bandwagon, my life would simply be a product of evolution that appears via chance, survives through being fit, and eventually dies to annihilation. My life would have no more meaning than what I can observe on earth. I do not believe that this is all there is. I just feel deep within myself that I came from a God of love, and I will return to that God united with my loved ones. I hope I am right."

Shelly's aunt takes a simpler and quieter stand toward her religion and its services. She can accept, avoid, perhaps deny, and detach from the inconsistencies and contradictions of her church, so that they do not bother her much. She participates in religious services because they help her make more sense of life and to live a better life. She is wise not to let theology and religion impede her spiritual experiences of God.

Hilda's religion is less heady and contentious that her niece's is, but at least just as important. Hilda lives her lay theology, and her God is essential and perhaps paramount in her life. One could argue that her view of and relationship with life and God are subtly profound. Her God and religious practices do not harm her health, but rather help her to be stable, secure, and serene—healthy.

"Hi, my name is Chick, and I am an alcoholic. I have come to admit that I am powerless over alcohol and that my life became much less manageable than I thought. I also know that only a Power higher than I can restore me to sanity. I have surrendered my life and will to this greater reality that I call God. Without God and the AA fellowship, I would be a physical and psychological mess, dead, or in jail. Thank God that I found a better way of living.

"For most of my life I was an active church member. I served on many committees, was a member of a Bible study group, and did charitable work. In short, I was a religious man, and I was an alcoholic. Looking back, I did the right thing more out of compliance than conviction. Currently, I do not partake of formal religion, for it does not help me very much. Maybe someday I will return, for now the God of religion does not touch me. As they say, religion talks the walk, and spirituality walks the talk.

"I wish my church was more like A.A. Unlike my church, the fellowship is welcoming. I feel accepted and at home. The members do not judge or set me straight, and they really understand my sharing as well as share their experience, strength, and hope. To be sure, the anonymous people of A.A. meet issues head on with open hearts—and, they hold themselves and me accountable.

"A.A., not my religion, has saved me from desolation. In A.A., I have found a God who comforts and consoles me as well as directs and guides me. I thought I would never say that I really live a God-centered life. Ten years ago, I would have said that that is sentimental mush, or hokey at best. Now I can say that I am grateful that I have found God. I know no matter what, I am never alone.

"I cannot tell you what happened to me to turn my life around. I do know that without my Higher Power or God, I would not have recovered and continue to stay sober. I cannot know who or what this God of my understanding is; in fact, I avoid religious intellectualizations. I try to stay out of my mind, and listen to and reside in my heart. I know that alone or relying simply on my inflated ego, I would not be sober. With God and my fellowship, I continue to grow in sobriety.

"I find it interesting that A.A. started with the Oxford Group that strived to rekindle the basics of Christianity, and to make Christianity more significant and practical in one's life. Although A.A. became a fellowship of its own, its 12 steps largely come from the religious, Oxford fellowship. Nevertheless, A.A. does not officially subscribe to any one religion or conception of God. It does propose that you must surrender to a Higher Power in order to get sober. Most people conceive this Higher Power as God.

"Surely, my past religion has influenced my concept of God, but I try to avoid religion and its God. Nevertheless, I have come to believe and trust a God of my understanding, which is not quite the same as the God of my religion. In fact, I try not to think very much, for thinking seems to get in the way of my God. Whatever or whoever this God is, I know that I am better off with this God. I do not have to explain it; I have to live it."

Like, Hilda, this recovering alcoholic lives a God-centered life. He would probably say that God and the A.A. fellowship saved his life. Like many A.A. members, he avoids intellectualizations and religious concepts about God, for he found them more harmful than helpful.

Chick indicates that too much thinking and religion can impede our experience of God. Indeed, you can be a doctor of theology so that you know all the concepts and proofs of God, but have little experience of God. You can know the what, but fail to experience who God is. In one sense, religion and theology are matters of the mind, and spirituality is a matter of the heart. From a distance, Hilda and Chick are quite different, but they are similar in their relationship to God and life.

We will see how religion and conceptions of God can help or hinder our spiritual life and relationship with God. Instead of harming our health, our mind and its religion can protect and nourish our health.

Chick knows from experience that there is a reality more powerful than he is, and when he surrenders to this Higher Power, which he calls God, he functions better for others and himself. With God and his fellowship, he is healthier. Although Hilda is not a recovering alcoholic, she too finds that with God and her fellowship/family, her life and health are better. Empirical research shows that religious and God-centered living can help people live healthier, happier, and longer lives.

Some health professionals would disagree with this A.A. approach, contending that 12-step fosters dependency rather than ego empowerment. A counter argument is that accepting your powerlessness (having less power than you think) and surrendering to a Higher Power actually empowers you. Such empowerment enables you to cope better and to be healthier.

Listen to Helen, who, like Hilda, is also similar to and quite different from Chick, the recovering alcoholic. "I have not given too much thought to religion or God. Sure, some people and pastors have irritated me a bit, but overall, I trust that they are good people. I don't give much attention to the negative, for it doesn't get me anywhere. I'll leave that up to the pastors who know better than I. Besides, that's what they are educated and paid for. I guess this sounds pretty simple or stupid. Maybe it is, but it works for me.

"I go to Sunday services, and during the week I am involved in other church activities. I say my prayers, follow the services, try to sing the hymns, and put money in the basket. Furthermore, I help to clean and decorate the church, volunteer with fundraisers, and am active in several church organizations. I guess one could say that I am a church lady.

"I wanted to be married, but never met the right man. It may sound corny, but maybe the church was or is my spouse. I know that with my church and God, I feel less lonely, and stronger and more complete. With God and church, life does seems to make more sense.

"I go to church early so I get my seat, and I can see some of my friends. I feel that this is where I belong. However, I must admit that far fewer people go to church than when I was young. This worries me. Still, church differs from a supermarket or even our card club. Something different happens. It is more than a social event.

"I try to listen to the word of God. I am fortunate in that most of our pastors have done a good job at making the word of God touch me. They have helped me. Somehow, something, or someone touches me, and it makes a difference in my life. When I miss services, I feel I have lost something. I feel less than when I do go.

"As I listen to myself, I guess I am a simple and lonely soul. I can only say that praying to God and worshipping Him helps me to live a better life. Religion helps me to believe that there is a life after death, and that my life will not end when I die. When I pray to God, I feel that I am not alone. I feel comforted and consoled. I feel that someone is watching over me, and that my life has made a difference. When I die, I feel I will have done the right thing."

Unlike Chick, and like Hilda, Helen subscribes to a religion and its services. Like them, she does not theologize or think much about religion or God. She has a simple faith, one pure of mental machinations. Helen knows that when she worships God, her life makes more sense, and she functions better. That is good enough for her. Again, with God she is probably healthier than without God.

We will see that Helen is not so simple and certainly not stupid. Indeed, intellectuals could rip her religious beliefs and practices to shreds. They could say that her religion is on the level of a child, that her God is simplistic or an illusion, and that group therapy would give her the benefits of her religion. They might say that she uses her church activities to fill her lonely heart, that her religion is psychic opium to lessen her anxiety and loneliness.

However, we will see how Helen may "know" more than the smart people who criticize, tolerate, or pity her. Perhaps, Helen is a happier and better person than they are. Perhaps her God and religion have something to do with it. Perhaps she does not live an illusion or imbibe in Marx's opium, but rather her religion and God help her to manage realistically and to live serenely. Perhaps being single is not so bad and sad, or inferior to being married. Listen to Professor Jim's view toward his Aunt Helen.

"Look, I neither tolerate nor pity my aunt. If her religion and its God float her boat, I give her kudos. Clearly, it keeps her in order and on a good path, lessens her anxiety about death, and helps her to socialize. Her religion promises her an eternal reward for living a good life, and I hope she gets it. In short, it gives purpose to her life, which probably has had suffering; it helps her to make sense of this mess called life.

"Aunt Helen does not irritate me; in fact, I admire her simple faith and life. I wish I had her contentment. However, religion and its leaders do irritate me. They take this poor woman's money to subsidize their sham. They exploit her time and energy to work for them. They patronize her, talk over her, and fail to honor her. They offer her their magic elixir that ameliorates her anxiety, clouds her reason, and keeps her in a position of servitude. I have compassion for my mother's sister.

"Is Aunt Helen's God an illusion—a constructed hoax to control her and her friends? Is religion a tranquilizer to calm the masses? Is religion simply a way to keep order and prevent chaos? Is religion a way to give a few the power to control many? Do the purveyors of God really live good lives? Is religion, like science, simply a theory to make sense of life, or to lessen the sting of absurdity? Is religion and God the best mass appeal that we have to offer?

"I am happy for Aunt Helen, but I cannot follow her way. The mirror of reason reflects the glaring limits and defects of religion. The hard and soft sciences can give me just as much security and guidance as religion.

Moreover, I think science has less of a hidden agenda as religion; in other words, it is purer and more reliable. Science has less smoke and mirrors, is more likely to field questions and admit its limits, and is overall more open and honest.

"Thus, I trust science and its advocates more than religion and its purveyors. To me, God is an unnecessary concept, a hypothesis that has little data to support it. God is an illusion that helps one to make sense of and cope with life, especially its suffering and unfairness. Clearly, as people become more enlightened through education, they give up on or seriously doubt the validity of religion and its God. They come to see that they can be as good and live as well as their religious brothers and sisters.

"Life without God can make sense. There does not have to be a creator or a savior; life can just be what it is. When we die, we turn into energy. In this sense, we live forever. Good is better than evil, crime, or pathology because it works better. When you are good, healthy, and keep the law, you cope well, are better with intimacy, and overall the world is a better place. You can do this and more without a religion and God.

"Nevertheless, I respect and love my religious brothers and sisters. I accept and admire the twelve steppers who surrender to a God of their understanding. I marvel at the men and women who commit to a true religious life. Buddhist and Trappist monks fascinate me. We need more Aunt Helens in the world. In spite of this, I see no good reason for a God and its religions."

Jim is a good man. We can learn from him, especially his criticisms of religion and its conceptions of God. We will show how that he and others like him speak much truth of which we can benefit. We will show how religion can impede and violate mental health as well as how it can foster it. We will show how atheism and agnosticism can help us live a God-centered and healthy life.

We will show how religion is deceptively easy to dismantle and how valuable such deconstruction can be. We will also show how Jim errs not so much in what he says but in what he does not say. We will see that when we reduce life to physical and functional (ego) dynamics, we construe life and health differently than when we also include spiritual and God dynamics.

Jim may have experienced or observed some people, like the following man, who is more a victim of unhealthy religion. Listen to Damon who suffers severely from scrupulosity. "Will I ever find peace? I go round and round, seeking the right answers, trying to tie the loose ends, and eventually end up in the same place—in knots and at odds with myself. I try so hard to be good, yet I feel so bad. I try to do God's will, but I feel I am always transgressing it. Sometimes, I feel I am going to go crazy.

"Let me give you an example. Recently I was watching a movie that showed a couple passionately kissing. I can often get through it without much difficulty, or I walk away. This time my imagination went wild. Before I realized, I found myself taking the place of the man, undressing the woman, and getting aroused. Oh my God, here I go again.

"My mind shackles me with moral doubts. I should not be thinking this way. Did I touch myself impurely? Did I plan to do this? Did I put myself in a near occasion of sin? Did I commit a mortal sin? How can I be sure? To play safe, I better get to confession, make a firm purpose of amendment, and do penance. But I went to confession last week, and here I am again. Am I mocking God? Was my last confession valid?

"Almost all the priests are kind and compassionate. Sometimes, I get one who seems irritated with me, and I think a priest once told me that I should avoid such movies, for I am putting myself in an occasion of sin. At least, I think that is what he said. I felt myself getting angry with him, but I kept quiet and did my penance. Then I questioned if I sinned by getting angry with the priest. Was this a sacrilege? I go to confession to get some relief.

"Sometimes I have a couple of days when I am free of almost all doubt. What a good feeling that is. Finally, I feel peaceful and free. Indeed, it does not last long. I can sense the demons of doubt lurking in the shadows. Sooner than later, I will find something to obsess about. I can understand why some people call my condition the doubting disease.

"It really gets bad when I cannot get to confession, or when I question if I told all my sins. I question if I got the priests to understand the gravity of my sins, especially when he seems to take them lightly. Then I feel guilty for doubting the priest. On the positive side, scrupulous anonymous helps me to cope, have hope, and not go crazy. It helps me to avoid drowning in my vortex of scruples.

"Often I feel compelled to do my own penance, and of course: perfectly. For example, if I say a rosary, it must exclude all impure thoughts. If a sexy woman crosses my mind, I must start over again. Sometimes it takes me hours to do it right.

"After confession, I can feel clean, like I have taken a spiritual shower. But, I know that it will last only for a short time. I pray and pray to ask God to give me a clear conscience. I pray that I will not go to hell, and somehow go to heaven. It seems the more I try, the worse it gets. Will I ever be free from these nagging doubts? I know I am scrupulous. I know I see sin where there is no sin. That is what the experts tell me. How can they be sure? Maybe they are wrong."

Damon suffers from an obsessive-compulsive disorder in the moral realm. He is scrupulous—a condition that not only wastes enormous time and energy, but also impedes healthy religious growth. Damon's God is judgmental and vindictive, not an accepting and loving God. In his case, his concepts of religion and God harm his health.

Indeed, religion can be a means to control people, to program them to do ethically horrific acts. Presently and in the past, we have seen how people can torture and kill in the name of God. Religious leaders war against each other as well as exploit their followers for their own selfish gains. Clearly, religion can hinder and violate mental health, particularly when it is restrictive, authoritarian, and malevolent.

Moreover, most people have some religious grips. Some hold grudges because their pastor failed to attend to their dying mother. Some are angry at their religious education, blaming their religion and its leaders for making them guilty, repressed, and generally messed up. Others leave their religion because of financial expenses, too much work, poor homilies, a bleak future, lame ministry, incompetent communication and leadership, lack of enthusiasm, elderly majority, liberalism, conservatism, authoritarianism, clericalism, double standards for clergy and laity, clergy perverts, etc., etc.

Nevertheless, research offers considerable evidence that religion highly correlates with mental health when religion is positive and benevolent as well as offering communal support and healthy direction. However, when religion is negative, judgmental, and manipulative as well as suppressive and isolative, it fosters unhealthiness. In short, religion can liberate and engender health, or it can impede health and cause unhealthiness.

Rachelle for a long time thought little of religion and felt she had no need for a God. Unlike Damon, she dropped out of religion, but took a circuitous journey to a very different religion. "Hello. My name is Rachelle, and I am a religious sister. How and why I got to where I am is much too long of a story to tell. Suffice it to say, it was not an easy journey, but it was worthwhile and perhaps necessary. Let me give you a few of the highlights.

"I graduated college as a confirmed agnostic and budding atheist. I quickly rose to a high position in my profession, and I lived a free and fun life. In my early thirties, I got married, had two kids, and ten years later got divorced. My divorce was very contentious, and I vowed never to marry again. Once was one too many.

"However, my pledge to be single included many sexual relationships. Some were somewhat meaningful, and most of them were recreational with no strings attached. They served to take the edge off, but admittedly, the hole in my soul remained empty. When the children left the house, I found myself as a middle aged, lonely women with little meaning and direction in life. Although I had plenty of money and possessions, I was poor in spirit. I neared the precipice of suicide.

"I sent my children to private schools because they were better academically, and I wanted them to be exposed to solid character formation. Although I attended church with my kids, I never got into religion. Religion and its ministers never helped me; moreover, too many parts of my life went contrary to their values. That changed when a friend cajoled me into going on a weekend retreat at a Trappist monastery.

"Initially, I really felt out of place. Keep in mind: I am not a Catholic. The place was spooky, and the monks initially seemed to be out of touch with the real world. Yet, I had to admit that there was something strangely attractive. Their pious prayer at ungodly times as well as their beautiful and haunting chant lured me to an unsettling yet comforting place. Who would believe that I found these odd men enchanting? With a veiled smirk, I reminded myself that Carl Orff used the Latin and German poetry of thirteenth-century Benedictine monks for his sensuous and sacred choral symphony, Carmina Burana. Perhaps these humble monks had more to offer than my eyes could see.

"Well, I requested to meet personally with a monk who for whatever reason had a special attraction for me. That interview turned out to be what the Greeks called *Kairos*—a sacred time that made a significant and lasting difference in my life. I never met a person who was so purely present to me; he did not have any hidden agenda. To my surprise, he agreed with most of my criticisms of religion, but he gently and respectfully challenged me for what I did not say. In short, he broadened and deepened my vision.

"He did not preach or patronize me. He honored my questions, and encouraged me to question more. He not only engaged my mind, but also touched my heart. I found myself sharing my story, and he really understood. He even shared some of his life, stating that he was a very successful stockbroker who made millions. This may sound hokey, but he said that since living a vowed life, including poverty, he is richer than ever. I believed him.

"After the retreat, I wanted to find the treasure that this man had found. Clearly, the things that I tried did not work. They left me empty, not fulfilled. Incredibly, I found myself looking into the religious life. I wondered if I were going mad. Indeed, some of my friends thought I was a bit off my rocker. Maybe I was losing my mind, but something or someone was enticing me in a way I never experienced.

"In service of my heady self, I did considerable research on the religious life, and I lived for several months in three religious communities. Being my pragmatic self, I said what the hell; I'll give one a shot. After all, nothing else worked. Here I am, ten years later—a Catholic nun who has taken permanent vows.

"I have learned to accept the limits of religion, and to use what helps me. Its liturgies, scripture, spiritual literature, communal and private prayer have helped me become a better person who centers her life on God. I never thought I would say that I believe in and am closer to God, others, and myself. Although I doubt if I am as serene and settled as that wonderful Trappist monk, I am infinitely better than ever.

"My children and four grandchildren visit me, and I visit them. They have learned to accept and even appreciate their weird mother and grandmother. I do wish that I could enjoy more time with them, but every life has its limits. Their Dad, my ex, has finally grown up, and has become a good father and grandfather. Moreover, his wife is a good woman who treats my kids and grandchildren well. Actually, we have become friends.

"Perhaps with the exception of my children and grandchildren, I am more intimate with my community sisters, and actually with life. The business side of my head says that I am living in a fantasy world. I was a rich, independent, and sexually active woman, and now I am happier and healthier as a nun who lives the vows of poverty, obedience, and celibate chastity. Wow!"

Wow is right. Although Rachelle has a very different lifestyle than Chick, the recovering alcoholic, they are similar in that both of them radically changed their lives. While Chick minimizes religion, Rachelle nurtures the religious life. Both center their lives on a Higher Power, or God. Some would say that they had a conversion, or that they turned their lives around to a new way of living. It is not easy or common to make a significant and positive change in your life. Some do.

There are people who freely choose to give up the ordinary pursuit of pleasure and power, and center their lives on more extraordinary spiritual concerns. Rachelle dealt with her desire for God by leaving a highly successful life and entering a religious life that is relatively abnormal. She has discerned that the religious life is the best way to live the rest of her life. Indeed, it is a road seldom travelled.

These vignettes indicate that "God" seldom goes unattended. The overwhelming majority more or less grapple with the issue of God. Indeed, every person has his or her individual way. Some are very similar, while others are very different. Some are relatively clear, certain, and settled in contrast to others who are more clearly unclear, certainly uncertain, and settled in their unsettlement. Let us continue our journey.

2

BEING WHOLLY HUMAN

To reiterate, personality theories do not include the spiritual and God as essential components of health. As mentioned in the preface, William James wrote a classic book on religious experiences, but he did not propose an explicit theory of personality. Along with James, Carl Jung came closest to making spirituality and God integral to health. Although Alcoholics Anonymous excludes overt theories of health, it does follow a wholistic model that affirms the spiritual and God as paramount to recovery, or health.

Indeed, academics and clinicians educate future health providers to respect and process religion, prayer, 12-step programs, and other practices that include God or a similar reality, but only when the patient/client talks about them. Seldom or never do they encourage them. They are prone to see these God practices as adjuncts that may help or hinder but are not necessary to healthy functioning.

In short, the way we construe health highly influences how and why we live. My contention is that when we reduce health to physical (id, needs, feelings, neurology, biochemistry, temperament, evolution, pleasure, satisfaction, contentment, safety, security, etc.) and functional (ego, cognition, self-concept, coping, productivity, esteem, individuality, self-sufficiency, success, power, possessions, etc.) constructs and dynamics, we have a fragmented and incomplete view of health.

To be sure, the aforementioned prerational and rational perspectives are essential to mental health. However, when we exclude spirituality and God in our health models and practice, we treat others (and ourselves) as less than they are. When we include God and spiritual dynamics along with the physical and cognitive ones, we have a more realistic vision that helps us live better and healthier lives.

To that end, let us begin to explore spiritual and God dynamics—the ones that professionals tend to exclude, tolerate, minimize, or forget, and rarely include, foster, maximize, and remember.

Our Spirit

Our spiritual self, along with our physical and cognitive dimensions, is integral to our being human, and therefore, essential to health. Rather than being harmful, immature, unnecessary, or simply an adjunct, we will see how our spiritual dimension is our most practical and significant mode of behavior. What is this life of our Spirit?

One way to understand spirituality is as the art of maintaining and promoting good and transrational experiences. Let us reflect on what this definition means to living a good and healthy life.

First, spirituality is not primarily a science, but more so an art or a way of living, more experiential and formative than theoretical and informative. Spirituality pertains to practical and everyday living. Thus, one can have a doctoral degree in spirituality and not be very spiritual—and, a person who never graduated from elementary school can be a saint. Spirituality deals with walking (being and doing) rather than talking (thinking and theorizing).

We must consistently behave in ways that maintain and foster ongoing growth; otherwise, we begin to regress. This is true for any human endeavor. If we want to keep in good physical shape, we must regularly eat healthily and exercise. If we want to progress in our career, we must study and work. Good parenthood is not a haphazard event, but we must consistently think about and practice it.

Likewise, we must continually use our minds (ego) to structure our time and space (body) for spiritual growth. Unlike the constant reminders and reinforcements, via culture, mass media, and education, to get and stay in good physical condition (body) as well as to succeed functionally (ego), we get relatively little cultural help for but often impediments to spiritual growth. Thus, we must be vigilant in remembering to practice what we value most.

Along with our personal efforts to counteract this secular thrust, we have religions and their communal worship sites that remind us of God as well as offer ways to learn about and to practice the spiritual life. However, fewer people actively practice their religion, and religion has less of a voice in the public forum than it did in the past. Clearly, religions have much less influence in politics, media, education, and society in general.

As we have seen, many people feel that they can be spiritual without religion and its leaders. A caveat, however, is that when we separate from or avoid religion, we risk having little guidance, encouragement, and communal support and reinforcement to develop our spiritual life and therefore our health. The (ego) illusions of individualism can seduce us into thinking that we can be self-sufficient and have no need for spiritual support, information, and formation. Actually, research indicates that communal recognition of and dependence on a benevolent God or a Higher Power fosters our health.

We can also understand the spiritual as our most intimate, creative, and fulfilling self. It is similar to (but not the same as) Maslow's actualizing and peak experiencing self, or Jung's spiritual self. Consider, for example, a spiritual experience of a beautiful sunset. Our experience differs radically from our everyday and functional ones. We may have an uncanny feeling of being one with the sunset so that in our purest moments, we do little, if any, thinking. In fact, the more we think (ego), the more we distance ourselves from the experience.

Spiritual experiences preempt rational analysis in favor of intimacy and self-surrender. In our (aesthetic-spiritual) example of the sunset, we respond to the mystery of reality, and in awesome reverence, we experience a certain kinship with nature. We know intuitively that we are most uniquely ourselves in being one with reality, or that our singularity stands out in clear relief while being in communion.

Experiencing a paradoxical and mysterious encounter with the sunset, we may experience joy and dread, pride and humility, feeling freely dependent, and significantly insignificant. We may feel confident and strong, free and independent as well as small, weak, and dependent. We can experience ourselves as being one with the universe and simultaneously as a very limited part of an unlimited whole.

Imagine the physician who periodically would spend a couple of weeks giving (pro bono) medical help to third world people. Eventually, he became despondent and discouraged with the stark poverty and pau-city of things we take for granted. One night when he was sitting outside of his poor host's hut, his host said, Look! Look at what? the physician said. Look at the stars, at the universe, at the beauty that God has given us. Life is so good. We have so much to be grateful for.

This simple experience changed the physician's life. He no longer looked down, but he looked up. He no longer took things or life for granted. He no longer fixated on what is absent and negative, but what is present and positive. Like his very poor friend, he learned to celebrate the richness of life. His expanded vision and appreciation enabled him to cope more effectively and to be more at peace. The poor, uneducated man taught the rich, educated doctor how to be healthier.

From a rational perspective, life is a series of problems to cope with and to solve. From a spiritual perspective, life is more of a mystery to cel-ebrate and suffer. To solve problems is definitive; to experience mystery is inexhaustible. Indeed, the satisfaction of our prerational (body) and the success of our rational (ego) functions are essential to mental health, but they are temporary in contrast to the permanency of our spirit.

Transrational (spirit) functions and knowledge are inexhaustible and unending. Consequently, when we foster our spiritual life, our life is never boring or sterile, but it perpetually gets better. Instead of living a constricted life, we unendingly know, suffer, and celebrate life. Like the poor peasant, we can see and be grateful for the richness of life. Spiritu-ally, life is never boring; it is full of unending wonder and meaning.

Too often, however, we fail to see, appreciate, and act on reality's infinite field of possibilities. Look at and see, for example, a simple reality, like a tree. You can see a tree as beautiful, a certain species, a source of shade, a seasonal message, evoking happy and sad memories, a sign of strength, aging, and dignity, a spiritual symbol, an opportunity for play and rest, a reminder of loving experiences, ad infinitum. We can be open to meaning that gives us life.

However, with light comes darkness. When we are spiritually open, we are neither naive nor exclusive. Spirituality is both diverse and inclu-sive. We see not only the good and beautiful but also the bad and ugly—in self, in others, and in the world. We cannot have one without the other. The unending challenge of the spiritual life is to keep perspective and to invest our spiritual energy into healthy activities rather than unhealthy ones.

Facing darkness can be very daunting, so much so that we avoid exploring life's mystery. For instance, we may fail to grow spiritually because of our fear of or inability to see and deal with the dark side of life. Thus, it is unwise to force people to grow spiritually, for they may be unable to cope (ego) with the feelings (body) that spiritual awareness (spirit) evokes. A wiser way is to help with motives of appeal, not force.

Our call is to face and conquer the bad with the good, evil with love. Psychotherapy and religion should help us find the courage to name and claim, cope with, and learn from our faults. We can face and transform the power of our dark shadow self to help (and not hinder) us to become enlightened and compassionate persons. Clearly, this dovetails with and fosters health.

Keep in mind, possible vice often elicits and challenges the opposite virtue. For instance, impatience (or fear, dishonesty, selfishness) often challenges and strengthens patience (or courage, honesty, charity). In chapter 4, we will see how the apparent negativity of nothingness is part of and can lead to a positive and fuller presence in everything. If we stick to a rationalistic model of health, such a statement may not make much if any sense. Spiritually, however, it makes healthy and necessary sense.

When we say that our spiritual self is transrational and transcendent, we do not infer that we are irrational or anti-rational. Rather, we go beyond and incorporate prerationality (body) and rationality (ego). Our spirituality is immanent (interior), communal (interpersonal), and transcendent (more than us). Since the experience of transcendence is a key dynamic of spirituality and to personal health, let us reflect on it.

Transcendence

Some think that transcendence means that we go out of the real world, escape into fantasy, exercise magical thinking, or go beyond the limits of experience. To the contrary, transcendence means that our experience is true, realistic, and concrete. In fact, when we transcend, we experience the deeper and truer nature of reality that can be very helpful in functioning more effectively. Unfortunately, health providers seldom employ transcendence, falsely assuming that it is off limits or irrelevant to health.

From an academic perspective, we do not presuppose an outdated, dualistic metaphysics that posits unrealistic dichotomies, such as transcendent vs. immanent, spirit vs. body, human vs. divine, natural vs.

supernatural, up vs. down, presence vs. absence, light vs. dark, being vs. nothingness, man vs. woman, West vs. East, black vs. white, young vs. old, or we vs. them. We construe transcendence radically differently than such a common and dualistic model. We will see that when we transcend, rather than separating, we unify these realities.

Our meaning of transcendence originates from the Latin *trans* = across and *scandere* = to climb. In transcendence, we "climb or move across" from our ordinary (body and ego) experience to an extraordinary (spiritual) experience of reality. We go beyond (extra) our everyday (ordinary) perceptual range to discover that we are integral parts of a dynamic whole that is part of and greater than everyone and everything (extra ordinary). Let us pause and reflect on this seemingly ponderous statement.

In transcendence, we experience life's radical unity that sustains and integrates everything and everyone. This simply means that we experience life's interconnectedness. Metaphorically, we experience all human beings as being different sized, colored, and aged threads of the same tapestry. Strong and beautiful threads weave a strong and beautiful tapestry, and weak and ugly threads make for a weak and ugly tapestry. Likewise, good and healthy individuals create a good and healthy community, and bad and unhealthy individuals form a bad and unhealthy group.

Indeed, our human reality is a tapestry of the strong and weak, fortunate and unfortunate, good and bad, healthy and unhealthy, helpful and hurtful, kind and mean, compassionate and narcissistic, and so on. We are not separate from one another. Rather, we are a dynamic web of related similarities and differences as well as infinite possibilities. When we take and follow this perspective, we manage and live more effectively and humanely.

We experience all people as being our brothers and sisters. Clinically, this means that we interact and treat people differently than when we see them only from a rationalistic point of view, that is, as being separate individuals, as if I and you, we and they are separate from each other. Such individualism militates against health.

Spiritually, we know that we are not separate from one another but rather are essentially interrelated. Thus, we realize that whatever I, you, or we do affects one another. You and I keep in mind what is best for us, not just you or just me. We strive to do what is best for "us" so that both society and we benefit. Our ongoing and ultimate goal is unity and its peace.

Spiritually, we see and act differently (than when we deny or forget the spiritual). For example, when I see a derelict, a prostitute, a drunk, or a criminal, I do not see them only as problem individuals, but also as my brothers and sisters. I experience them as integral members of the same human community of which I am a member. Our spiritual vision moves us to help these marginal, sick, sinful, or criminal people. One might criticize this approach as naive, simplistic, idealistic, or stupid. To the contrary, it is realistic, complex, realistic, and smart. Moreover, such a spiritual approach fosters both individual and societal health.

In short, we experience the underlying unity of reality's different parts. This means that we appreciate how everything and everyone inter-connect, and we respond to the problems and limits of self and others in ways that differ from an individualistic (primarily ego) approach. Rather than being impractical, transcendence enables us to cope effectively, lessen stress, and bring new and richer meaning to everyday living.

We can see that the way we use transcendence is far from being dualistic, unknowable, individualistic, disembodied, or the opposite of an immanently knowable way. Our reality is beyond dualisms (ego). We are communal people (spirit)—and, this is our most immanent reality.

Another way of explaining our transcendent dimension is to say that there is a centrifugal force in our spiritual self that propels us to go beyond our needy (body) and individual (ego) self. Our spiritual self urges us to seek union with reality, people, self, and God so that we experience one another as a community, as living members of the same body. Spiritually, we desire to be one with one another, and, as we will see, one with our source and ultimate destiny—cocreating, uncreated, perpetual, and perfect Love, or the original and ultimate centrifugal force.

This spiritual desire to be one moves us to be respectful, reverent, and compassionate with others and ourselves. Looking beyond and through the physical and functional, we are inspired to respect or take a second or different look (from the Latin, re-spectare: to look again) at reality—a view that resonates with our spirit. With reverent awe, we appreciate the infinite worth of human beings. Once again, we see saints and sinners, the healthy and unhealthy, the lawful and criminals as threads of the same human tapestry. The spiritual beckons us to bow to the Reality where we are one.

Spirit-and-Ego

A basic premise is that our ego and its individuality are second in priority to the primacy of spirit and community. Contrary to popular and professional assumptions, we are not primarily individuals (ego), but rather interrelated members of a community (spirit). In contrast to most models in psychology that give primacy to ego/cognitive functions, our health model affirms the spiritual as paramount.

This means that who I am and what I do affect you. We are not separate from one another, but rather we matter to and affect one another. Simply stated, when I love you, I help you, and when I hate you, I harm you. Moreover, when I love or hate myself, I help or harm you as well as myself. To wit, since we are interrelated parts of the same community, what you and I are and do helps and/or harms us.

We will see that ego/individuality divorced from spirit/community can lead to narcissism, alienation, and even personal and social deterioration and destruction. Ego without spirit and spirit without ego always diminish one's life.

Our cognitive/ego attitudes are important, for they influence how we feel, choose, and act. For example, since we are interconnected, you can make me angry, but how angry I become and what I do with my anger highly depends on my individual values, attitudes, and coping skills. From this cognitive behavioral perspective, the beliefs, thinking, and other cognitive functions of my ego highly affect how I feel and behave. Still, my individuality (or "I") originates from and is contingent on community. From a developmental perspective, there is no ego and its functions without community.

A common problem is that this spiritual paradigm of community can be countercultural insofar as much of our (Euro American) mass media, education, politics, and social sciences overemphasize individuality. For example, in our Western world, we divinize "self"—self: satisfaction, gratification, actualization, sufficiency, efficacy, esteem, enhancement, achievement, autonomy, independence, fulfillment, etc. We often assume that independence, control, and freedom-from are primary and more important than interdependence, surrender, and freedom-for.

As its etymology indicates, individuality implies that we are separate and independent units. As individuals, we look out for number one (ego). Getting as much as we can, doing our own thing, success at any cost, entitlement, diversity, greed, envy, ad infinitum can be symptomatic of our conventional narcissism, or inflated ego. The bottom line is I, me, and mine, not we, us, and ours.

Yet, contemporary physics, chemistry, biology, and some social science support that everyone and everything are interrelated and influence one another, and that we are not primarily independent of one another. Thus, for example, social, political, economic, and environmental changes—micro, macro, local, national, universal—more or less make a difference in our lives.

Likewise, how we care for or abuse ourselves affects others. To do good for myself is good for you, and to violate myself violates you. Moreover, to be good with others is beneficial to me as well as to others. For example, when I isolate (via drugs, cybersex, etc.), I harm others and myself. When I do kind acts, I help both others and myself. In short, we are not isolated units, but rather integral members of the same body of humankind. Again, our emphasis is on "us," not on "me."

If we assume that we are primarily individuals or that life should be in service of me, then our responsibility is primarily to self, not to community. Our ethic is that we look out for self rather than both self and others. There are serious consequences to these different views of being human.

For example, in spite of having a contagious illness, I go to a party because I am more concerned about my own satisfaction than about making you and others ill. I may rationalize that you probably will not get sick, or I may simply state that this is your problem, not also mine. I care about me, not you. I fail to admit that how I am in the world, healthy or unhealthy, more or less impacts on you and others—on us.

In the psychological and social realms, I (ego) may strive to succeed at anyone's expense. I may be a self-centered workaholic who puts spouse and family second to my individual success. I may place my needs and goals before the needs and goals of community. I may assume that my body is exclusively mine, and consequently what I do with it is my business. I may state that what I perceive, feel, or think to be right is right.

Ironically, this kind of thinking is not contemporary, but at best, it assumes sixteenth-century Cartesian dualism. Current philosophy and science simply do not support these kinds of dichotomized attitudes and behaviors. The critical caveat is that such dualistic models engender unnecessary problems such as mind-body dualisms, overemphasis on individuality, and incomplete models of health.

When I make such false assumptions, I live as if I am an individual who is separate from and has little or no responsibility to fellow human beings. I may mistakenly assume that what I do in private will have no impact on you. I may unjustly use others to achieve my goals regardless of the cost to them. I act as if I am not radically interrelated, or I reject the fact that whatever I do more or less and eventually affects others.

In short, I care about me, not us. We can argue that many of our problems are due to fostering individuality at the expense of community welfare. When we make need (body) satisfaction and functional (ego) success paramount, our lives are truncated or less than whole and healthy. When we fail to integrate the spiritual in our lives, we harm our communal and individual health.

Such health professionals as William James, Carl Jung, Erik Erikson, Lawrence Kohlberg, Carol Gilligan, and James Fowler have challenged the primacy of individuality. James analyzes the importance of religious experiences, Jung includes spirituality and the archetype of God, Erikson writes about virtue, Fowler and the later Kohlberg speak of functions that go beyond the ego, and Gilligan emphasizes the interconnectedness of care. In brief, healthy, unhealthy, right, and wrong behaviors are not only functions of individual satisfaction and success (ego) but also of communal care and goodness (spirit).

Our intention is not to minimize the importance of individuality or ego psychologies, but only to affirm that they are secondary to community or spirituality. As we have indicated, our ego and its functions are very important, and we will see how they are essential to mental health. Nevertheless, when we think that cognition, independence, and self-efficacy are primary and sufficient, we delude ourselves. Such models of health are less than healthy.

To be sure, our actions should not be simply in service of others, nor should they be just in service of self. Both empathy and self-concern err in the extreme. The criterion for healthy decisions and behaviors should be what is best for us—for community. From this perspective, we reflect on and decide what the best (imperfect) course of behavior is. We think, choose, and act not just for me or just for you, but rather for both you and me, or for us.

Another primary tenet is that we are dynamic persons who are constantly striving to be our best selves, or to perfect community. Because we are spiritual and not simply functional people, we never arrive in that we are always realizing our ideals. We are always growing imperfectly in perfection; we never permanently reach a peak. These statements may sound like platitudes, but they too have clinical significance.

In a certain sense, physically (body) and psychosocially (ego) it is possible to arrive, peak, or get "it." We can satisfy hunger, get sufficient rest and shelter, stay in good shape, make so much money, acquire certain possessions, or achieve a particular status. We satisfy our needs, and we often achieve our goals.

Spiritually, however, we never definitively arrive. Being embodied spirits, we strive for the infinite in finite ways; we desire the unlimited in limited ways. We are restless and restive, always becoming more of who we are. Since our being is in a perpetual state of becoming, our nature always encourages us to become better. It is wise to accept and grow from our healthy dis-ease.

Nevertheless, we often mistakenly assume that there is a way of getting the spiritual "it." For instance, we think that certain (ego) skills or education, or power, money, or (body) pleasures will enable us to get it—happiness, serenity, freedom, honor, dignity, love. Our mistake is that "having" marks the measure of our worth, not "being" and "being with." We mistakenly assume that our pleasures, power, and possessions are adequate responses to our spiritual desires.

The truth is that spiritually we are perpetually arriving. We are never completely happy, healthy, holy, fulfilled, peaceful, free, but we are always growing in happiness, in healthiness, in holiness, in fulfillment, in peace, in freedom. This means that we are always more or less happy-unhappy, fulfilled-unfulfilled, and peaceful-restive.

We are on earth to compose a symphony. The frustrating and satisfying experience is that our symphony is unending, never completed. The more we compose, the more melodies, rhythms, and instruments we hear; we feel more timbres, movements, and instruments; and we see more meaning, measures, and notes. We sing and dance to an ongoing symphony that takes us to profound and life-giving depths and heights. Only in death is our symphony finished.

This is good news, for our spiritual journey is unending and inexhaustible. Consider elderly persons who are past their physical peak, and have achieved most of their goals or no longer have the opportunity to do so. However, they are still realizing their spiritual selves, like becoming more compassionate, patient, and loving as well as enjoying and celebrating life. Spiritually (even when there is brain/ego damage), we need never stop growing—we never "get it"—or, we are always getting it.

Seeing others spiritually as brothers and sisters, we desire to help them bear with life. In this respect, our Spirit evokes compassion as well as hope and courage to be one with and to help others. Rather than manipulating, exploiting, or withdrawing, we feel a centrifugal inclination to accept, honor, and understand. In short, our Spirit moves us to Love. Let us continue our spiritual journey that will lead us to God.

Spiritual Living

Love is the paramount dynamic of the spiritual life. From our perspective, we describe love as a way of being with others wherein we choose as best we can to promote the optimum welfare of self-and-others. Love is our spiritual willingness to do what is best not just for "me" (narcissism) or just for "you" (empathism), but for "us" (love).

Our love always includes feelings, for we are incarnated spirits. Thus, we may feel intensely in love, or our feelings may be mild and mute. Although we more or less feel love, our love is not primarily an emotion. Our love includes and goes beyond our bodily emotions.

Neither is love simply an ego function. When we love, we do not systematically gather knowledge about a possible beloved, analyze the data, and then decide whether to love that person. Love is not so impersonal and controlling. Although love is not primarily a function of our rational powers, we can use our ego functions to reflect on and discuss the health and prudence of our love. We can also use our minds to foster, protect, and implement our love (spirit).

Love comes primarily from our heart, not our body or mind. Being a function of our spiritual self, love is more of an imminently transcendent gift—one that is within and beyond our power. In love, we desire to be one with one another, and consequently live in intimacy and peace. In our model of health, love is our optimum way of being. Indeed, love or healthy interpersonal relationships are paramount in many models of health; however, they do not see them as a function of our spiritual self.

In our more intimate moments of love, we take off our everyday masks to be open to and for another. Our giving is pure in that it has no hidden agenda. It is an end in itself, and not a means toward another end. We do not place conditions on people to satisfy our feelings (body) or to achieve a goal (ego), but our best love (spirit) is unconditional.

Because we are in love, we choose, with our body, mind, and spirit, to promote the health and welfare of everyone concerned. We ardently want to say and do what is best for "us." Sometimes it is easy to love, and sometimes love is very difficult.

Consider, for example, the decision to remain in or separate from a toxic marriage. Seldom is there an easy answer. Our challenge is to remain in and foster love, but the way we choose is the daunting decision. Because of financial matters or young children, it may be best to remain in the marriage. On the other hand, out of love it may be better to separate for the better good of all concerned.

We also know that love is risky, for in love we reveal and offer our most intimate (spirit) and vulnerable (body) self—our soul. Consider when we are hurt in love. We may retaliate with hurt, react with pleasing, or simply withdraw. Moreover, if we wait for guarantees of not being hurt, we can go through life rarely risking ourselves in love. Although such reactions are understandable, our destiny is to stand in Love no matter what.

The truth is that if we live a life of love, we will be hurt. Indeed, love is the source of our greatest joy and our greatest sorrow. Although periodically painful, there is no better way. Our greatest misfortune is to avoid love, and our greatest feat is to die in Love.

Still, it is difficult to practice such a mission of love, for sometimes it necessitates a "suffering love"—a willingness to suffer for our best sake. When we are hurt in love, we can choose to avoid reacting negatively. We can deflect negatively and respond positively in and with love. Such love makes good spiritual and clinical sense, for we strengthen the fabric of community, and thus we help both others and ourselves.

For example, if you discover that someone you love has betrayed you, you will be terribly hurt, disillusioned, and probably enraged. It is natural to want to retaliate, to demand justice, or to even the score. The problem is that these and similar reactions rarely resolve anything, and often make matters worse. With love, you can learn to set appropriate boundaries, to survive, heal, and to renew your life.

To further our understanding, think of our ordinary behavior. Most of it involves our body and ego functions, while we express our spiritual selves indirectly. For instance, we would usually avoid expressing ourselves spiritually in business transactions, cleaning the house, doing taxes, or fixing something.

However, if we neglect our spirituality, our everyday behavior becomes too functional and without significant purpose. Ideally, it behooves us to be spiritually mindful, for then we respect our bodies, and our work becomes more meaningful. Moreover, if our routine should change and become more personal, we are ready to express our spiritual selves more directly.

We usually relegate overt expressions of love to certain situations and to particular times. Even if we tried, we could not always love overtly, for love is too intense to be constantly explicit and, besides; most situations do not call for such love. Still, our challenge is to express our love implicitly in all our behavior, or to live always and everywhere in and with Love.

For example, a nurse who functions only on an ego level may be an efficient but poor nurse. We can say that nursing techniques (ego) without concern (spirit) make for efficient and cold nurses, but that techniques used to express and implement care (spirit) make for competent and compassionate nurses. Indeed, people experience good nurses as trained (ego) persons who care (spirit). We can say this about any worker, especially those in the helping professions.

Professionals who treat mental health problems only with biological or psychotropic medications can help patients meliorate their symptoms and thus feel relatively better. However, medications do not teach them how to cope more effectively or to have purpose and meaning in life. A lack of problems or psychopathology is part of but not the same as true happiness and health.

Likewise, counselors who help clients to learn to satisfy needs and to cope better and achieve success as well as to get along with others are certainly valuable and part of mental health. Still, when they do not proactively help their clients spiritually, their clients do not learn how to connect with their spiritual resources.

Consequently, they are prone to forget or exclude their Higher Power, Love, or God, and therefore do not empower themselves. They may learn to satisfy their needs and achieve goals more effectively, but lack enduring power and meaning within themselves and with others. Internal serenity, security, and safety are lacking—and, so is health.

Some critics have proposed that religious leaders, often with good intentions, also displace personal spirituality with impersonal functionality. They opt for that which is expedient and politically correct rather than standing up for justice and truth. To avoid so-called scandal and a loss of church members, they cover up the truth or tell half-truths instead of proclaiming the whole truth. They rationalize that they have to sacrifice a few people for the sake of the common good. Some of these critics would say that such ungodly thinking and behavior were at the basis of sexual and financial crimes and sins.

We will next discuss our meaning of God and the relevance of God and religion to mental health. We will see that how we understand God and religion says much about how and why we cope and live. Let us proceed to see how religion and God fit into our model of health.

3

GOD, RELIGION, AND PSYCHOLOGY

M ANY STUDIES HAVE SHOWN that the overwhelming majority of Americans believe in a God. Froese and Bader (2010) have shown that most Americans construe and worship Gods that fall into four categories: the Authoritative God, the Benevolent God, the Critical God, and the Distant God. Actually, every person conceives God in his or her way. In this sense, there are as many (conceptions of) Gods as there are people. Indeed, our conceptions of God say more about us than about God.

Most believers seem more satisfied with more concrete and personal notions of God than abstract and impersonal ones. As we have indicated, we will see God/Love experiences more personally through the lenses of Love, of I-Thou and not I-it relationships.

Whatever your conception, including my own, it will fulfill and frustrate your spiritual desires and experiences. Our minds are woefully inadequate to describe who beckons us and whom we desire. With these caveats in mind, let us first engage people who deny, doubt, minimize, or exclude the relevance of God to health.

Criticisms of God and Religion

Although most people in Western societies believe in God, no longer do they regularly attend religious services. Moreover, health providers and educators do not consider God as essential to health. Clearly, in society, politics, education, health professions, mass media, and in everyday life, religion and its God as the paramount reality in life is waning and often excluded.

Furthermore, the number of atheists is increasing. Recently, atheists have written best-selling books that argue that belief in God is unnecessary and not rational, and can be an illusion or even a delusion. They would argue that the notion of God and its religion is not conducive to mental health. Agnostics wonder about and question similar atheist issues but are open to the possibility that there may be a God. They are not so sure. In this respect, some would contend that most people are at some time in their lives agnostic. Let us take a closer look at some of their arguments.

Although Freudian theory (and practice) is no longer the principal school of thought, many would contend that it is the mother of psychotherapy. Moreover, Freud wrote considerably about religion and God, and his arguments are still popular.

Strict Freudians as well as many atheists believe that we construct God or a supernatural being to protect ourselves from and to mitigate our anxiety, helplessness, and weakness. They see God as an illusion coming from our minds, not from objective reality. God is a projection of our imagination or our wish for a divine father figure who gives us security and comfort. When very afraid, anxious, or stressed, we run to our father who art in heaven.

There is not much doubt that some and perhaps many of us use religion and its concepts of God and heaven to ameliorate fear and stress. When threatened and afraid, we may seek religion and God as sources of safety and consolation and as ways of making sense of our suffering. However, when our suffering dissipates, we tend to forget about God, or not be as actively involved with God.

In a similar manner, many of us hold notions of heaven that help us cope with our fear of death. Heaven is a promise that we live forever, reunite with our loved ones, and when and where everything is all right. In heaven, there is no more suffering, and everything makes sense. Even though life on earth is miserable, heaven offers eternal reward. Without the coping strategy of heaven, we may deny, rationalize, or use addictions to mitigate our dreadful feelings of mortality.

Maybe such thoughts and behaviors are true. If such notions of God and religion promote good living and a just and orderly society, and as Freud would agree, it is better than personal and social chaos. However, Freud contends that ideally we should use our (ego) reason instead of such immature wish fulfillment. In contrast, a thesis in this book is that our vulnerability, dread of death, and liminal despair can evoke a healthy desire for and experience of God.

In our paradigm, such critiques of God and religion do not include the spiritual and God dimensions in their explanations. In other words, they reduce and explain everything in terms of the id (body) and ego. When one excludes spiritual dynamics, it makes logical sense that God is an illusion, and religion and its teachings are unnecessary for a healthy adult.

Similarly, advocates of scientism and scientific naturalism reduce everything to that which is observable and measureable. They reject or deem as foolish what does not fit into their scientific method, like faith and God. They mistakenly assume that science and reason are adequate to fulfill our deepest desires. They too exclude the spiritual dynamics and experiences of God, or they reduce them to body and ego dynamics.

Some social scientists explain religion as a way that the powerful and educated control the powerless and uneducated. They give as evidence the negative correlation between education and religious practice, i.e., the more a society becomes educated, the less people subscribe to a religion. Enlightened people know that reason (ego) is sufficient to live a healthy life, so that faith (spirit) in God is unnecessary and counterproductive.

They argue that the majority of religious followers are relatively un-educated, gullible, and insecure. Religion offers them a meaningful and social way of living that gives them a framework to make sense of life as well as the security of salvation and eternal life.

Some critics point out that most religious instruction is on the level of an early adolescent, or that it falls short of the formal cognitive (Piaget), post-conventional morality (Kohlberg), and transpersonal faith (Fowler) operations of a mature adult. Like mass media, religious discourse addresses a sixth-grade mentality. Such an approach, though valuable to many, is inadequate for others who use formal cognitive and post-conventional, transpersonal functions.

Thus, adults who ask questions that go beyond their pre-formal, conventional, transpersonal framework feel frustrated or even disillusioned. Instead of pursuing answers for their questions, or challenging their religions and its leaders, they drop out, or become marginal members. Compounding matters, some religious leaders force them to fit their inadequate paradigms. From this perspective, religions are dreadfully inadequate for inquiring minds and desiring spirits.

Another approach draws on learning/conditioning, cognitive, and social psychology theories. One could argue that people come to a sincere belief in God through frequent and consistent spiritual practices, especially prayer. They imagine in their minds through repetitious practice the invisible God who becomes increasingly real to them. The internal becomes external, so much so that some would say that they hear and have even seen God. Simply stated, you perceive, act, and feel the way you think and believe.

These critics would say that the religious (church) leaders promote and reinforce such imaginative exercises as well as consequent emotional behaviors. Behaviors that are congruent with their conception of God and religion are socially celebrated and reinforced or rewarded. One could say that the congregants are in collusion. Those contrary actions and sometimes thoughts are not rewarded and even punished. Confession, penance, and amends are ways of getting back on the right track. Once again, one is apt to act in ways that are reinforced and in sync with their beliefs.

Think of a church assembly where people gather as a community to worship God. For the most part, they are in union, particularly experientially, with one another. More than less they believe in God and most of their religion's teachings and practices. They listen to their pastor's sermon more as a witness to God than to understanding theological concepts. In fact, if you asked the people what the pastor said, most would not have much to say, yet they would say that overall they benefitted.

Look again. Most of the congregants are more than less focused on what is happening. One could argue that there is social contagion when you sing, pray, listen, respond to the minister, receive communion, or whatever you do together with others or in union. Such practices are contagious; you feel encouraged to join in, or feel out of it if you do not comply. You feel the security and strength of being an integral member of a vital community. Clearly, there is individual and social reinforcement to do what you are doing. Something is going on, and you want to be a part of it.

Moreover, the more you practice such behaviors, you come to believe in how you are acting, and your behavior reinforces your beliefs. Then the pastor and leaders encourage you with eternal rewards to practice every day what you are doing in church. Eventually, you consistently act on and manifest your religious beliefs.

Some critics would also say that church members are encouraged to evangelize, particularly when church attendance is waning. They would argue that fewer members mean less money and power for its leaders. The church's hierarchy becomes especially anxious when they see that the majority of their members are in their elderly years, and that the children of the younger congregants have little religious formation. They get the queasy feeling that their church is dying.

In contrast, other professional and lay pundits would argue that with the exception of some religious hierarchy, most ministers of religion are far from wealthy, and most use their power for positive results. Although there is a broad spectrum of talent, interest, and motivation, most clerics are sincere, try to be good as well as do a decent day's work. They might contend that the church's dying is not unusual, but has happened periodically throughout history and has served as an occasion for renewal. In this sense, the difficult times help us to become better.

One cognitive psychologist could say that God believers base their repetitious practices on false beliefs that they come to believe and behave accordingly. Another psychologist might argue that if this belief helps the person to live a decent life, then it is acceptable, though not fostered. Still another therapist might hold that the client's God belief is essential to health, and therefore fostered.

Others explain the positive correlation between religious involvement and mental health to religion offering reliable and affirming social interaction, not because of the reality of a helpful God. Although considerable studies strongly indicate that most religious people are healthier and live longer than nonreligious, they give psychological and social reasons, not spiritual ones, for this phenomenon.

Moreover, they point out how people use and have used religion and its God for destructive, political, and unhealthy purposes. They contend that religion has caused more harm than good and that too many people have murdered in the name of God. They agree that Godless people have also murdered in service of their will-to-power or other such goals. They contend that both these religious and irreligious people are disillusioned, unhealthy, and bad.

Those who subscribe to solely rational explanations assert that there is no valid reason for them to need a mythological god or a religion. They need no God, and they can take care of themselves as well as understand the why and how of living. From their perspective, there is no room for divine faith in the house of reason.

Many clinicians (in their professional practice) consider the traditional conceptions of God as myths or anthropomorphic wish projections. Some propose that God and religion helped people in pre-enlightenment times to understand and cope with life as well as to give life and suffering a meaningful explanation. Once again, religion is the comfort, consolation, and direction for the unenlightened masses. Thus, if we are enlightened, we do not need God to be healthy.

From such perspectives, one can easily criticize or even mock people who subscribe to simple and repetitive religious practices. Indeed, religious people may have childlike conceptions of God as well as little or simplistic explanations for what they do. In fact, most of them do not care or try to give explanations of why they do what they do; they just do it. Such so-called blind faith baffles rationalists. Nevertheless, we will show how their repetitive and rote prayers, simple singing, and blind and mindless adoration may have more spiritual depth and value than our (ego) analyses can grasp.

Indeed, their religious practices and experiences of God (spirit) may go beyond enlightened comprehension (ego). Their mindless repetitions may enable them to transcend their ego to spiritual experiences of God. Their childlike experiences and explanations may make more sense than fits into the confines of hyperrational minds. Perhaps simple people who know little theology and science but practice a God-centered life may be wiser and happier than the more erudite scientists and theologians who explain God away and fail to live God.

Nevertheless, we should not dismiss but rather discern criticisms of religions and God, for they usually contain truth. From our perspective, they often describe inauthentic or immature forms of religious and God experiences. For example, some people do see God as a (projected) father who protects them especially when threatened, suffering, or afraid of death. For some and perhaps many people, religion is, at least partially, a superego function that prevents chaos and offers a safe and comforting haven.

We have indicated that critics argue that religions and their beliefs are premodern and irrational myths and illusions that are no longer necessary to understand and cope with life. They contend that enlightened modern and postmodern man can replace such faith with rational explanations and behavior.

Indeed, this makes sense when you exclude the dynamics of the spirit and sacred and only use those of the body and ego. However, when you include the spiritual, you make different sense and judgments of people who practice religion and practice a God-centered life. From this perspective, so-called simple, unenlightened people may be better off.

Rationalistic reductionism makes it relatively easy to debunk religion and God. When we reduce the dynamics of the spiritual and of God experiences to those of the body and ego, it logically follows that God and religious experiences are machinations of the mind (ego), illusions, or even delusions. Thus, health providers may debunk a client's beliefs, or more likely passively accept them and not foster them.

In summary, the fundamental error of such approaches is that they fail to account for factors and dynamics of spiritual experiences in general and of God experiences in particular. Those who accept the rational and reject the spiritual only incorporate the constructs and dynamics of body and ego or similar and related constructs. They try to explain spiritual and God experiences in terms of the body (id, emotions, etc.) and ego (cognition, social self, etc.).

In my opinion, this is a primary error of health providers and educators. Health criteria and outcomes only include the dynamics and goals of the body and ego. Such reductionism fragments clients and in general fails to treat the whole person. With their paradigm, providers cannot make good sense of religious, spiritual, and God experiences. Although they accept and listen to such spiritual thoughts and behaviors, they seldom pursue, evoke, and foster them, or see and treat them as essential.

God as Love

Religions, man's handmaids of God, are our clumsy and courageous efforts to understand our origin and destiny as well as to make sense of life, especially its suffering, evil, and overall injustices. To that end, we draw on divine revelation, tradition, and theology. Indeed, our attempts to grasp (ego) God (Spirit) fall terribly short.

Our approach does not draw from theology or religion, but rather from psychology and spirituality. In our model, experiences of God are primarily a function of our spiritual dimension. "God" is a word, construct, or mental construction (ego) that we use to help us make sense of our spiritual questions and desires. Theoretically, we construe God as the object of our (subject) experiences that we call holy, religious, divine, sacred, ultimate concern, or those of a greater (spiritual) power than our ego.

In our model of personality and health, we conceive "God" as uncreated, cocreating Love, or the uncreated and cocreating energies of Love, or Love (object-pole) to whom we (subject-pole) relate beyond and within ourselves. When referring to God, we use the personal "who" rather than "what" because our best experiences of Love are interpersonal. Moreover, Love with a capital L will refer to God.

In short, we see God as uncreated, cocreating Love who is part of (imminent) and beyond (transcendent) us. God/Love is our uncreated, cocreating source in giving us life, sustaining us, and motivating us to be and do good until we die to attain our destiny—Love. Thus, our destiny is to return to our origin.

A major tenet is that God who is uncreated, cocreating Love and who dwells within and beyond us is our most important resource. To deny, rationalize, or forget this reality is foolish and sad, for our energies of Love empower us to cope better and to be healthier. Carl Jung said that whether we admit it or not, God abides within and beckons us. Fortunately, God hounds us to death to be in Love.

Another major and recurring thesis is that God-you-I are essentially interrelated. Our human condition is a web of interconnectedness (which is a basic tenet of quantum physics). God is in us, and we are in God—and, we are in and with one another. Without God and others, we do not exist—or in existential parlance, our existence is coexistence.

As we have seen, a consequence of this reality is that whatever we do and become always involves and affects in some way others and God. We are not primarily individuals (ego), nor do we follow dualistic, Cartesian scripts. We are primary, integral members of the human community (spirit) so that whatever we do impacts others.

It is reasonable and important that counselors acknowledge that Love/God is significant in learning to cope effectively and to experience ultimate and enduring meaning. For example, if a client lacks purpose and meaning and is consequently depressed, anxious, or lonely, Love (or

the God of one's understanding) would probably be relevant. Alcoholics
Anonymous gives testimony and evidence to the importance and efficacy
of this therapeutic Power.

When we make our ego and its individualism primary, we can alienate ourselves from our powerful community of Love. Moreover, when we
reduce God to monistic explanations or dispel God with scientism, we
impede our health. Indeed, we must deflate such ego inflation to come
to experience God. (For example, the various methods of Eastern and
Western meditation and contemplation are ways to go beyond our ego
to our Spirit.)

Think of when we forget or separate ourselves from God. We lose
power and diminish ourselves. For example, our addictions to ego (power, work) and body (sex, drugs) militate against spiritual experiences of
God/Love and health. In fact, they are often displacements of God, and
therefore of ourselves. Displacements of God, like power, money, sex, and
drugs in themselves, simply do not foster health.

Once again, it behooves the counselor (and client) to be aware of
and deal with such dynamics. Take notice of people who practice 12-
step programs (like Alcoholics Anonymous and Al-Anon). They make a
Higher Power, or the God of their understanding, the core of their recovery. As 12-steppers say, "it works."

Finally, we must be careful that our words and images do not cover
more than reveal God. Ironically, we can harm ourselves when we try to
be too exact, for our efforts can lead to restriction, reification, steriliza-
tion, and even falsification of whom we desire to experience.

For instance, a doctor of theology may give you a plethora of theoretical proofs for the existence of God, and he may give erudite lectures
and eloquent homilies about God. His heady proclamations, however,
hardly ever touch people's hearts, or help them deepen their experience
of God. When students or parishioners ask him questions, he may respond only in ways that fit in his theology box. Furthermore, although
he seems to have all the answers, he himself may have little experience of
God. Thus, he shares ideas (mind) rather than experiences that appeal to
the heart.

Meanwhile, when asked what the doctor said, the couple in the back
row who never graduated from high school smile, shrug their shoulders,
and say little. We know simple and humble people, like this couple, who
despite their lack of pedagogy or perhaps because of it, seem to experience

God. As the lyric in the musical South Pacific says, fools give you reasons, wise men never try.

Consider the doctor of psychology who has no use for the theologian and pities the couple. He may see the theologian's beliefs as false, unnecessary, and perhaps dangerous because they impede people from dealing rationally with reality. However, he may reluctantly accept his clients' religion and God because they help to keep them in order and give them some social interaction, control, and security.

Although this psychologist helps his clients satisfy their needs and manage better, he is clumsy at helping his clients make lasting sense of their lives. He senses that bodily satisfaction and functional success fail to fulfill his clients' and his deepest desires. He avoids and rationalizes questions about one's reason for being, suffering, injustice, evil, goodness, God, and afterlife. "What's it all about?" goes unheeded.

To avoid describing and responding to divine experiences can also be foolish. Although our experiences of God (faith/spirit) include and are beyond our rational grasp (reason/ego), they are real. Surely, not all people who claim to experience God are naive, immature, stupid, or sick. A refusal to reflect on and articulate our holy experiences could be a denial of reality, which is not very perceptive, mature, smart, or healthy. In short, God experiences are primary, and their explanations are secondary and in service of experiences.

The theologian can face his own questions, doubt, ignorance, and darkness to which his theories fail to respond adequately. His experience can challenge his theories so that his theories are in service of (his own and others') experience, not vice versa. He can humbly admit that he does not have all the answers, and he can learn from his followers.

The psychologist can stop avoiding or reducing spiritual and God inquiries to the confines of the body and ego. Instead, he can listen to his clients' (and as his own) spiritual questions and desires so that he includes the spiritual and God in his therapeutic models and approaches. He, too, can honor and learn from his clients' search for God.

In short, the doctors' theories and approaches should help and not hinder people's desires for health. In the following chapters, I will try to be mindful of these problems and possibilities.

4

EXPERIENCING GOD

SINCE MY APPROACH INCLUDES the spiritual along with the body and ego dimensions, it differs from much of mainstream psychology. Why do I include the spiritual as well as experiences of God? Here are some reasons.

In my clinical experience with individuals and small groups, people frequently expressed a genuine concern about and desire for God. They wanted to explore the relevance of God to their health. In and out of the classroom, students desired clarity, concreteness, and relevance in regards to God discussions. They shared their thoughts and experiences, and I listened to and learned from them.

I also asked people to write spontaneous descriptions of an experience of God. I had them describe their holy experiences as openly as possible, without using theories about or explanations of God. A phenomenological analysis of these descriptions as well as those from literature also helped me to understand what people called holy or God experiences.

Personally, literature also evoked questions about and shed light on the issue of God for me. Fiction and nonfiction writers as well as mystical and spiritual writers inspired, evoked, and provoked me. Finally, I listened to my own spiritual experiences, especially those of intimacy, and tried to explicate what happened.

The purpose of the following analyses is to present the common factors of these direct and indirect experiences of God while remaining faithful to each experience. My project is to describe the necessary and sufficient constituents of God experiences. Keep in mind that all the factors are interrelated parts so that each one implies the others as well as the whole experience.

This means that a particular person may emphasize one or more qualities in their experience while minimizing or being unaware of other factors. In other words, different people will experience the same reality differently. For example, one person may focus on imminent transcendence, while another emphasizes sacredness and worship, and a third person speaks of mystery and paradox.

Divine Desire and Attraction

"If you asked me if I think that there is a God, I would say that I believe that God exists. After all, my parents are devout Christians, and they, along with Sunday services and Bible schools, taught me the Christian ways of God. I am glad that they did what they did, and my wife and I gave our children a religious education as well.

"I never really doubted God much; I rather took God and religion for granted. We regularly attended church services, and were relatively active in church affairs. Over all, it served us well.

"Moreover, I have been very successful in my professional career, my marriage is good, and our children are doing well. We have enough money to get what we want—things, vacations, good schools, cultural events, etc. More importantly, we have family and friends. We are better off than most people are.

"However, it seemed like when I got in my forties, things started to change. Then I heard in the recesses of my mind Peggy Lee singing her haunting words: 'Is that all there is? I still haven't found what I'm looking for.' My success, pleasure, power, notoriety, wealth, family, friends, and religion have not filled the nagging hole in my soul. Where is this peace and joy that is supposed to come with a belief in God?

"I started to wonder if I really experience God. I know God is not the God of my childhood, a judgmental, omniscient, supernatural father. I have let go of my anthropomorphisms of my youth, but irritating questions remain. Is God a he, a she, or whoever or whatever? What or who do I really experience. Better yet, do I really experience a person, or anything? Is God just a thought, a belief, a desperate attempt to make sense of life? Is God a result of my persevering wishes, programming, and study? Do I really experience a God beyond myself? Is God a projection of my thinking? Is God an illusion?

"I have read many contemporary and classic books on theology as well as atheism. They make philosophical and scientific sense, and they raise important questions especially about faith and suffering. Although they challenge my mind, they do little for my heart. I have also read many authors of novels and spirituality. They wet my appetite, intrigue my mind, and stir my heart, but I still desire to understand and experience more.

"Not only do Peggy Lee's laments haunt me, but also the words of St. Augustine resonate with me—my heart is restless until it rests in Thee. Who is this Thee whom my heart seeks? I have read the lives of saints and other good people who centered their life on God. I have been fortunate to know several Christian and Buddhist monks who seem to have found what I am looking for—to live freely and serenely.

"I want what these people of God have found. They seem to have purpose and direction in their lives. Life makes abiding sense to them. I want to respond to Peggy Lee's question, and say that there is more to life. I want to say that I have found what I am looking for, not just in my mind but also in my life. Religious beliefs are not enough.

"I desire to experience God. But, maybe there is no God to experience. Maybe God is a religious deception, or simply an illusion. Still, I cannot get Peggy's chant out of my mind—and, out of my heart."

This man is probably around the midpoint of his life. Until recently, his God, religion, and its practices have served him well. Now, he longs for more. Although he questions his beliefs, he has not given up on them. He yearns to experience what he believes. As he said, he wants to experience his God. He desires more than what he has. Perhaps in the Peggy Lee song, he hears God calling him.

Like this man, perhaps you too are looking for more. Perhaps, your heart is also restless and yearning for more than you have. Perhaps, your pleasurable satisfactions, successful achievements, and other such fulfillments have left you unfulfilled and wondering if this is all there is. Perhaps, your religion and theology give you information about God, but not formation in God.

Many of us have met, read, or heard about people who seem to have purpose and serenity without having many possessions and worldly power. Somehow, they experience a reality that appeals to and intrigues us. They may be saints, noble men and women, consecrated religious, or simple and humble people serenely living a God-centered life. Such people evoke and affirm a desire, an ambivalent and ambiguous one, to find and follow what they have found.

How can we satisfy our heart's lasting longings? Actually, we will see that our desires for and questions about God are part of our experiencing God. How can this be? If we look at the nature of such desires, we may find some clues.

Interestingly, the Latin derivation of desire literally means from the stars. In our framework, desire means that we are perpetually reaching for the stars, or that we long for something or someone more than our body and ego can give. When we (subject) desire, we yearn for something or someone (object). We desire more than the ordinary (body and ego); we desire the extraordinary (spirit).

This means that our spiritual desires affirm a spiritual reality that is more than the objects of our body and ego desires. Even if we cannot verbalize it, our spiritual desires involve an adumbrated or implicit presence. Without conscious awareness, our restless desires for and questions about God seek and verify a divine reality. Our restless emptiness desires a serene presence.

We can come to say to St. Augustine and others that our hearts are restless until they rest in a spiritual reality. We can come to say to Peggy Lee that there is more than our everyday (body and ego) life can give. We can come to say with Karl Rahner that all our human symphonies are unfinished. We can come to proclaim a healthy incompleteness that gives us hope, purpose, and meaning. We can come to say that our ontological dis-ease is the source of our health.

Another way of looking at spiritual desires is from a Jungian perspective. We can understand spiritual desires—or if you will, divine desires for God—as archetypes. We have innate, universal desires to face and respond to a divine reality who demands integration. By nature, we hunger for and are attracted to and by a reality that many call God.

It is reasonable to say that our divine desires include a God who beckons us, or that our persistent longings indicate a sacred reality or God. That is to say, our desire for God implies a God (or Love) who desires us. We feel a divine attraction, a summons to Love. Love invites us to surrender to Love, to leap with faith and trust in Love.

Critics might say that this so-called divine desire is really a subjective need to ameliorate anxiety, fear of death, or some form of pain. An objective God does not really exist. They argue that most people go to a God when they are afraid of a catastrophe or impending death to self or a loved one. In short, people manufacture or project a God to comfort themselves and to make sense of absurdities.

Indeed, this may happen. Nevertheless, such evidence does not disprove that an innate desire does not exist. A subjective projection does not necessarily exclude an objective God whom other people experience. Because some people project does not mean that all people project or live in an illusion. Moreover, coping mechanisms like projection may be circuitous and adumbrated ways to come to a healthy experience of God.

Consider that sometimes our desire for our beckoning God suddenly makes sense. For instance, this may happen in and through considerable suffering, or in and through love. We have a breakthrough experience where things come together, and we can say yes to life. In an uncanny way, our problems seem to subside, and life makes ultimate sense. Finally, we fulfill our desires, and we are happy.

Maslow might call this a peak experience toward becoming your self-actualizing self. Jung might analyze such an experience as facing and integrating an archetypical drive toward being your whole self. Some religious leaders may refer to a spiritual awakening. Others describe it as a breakthrough or conversion experience. A.A. members may describe it as hitting bottom where you accept your powerlessness.

For a time, our hearts settle and are no longer so restless. Although our intense experiences soon dissipate, they still linger in our minds and hearts. This unusual event makes a significant and lasting difference.

Another way of validating this desire for a perpetual Love is one that many of us are hesitant to admit, yet is more common than we may think. Many and perhaps most of us catch numinous glimpses of what we yearn for. We intensely sense a reality that is beyond and part of us, a reality that engenders a serene sense of being one with self and others.

So-called mystical experiences are not just for mystics. We experience them, have a hint of them, or sense their presence in absence. During the experience, it is not important to name, explain, or justify it, for it is too real and unmistakable. We know beyond rational explanation what we yearn for. We know deep within us that this "Hound of Heaven" will not give up pursuing us. This reality—God—will not abandon us.

In the midst of all the noise and distractions of busy living, we can step back, be still, and listen to the sounds of silent music and see more than the ordinary. We can feel an extraordinary beckoning. We can see, hear, respond to, and manifest the Love who is in, between, and beyond us. We can honor and bow to the presence of Love where we are one.

Many of us come to admit to our desire for and summons by God when we experience our vulnerability. Simply stated, we feel drawn to and by God in the midst of our suffering. Our limits reach for the Unlimited. We sense a reality that gives us hope, a Love that asks us to trust that there is more to life and that somehow or ultimately our nonsense will make sense. Some critics would argue that such experiences are desperate attempts to ameliorate pain and fulfill wishes.

Others would suggest that Love's magnetic force draws us to a place of hope and possibilities, to a life that makes more sense than is apparent to our body and ego. They argue that this divine magnetism calls us to trust that life will make ultimate sense as well as invites us to a presence that comforts and consoles. When we respond to the welcome of Love, we feel uncannily at home.

Still, we can use our experience as a temporary mechanism to ameliorate our pain. As we have stated, many of us strongly seek a God only when we are scared, threatened, or suffering, and maybe this is the best that we can do at this time. The danger is to forget about God once life settles and is less painful. Nevertheless, even if we do use or forget God, God still abides in and beckons us.

However, turning to God in dire circumstances need not be a psychological ploy. Even if it is a crutch, we still seek in our powerlessness a reality more than our body and ego can give. Precisely because our body and ego are weak, we are more open to life's spiritual dimension. No longer do our thoughts or mental defenses obstruct or silence our spiritual desires. It is as if life forces a divine awareness. Actually, our vulnerability (which is always present) can awaken and foster our innate desire for God. In weakness, our strength appears.

We can notice (and nurture) our desire for and attraction to and by God in many ways. Our desire for and appeal from God is especially intense and demanding in our experiences of nothingness. In the next chapter, we will see how our experiences of limits motivate us to desire an Unlimited God. We will show how our limited humanity affirms and evokes an unlimited divinity, and how the Unlimited evokes and empowers us to manage our limits more effectively. Surely, health providers can and should explore this fertile ground.

For now, it is good to realize that we do long to reach the stars, and that the stars guide and inspire us. We desire more than our body and ego can offer, and there is more, Spirit (Love), that attracts us. The beginning (and end) of our search for God is our desire for and attraction by God. Let us continue to explore possible factors in experiences of God. Listen to the following woman, Catherine, who focuses on mystery and paradox in her holy journey.

Mystery and Paradox

"I don't know if I can explain it, but I'll try to describe what happens to me. One of my most recurrent and pervasive experiences is feeling strange and uncanny and yet at the same time familiar and at home. I know that this may sound like nonsense, but it makes strange sense to me.

"Let me try to share a little more. Sometimes, it is as if I am out of my body, as if I am lighter or do not have the weight of my body. It is as if my body becomes part of a larger body. I feel so small and yet so immense; I feel humbly proud. I know it sounds crazy, but I feel saner than ever.

"In a similar way, I feel like I lose myself in this greater reality, and yet I feel most myself. I feel I am in a foreign land where I am at home. Although I am kind of scared and uneasy, I am okay, and even experience a soft and comforting joy. I feel I am where I should be, that this mysterious land is where I should reside.

"Sometimes I get scared, and hold back, or try to detach and observe what is happening. When I do this, I invariably diminish the experience. When I surrender and let the experience take me to wherever, I find myself in a wonderful place. It is as if I step over a threshold into another world.

"In this new and strangely familiar world, I often experience a personal presence similar to and more than being in love with my husband. Being in this presence is warm, safe, consoling, and simply good. Maybe this is God. I do not know, and I do not, not know.

"Call my experiences what you want. From a psychological viewpoint, I suppose you could call them peak experiences, or certainly uncanny. Some people may even deem them wish fulfillments, sensory overriding, or pathological. You could also call them simply different, extraordinary, or healthy.

"I do know that they are just as or even more real than my ordinary experiences, and they feel so right and so good. I do not think they are sick; actually, I think they are healthy, for they strengthen and console me as well as give me inner peace and perspective. For various reasons, I seldom talk about them."

Like Catherine, many of us have experienced a sense of mystery and paradox. An extraordinary reality envelops us. In light of our paradigm, we can say that her experiences incorporate an ineffably liminal quality that transcends normal problem solving (ego) and need satisfaction (body). Our ordinary (body and ego) world transforms to an extraordinary (spirit) world. What we might consider irrational or unhealthy makes significant, healthy sense.

One of the etymological meanings of mystery is to experience in an adumbrated or cloudy way—or, we know in a cloud of unknowing. This means that our spiritual experiences go beyond immediate satisfaction and rational clarity, but rather are numinous, liminal and blissful—or, they are rooted in mystery.

Spiritually, we cannot be completely satisfied (body) or "grasp" (ego) what is happening, for mystery points to an inexhaustible source of knowledge and growth. We simply cannot exhaust, define, or limit our spiritual desires. Thus, when we are too rational (and too physical), we risk taking the mystery out of our relationships so that our life becomes dry and boring.

Paradox also permeates our spiritual experiences, particularly those of God. Mystics, for instance, speak of their fascination and trepidation with God's allure. Especially in Love, we can feel that we are losing and becoming ourselves. We can know better than ever and yet know nothing. Logically, this is nonsense. However, experiences of spiritual paradox go beyond the limits and confines of logic.

Be aware, however, that our spiritual presence to mystery and paradox can present problems and challenges. The openness of our spiritual self is not biased, i.e., it includes both light and dark. Although we can rationally know this paradoxical aspect of reality, to experience it can be unsettling and challenging.

Indeed, our nature includes demonic forces like narcissism, lust, ignorance, and untoward power, and experiences such as dread, despair, and nothingness. Understandably, we may try to avoid and repress our dark side, for awareness demands attention and change. However, when we fail to face, embrace, and learn from our dark nature, our darkness threatens to control and consume us.

We must realize that health and goodness on earth are fictions without the possibility of unhealthiness and evil. To become stronger, freer, and healthier, we must journey with Love through both light and dark lands. To dance to light and dark music helps us to become stronger and freer. We can respond to vice with virtue and bad with good as well as become compassionate with the dark side of self and others.

A mysterious and daunting paradox occurs when we experience the absence of God as a fuller presence. Most of us find it difficult to sit still and silent in the presence of absence. We feel uneasy; our minds wander and want to be somewhere else. We may feel that God has abandoned us, or that God is a fiction.

Paradoxically, our emptiness may be a greater fulfillment. Our experience of absence may be a call to go beyond rational (ego) thinking and its conceptions of God. Indeed, our ego (religions and theologies) can explain and point to God, but our spirit desires to circumvent these rational detours to experience God more directly. In this respect, some persons with little theological education may be better off than some who follow reductionist theology.

This phenomenon of mystery and paradox can cause considerable problems for those who need clarity and control. We can be certain that we will lack certainty in our futile attempts to gain a definitive grasp of God. In other words, if we need certainty, clarity, and control, we will have trouble with the mystery, ambiguity, and power of God. The significant mistake is to allow our egos to get in the way of God. To let go and let God is not a trite statement.

Most of us have relatively little difficulty when we have certainty and clarity in regards to the existence or nonexistence of God. However, when we experience God as more absent than present, we can become anxious and seek premature closure. Consequently, we impede our God experiences that are sometimes more present in absence.

It behooves us to remember that this absence is a form of presence, to accept that the apparent emptiness of spiritual absence may evoke a presence that is beyond our rational comprehension. Being present in absence defies and challenges our rational (ego) grasp of God and calls for acceptance of transrational experiences. We come to realize that we cannot control God, or that we are not God. With patience, faith, and gratitude, we stand still and strong for God to be present beyond our rational grasp.

In short, our spiritual presence is a-logical, a-contradictory, and a-discursive. In contrast to our normal world of dichotomies, dualisms, certainties, problems, analyses, exactness, control, and individualism (ego), we experience paradox, unity, certitude, mystery, synthesis, liminality, surrender, and community (spirit).

From a reductionist rational perspective, this may sound contradictory or absurd, but spiritually it makes sound sense. When God is present to us in and as absence, it may mean that our experience has gone beyond our rational grasp to a fuller presence. To experience absence is to desire and experience presence.

Once again, when we take a reductionist rational approach, it is easy to debunk religion and theology as well as its God. Our mistake is to try to control what/who is more than we are. We may falsely conclude that what is beyond reason is unnecessary, an illusion, and less than healthy.

This approach is not anti-rational. Actually, we risk doing what we are criticizing—to be rationalistic. Our agenda is to be rational in service of the transrational. For example, think of being deeply in love with your beloved. When you try to control her (or him), you impede and even abort her unfolding. You obstruct being intimate with her, and will probably pressure her to withdraw. Conversely, when you love her unconditionally and let her be, she is more likely to share herself endlessly.

Love beckons and helps you to be purely present, to listen and respond openly, to feel renewed, and to surrender to be one. In the still moments of silence, when nothing is happening, you may be closest. Your connection goes beyond thoughts and words. The absence of ego functions ushers in a spiritual abundance, or ecstatic love. You communicate with the wordless language of Love.

Such experiences may sound like idealistic, unrealistic, or sophomoric fantasy. Indeed, they are extraordinary, but they are quite realistic, attainable, and mature. Once again, think of your deep experiences of love. To some extent and especially in their purest moments, you let go of much of your control (ego) and come to spiritual union. Paradoxically, in losing yourself, you feel most yourself.

In our holy encounters, we can experience the unity of joy and anxiety, pleasure and pain, closeness and distance, fascination and trepidation, knowledge and ignorance, pride and humility, presence and absence, life and death. We realize that our sacred stance becomes profane in that we are more deeply in the world, and that our profane stance becomes sacred because our world is holy.

Thus, we become more aware and appreciative of the many mysterious and paradoxical complexities and clarities of the spiritual life. We are careful that our ego does not limit, impede, or abort our spiritual experiences. In short, we gratefully accept that mystery and paradox are spiritual ways of knowing in and with Love.

Divine Dependence

"My name is Gary, and I am a sexaholic. Out of context, that sounds so clichéd, but in my life, it makes crucial sense. To admit that I am powerless over lust was and is the most difficult and important event in my life.

"Keep in mind that I have had a high position in the corporate world where power, in its good and bad forms, is at a premium. To recognize and accept that I had significantly less power than I assumed was terribly humbling. Yet, it was and is necessary to get down on my knees in order to stand up in an infinitely better way.

"To drastically abbreviate a very long story, after much guilt and shame, I came to admit that I am powerless over cybersex and that my addiction was hurting not only myself but also people I love, especially my wife and kids. I deluded myself into thinking that my many hours with sex on the internet were relatively harmless, after all, I reasoned, most guys did it. I rationalized that it was nothing personal as long as no one knew.

"Well, things got out of hand. I started to run up considerable debt on porn, and I extended my sexaholic activities at sex clubs and so-called massage parlors. In short, my wife uncovered our $135,000 debt, and soon after, what the money was spent on. To say the least, my wife felt betrayed, manipulated, and demeaned, and of course, trust was shattered. After much pain, she divorced me. I do not blame her. However, let us get back to me.

"I joined Sexaholics Anonymous, and for seven years I have been an active member. After much struggle and self-deception, I came to accept that I could not turn my life around on my own. I needed the insights and understanding of the fellowship; I needed and need their help. More importantly and harder for me was to admit that I needed the help of a power greater than I. Remember, I always thought that I was in control so that I could change or achieve at will. This was simply another example of my self-deception.

"To my surprise, I learned to surrender to a Higher Power, which I eventually called God. After more than a year of battles between my Higher Power and me, I turned my life and will over to the care of God. The paradox is that when I admit that I am powerless over lust and surrender to God, I become empowered.

"If I told my business colleagues of this metamorphosis, they would say that I lost my mind. In some ways, they are right in that I immersed my mind in a greater mind. I know that this may sound crazy or corny, but it has enabled me to be freer, stronger, and happier. My Buddhist and Hindu colleagues would smile in agreement with me.

"I never thought that I, an independent, self-sufficient man, would ever say that he was happy and grateful to be dependent. In some ways, I am just as autonomous as ever, but in an interdependent way. With the God of my understanding, I am definitely dependent and freer; thank God. Without God, I would be an addictive mess. Simply stated, I depend on God to help me maintain and progress in sobriety and serenity."

Gary speaks of a dependence that liberates him. From our perspective, he gave up his unhealthy (body) dependence and (ego) independence to connect with a greater (spiritual) power of inter-in-dependence. He let go of his body lust and ego self-sufficiency, admitted to having less (ego) power than he thought, and surrendered to a greater spiritual power. Paradoxically, his powerlessness engenders more power, freedom, and healthy management. His dependency on God enables him to live a freer and healthier life.

Clearly, Gary's dependence differs radically from infantile, immature, and unhealthy modes of dependency. Our dependence on God is not that of an infant who must depend on adults and who takes and cannot give willingly. Indeed, when we regress and act in a dependent (childish and needy) manner, we are less than healthy. In many ways, Gary's sex addiction to lust manifests this process.

When we harbor unhealthy dependency, we depend on others, places, or things to satisfy our needs, often at the expense of others. When our needs are not satisfied, we feel uneasy, inferior, angry, and needier.

Thus, we lead a precarious existence because our well-being primarily depends on events outside ourselves instead of our coming freely from within ourselves. In contrast, holy and healthy persons choose to nourish their dependency on God and their interdependency with others.

Divine dependence means that we admit that God is greater than (more powerful) and part of (empowers) ourselves. In the previous chapters, we proposed that we depend on God and others to live, or that our existence is coexistence. Simply stated, if God is our uncreated, cocreating Creator, we depend on God (and others) to live and to create a better life.

To concretize our understanding of divine dependency, let us follow Gary's lead and reflect on the first three steps of Sexaholics Anonymous. Following step one, we admit that we are powerless over lust (alcohol or other drugs, food, gambling, life, or whatever)—that our lives have become unmanageable. That is, we (ego) have less power over lust than we assume or would like.

In step two, we continue to believe that a Power greater than ourselves can restore us to sanity. In our framework, our individual ego is insufficient to cope adequately so that we need a higher power (Spirit/God). Following step three, we make a decision to turn our will and our lives over to the care of God, as we understand God. In short, we commit to integrate God and spiritual practices into our everyday life.

Instead of reducing our power to body and ego functions, we combine them (feelings, emotions, cognition, volition, coping, etc.) with a higher (spiritual) power—primarily the care (love) of God. In other words, we freely surrender (our body and ego) to the empowering power of Love.

These steps (and the other nine as well) are clinically effective ways to recover from addictions. Moreover, they are sound spiritual principles and practices. Actually, we can apply them not only to addictions but also to life, or as the last clause of the last step says, to practice these principles in all our affairs.

As we have indicated, our surrender to God or a Power (Love) greater than our individual ego affirms our divine and redemptive dependency. Our Spirit (or the God of our understanding) empowers our ego so that through being powerless we become more powerful. Some would say that through and with divine dependency, we become more independent.

Divine dependence confirms that we are powerless, not just over addictions, but ultimately over life itself. As we grow older, we realize more poignantly that life is not ultimately in our hands. Death moves us to affirm that life is beyond our (ego) control. Wisdom urges us to wed our body and ego to and with our Spirit.

However, ego power is very seductive. Using our rational reasoning, we may explain everything in terms of science. What does not fit in our scientific purview, we dismiss as irrelevant, unnecessary, superstitious, or neurotic. We may see faith as a defense against our fear of death or meaninglessness. We contend that it is foolish to escape into the fairyland of faith. We see no need for God.

To the contrary, it is foolish to depend exclusively on the limited power of our body and ego, and it is wise to bond with the unlimited power of our (Holy) Spirit who is greater than and part of who we are. The clinical fact is that when we reduce life to body and ego functions, we limit ourselves and cause unnecessary problems.

Conversely, when we accept the limitations of our ego, we are more likely to surrender to the Unlimited and manage our limits more effectively. When we depend on God, we tap an unlimited source of power, and thereby enhance our freedom, improve our coping, and secure our reason for being. As a psychologist, I try to evoke the Spiritual Power that resides within my clients.

Too often, we try to depend solely on others or ourselves. We deny or forget that God and no "one" else is our radical source of health. Radically and ultimately, God redeems us, not society, friends, parents, spouse, or self. Although this statement may sound like or be a religious belief, our intent is not theological but rather psychological and clinical.

From a psychological point of view, when we (as adults) expect others to be our primary sustenance, we become psychologically dependent, and are immature or unhealthy. We see people as gods, or sources of our well-being. We put them on pedestals and bind them to us as perfect idols. Soon they will resent our adulation, for they are unable to be perfect—to be God.

In contrast to dependency, we can behave oppositely. We can try to be completely self-sufficient, or to depend only on ourselves. We futilely try to avoid needing anyone, including God. Understandably, our detached and cold demeanor will likely alienate people, leaving us alone. Consequently, we will eventually become empty and miserable in our self-sufficiency. Total self-sufficiency is futile and sad.

When we depend primarily on God, we strive to love unconditionally. With God, we find the courage to risk in love and the strength to suffer in love. Our divine dependency gives us the power to love as well as the security to let others love us—the basis of both community and health. Especially when we are in the throes of pain, fear, and confusion, our dependency on God gives us the courage to cope in and with Love.

Although we can never force God (or others) to love us, we can take the initiative to increase its likelihood. For instance, we can learn to discern when we are more likely to respond to God's pervading presence. We can learn what places are more conducive for holy experiences. For example, a public place of worship, the solitude of our room, and a forest or seaside walk may facilitate a divine experience. Ideally, we can experience God everywhere and always.

In contrast to human beings, God is always available, for without God we would not exist. As we have indicated, however, God can be present in absence, and this can be unnerving as well as test our faith. With the certitude of faith based on reason, we can depend on God more than we can on people. We know that ultimately God will not let us down, as people (including ourselves) more or less will. We can depend on God to fill us with life, if for no other reason than God is the Source of life. Even (and especially) when God is present in absence, we come to trust God.

Finally, with humility and gratitude, we can acknowledge that God is dependent on us in that God is present most significantly in and through people. Without people, God does not exist for people. In this way, we are dependent on people and ourselves to see, hear, respond to, and manifest God. In this sense, we, humans, are manifestations of God. To be sure, we are not God, but we are and should be daughters and sons of God.

In short, divine dependency is surrendering to, in, and with Love, and thus becoming cocreators of life. With humility, we should be grateful for this gift of divine life. Let us listen to Jim who describes another aspect of God experiences.

Indebtedness

"As far as I can remember, I always wanted to help people. Some might call this need a classic case of codependency, and I would not be surprised to find some codependent elements in my life. Nevertheless, I think my call to help others goes beyond codependency. I try to be aware of my motives so that I can give without any expectation or need of return.

"My parents were and still are very good persons who enabled me to be and do the best I could. Although they were not religious zealots, we never missed Sabbath services, and they taught me and were models of values in the Jewish tradition. Even in elementary school and high school, I did considerable volunteer work and became an eagle scout. For whatever reasons, I have always chosen to give back some of what I have been given.

"In college, I majored in premed, and I joined a fraternity whose mission was to help the disadvantaged. For a time, I dropped out of formal religion, and became a secular humanist, or perhaps more accurately a reverent, agnostic Jew. In my senior year, I returned to Judaism in a renewed way. I went on to med school, specialized in emergency medicine, and met a med student whom I married.

"To say the least, we have much to be grateful for. Still, that boy who cared for others continues to live within me, and keeps me on the right path. I take one day a week to help street people, and my wife's full-time job is in a free clinic for the indigent. Furthermore, one or two times a year, we go to a poor country to offer our medical services.

"Our professional colleagues ask us why we do so much charitable work. On one level, our answer is simple: why not? We have loving children, are healthy and wealthy, can do practically anything we want, and we love each other. It is time for us to give back. You could say that this is our small way to help make a better world.

"To be sure, we have our challenges, like our youngest is autistic, yet in many ways he is our most precious gift. He keeps us living in proper perspective. Our oldest is gifted in other ways, especially intellectually. I can go on and on, but the bottom line is that life is good. We are very aware of how blessed we are.

"However, both my wife and I think it goes even deeper than that. We feel that, in a sense, we owe life, or if you like: G-d. It blows our minds just to think of the odds of simply being alive. As my older patients remind me, just to get up in the morning and start walking is such a gift. When I thank G-d, it helps me to keep perspective.

"From a spiritual perspective, we owe our life to the source of life, to G-d. The longer we live, the more my wife and I are gratefully indebted. It is as if within us there is an urge to be grateful for our gift of life.

Interestingly, we have noticed that when we give back to life, we become more alive."

Our proposal is that when we experience a spiritual connection with God, we often experience a subtle sense of indebtedness. Closely related to divine dependency, we feel and come to recognize that we owe our existence to God and others. Such a spiritual indebtedness moves us to return the gift of life primarily through love. In our God experiences, we discover a call to care that comes from and is a response to the indebtedness that resides within the core of our being. God beckons us to give back or cocreate our gift of life.

Like Dr. Jim and his wife, we become aware of being indebted in so many ways. Even if we are not nearly as fortunate as these physicians are, or even if we are destitute, we are alive. Think about it, the odds of not being born are incredibly greater than being born. We are in debt for the gift of life. Instead of taking as much as we can get, often at the expense of others, life calls us to care, to give back to life and its source, God.

Moreover, we recognize that God, parents, friends, and society have enabled us to be and to become ourselves. Without their loving acts, we could not have lived, let alone develop into persons. We have debts to pay for our many gifts, especially those from childhood and adolescence. Spiritually, our greatest gift is life and its source: God, for without God, we do not exist. When we are aware of our existential indebtedness, we want to give humble thanks for who we are and what we are given.

Think of when someone gives you "something," you are probably grateful. If the thing symbolizes the gift of another person, it makes the gift more meaningful, and you are more grateful. The best and truest gifts come from and manifest our love. Indeed, there is no greater gift than the gift of oneself in love.

My point is that when we forget our indebtedness, we forget to be grateful for and return our gifts of love and life. Our indebtedness reminds us to avoid body and ego fixations and to respond to our primary reason for being: Love. Indebtedness moves us to practice the attitude of gratitude.

We gratefully pay our existential debt to others and to God primarily by being good and loving persons. The purpose of paying this debt is not to receive a reward, for that kind of giving is business. If we should demand a return, we would make love a means of personal gratification. Even when we use love to get rewards of wholeness and holiness, we distort love and impede healthiness. Our best gift is the giving of our-selves in Love without the expectations of a return.

Once again, congruent with the mystery and paradox of spirituality, the more we give, the more we want to give, and the more we become. In this way, our indebtedness moves us to help others (as well as ourselves) realize their potential, most importantly to become good and holy people.

Some people experience their spiritual indebtedness with uneasi-ness and unrest. They feel that they are in a process of not-yetness or of always becoming, that they have more to give, do, and be. Actually, our anxious indebtedness reminds us not to forget to fulfill our destiny—to return our gift of life, to live in Love.

Along with being restless and restive, we may also experience exis-tential guilt. Unlike neurotic guilt, we feel guilty in that we are returning so little compared to what we have received and are receiving. We may feel that we are not adequately responding to God's call—to love, or that we forget or minimize our potential to follow God's way—to be one with and for one another and God. Such guilt can help us to realize our imper-fections and to strive to perfect our life of Love.

These discussions of feeling indebted, anxious, and guilty may sound negative, dismal, or burdensome. Psychologically, they may be un-healthy. Clearly, guilt and anxiety can be symptomatic of less than healthy behavior. For example, it is unhealthy to suffer the guilt of scrupulosity or the anxiety of repressed feelings. Putting a person in debt may be a form of unhealthy manipulation.

Spiritually, however, these feelings are healthy and even necessary for spiritual growth. Spiritual guilt and anxiety can motivate us to live a virtuous life that enables us to be good and become healthy. They keep us honest. In short, the restless and restive feelings of spiritual indebtedness are indigenous to holy experiences, and they move us to return love in and with Love. Reflect on what Jake has to share.

Faith-and-Doubt

"Part of me says that it's a little late in the game to start doubting what I've always believed. At 90 years old, should I be doubting the existence of God? Should I be wondering if religion and its God have been opiates to reduce anxiety and to control the masses? Are God and heaven fairy tales that we believe in order to avoid the reality that this is it, folks. Are religions and its gods, shams? Is God for the uneducated, naive, or for those who crave power? Is God simply the result of repetitious practices of religious beliefs, a projection of internal, cognitive programming?

"Before I retired from teaching, I never seriously questioned if there is a God. This may sound strange for me, a so-called scientist. Somehow, I managed to separate my personal and professional lives, and I took religion for granted. I have always gone to church, and have lived a decent life. As a university professor in the social sciences, I learned to question to seek truth, but not with religion. My religious life did not entail any conscious doubt; it was sort of a reliable place for celebrations, consolation and reflection. I did not have to think; I just believed.

"Moreover, my ministers taught me that if you really believed, you should have no doubt. When I shared my doubts with my pastor, he told me not to worry, that my doubts were the works of the devil, and to pray more. Part of me thought that he was sincerely trying to dupe me as well as himself. I do know that he did not want me to question or doubt. However, since my retirement, the ball game has changed.

"Questions about life pursue me. Part of it is the perennial question of unfairness and suffering. Why do horrendous things happen to good people, and why do some bad people seem to live more than contented lives? Why can you make children unhealthy, but you cannot make them healthy? Why did my innocent and precious wife die of excruciating cancer? Why did I outlive my children? Most people give me inadequate and inane answers. Regardless of suffering and injustice, I wonder if there really is a God, and if there is a heaven.

"A university colleague, a priest, listened to me, and responded very differently. He said that he was glad that I doubted religion and God. Initially, I was surprised, and yet relieved. Strangely, I felt a heavy burden had lifted from my shoulders, and I felt freer. I somehow felt better in and with my doubt. He said that it was good to doubt religion and God. He thought it was wise to cut through the cognitive crap of religion and come to its helpful truths. I liked his style and language. In short, my doubt could help me to deepen my faith. We talked many times, for many hours.

"This man, whom I thought would have no doubt, helped me to embrace my doubt, and challenge and deepen my religion and faith. He did not try to purge my problems, ameliorate my unrest, induce guilt, give me answers, or fix me. In fact, he encouraged me to doubt and explore my religion, faith, and God. Now, I welcome and even foster doubt, for I have come to know that, oddly enough, my doubt deepens and strengthens my faith in God. I am eternally grateful to this man who danced to different music."

Indeed, this professor emeritus has learned a wise lesson—that faith and doubt are natural dance partners. Contrary to popular opinion, faith and doubt are not mutually exclusive, but they need each other. When we separate them or see them in opposition, we impede our growth, and risk engendering unhealthy problems.

We should not feel guilty for doubt, or to try to purge it, but rather as the priest suggested, embrace it. We can see both doubt and faith as gifts that are necessary for healthy growth. Proponents of dialectical behavioral therapy would probably agree with this approach.

Like Professor Jake who lives on the threshold of death, we can come to accept, often with daunting uneasiness, that our faith needs doubt in order to develop. Doubt challenges, provokes, deepens, and strengthens faith. Doubt is the darkness that enables us to see and defend the light of faith. In short, doubt is necessary to become a healthy faith-filled person.

From our perspective, faith occurs when we accept experiences that we cannot definitively explain or control. Faith means that we accept or take in (the Latin ad-capere = to take in) experiences that include and go beyond our ego. In faith, we own up to our transrational and transcendent experiences (of love, truth, beauty, being, goodness, etc.) and "let them in" to our life. Instead of controlling and analyzing them to death, we let them come alive in us.

Faith is not fantasy wherein we deceive ourselves. Neither is faith a type of magical thinking wherein we make reality be what we do not want it to be, nor do we rationalize or justify what we do not experience. Faith is not a replacement for reason, an escape, or a *deus ex machina* when reason falls short of our questions.

To the contrary, faith is the dance partner of doubt. In faith, we embrace the liminal and transcendent (spiritual) dimension of life, while humbly admitting that we do not possess absolute certainty, or control (ego). Our spiritual life demands faith that defies and strengthens. In turn, doubt keeps us honest, and increases and fortifies our faith.

Faith is not certain or exact, but rather it is rooted in mystery and certitude. Instead of reducing our numinous experiences to rational explanations, or avoiding and forgetting them, faith means that we openly accept them. Indeed, we can rationally set the conditions that increase the likelihood of a faith experience, but faith goes beyond rational (ego) control. God's presence, or grace, beckons us to go beyond mere reason and take the leap of faith. Faith invites us to leap beyond reason into Love.

However, we are not simply people of faith, but also of reason and therefore doubt. Like ninety-year-old Jake, we will experience doubt. In fact, we can, should, and will question our beliefs and faith. Certainly, we should question our religion and its leaders, and doubt some of its tenets. Likewise, we can question the existence of God, or more concretely, God's presence. We can also be grateful to atheists and agnostics, for they help us to question, challenge, and strengthen our faith. Remember, doubt does not necessarily mean disbelief, but rather to question and thereby deepen our beliefs.

Our thesis is that such doubt is healthy and necessary to grow in faith, for it challenges the limits of our reason and deepens our faith. When people learned that the saintly Theresa of Calcutta lived with persistent religious doubt most of her life, many were bewildered. Actually, it is no surprise because this holy mother accepted doubt as a necessary part of her growth in faith. Without her doubt, she may not have grown in her extraordinary faith and have done so much good.

Actually, an absence of doubt could indicate a pious arrogance that excludes openness to and trust in the mystery of God. It could mean that we think we are self-sufficient in knowing and controlling everything. (In this regard, such a person is somewhat similar to a zealous atheist.)

Worse yet, we can manipulate people, with good intentions, to follow and serve us. So-called religious people who know it all, who have no doubt, and who have all the answers can come precariously close to playing god.

Healthy and holy persons avoid grasping God. However, we Westerners feel more secure and comfortable when we comprehend God, when we know exactly where we stand. When God is present to us, we feel secure. Yet, a stringent test of our faith is when God is beyond our comprehension, or when we are in the throes of doubt, absence, or nothingness. We have no problem when we bask in the light of faith, but we have trouble when we find ourselves in the darkness of doubt. A serious mistake is to run from the desert of doubt to the illusion of a land without doubt.

In our purest experiences of faith, doubt dissipates. Our peak experiences of God suspend and supersede doubt. (When we discuss unity, we will see how our dichotomies, like faith versus doubt, disappear or dissipate.) Later, our ego may raise its critical mind and question the sanity of our liminal experience. Again, such doubt can help us to grow in and strengthen our faith.

A ninety-seven-year-old Catholic woman, Margaret, asked as part of our conversation if there was a heaven. This woman participated in daily Mass, was active in church affairs, respected priests, and financially supported her church. More importantly, she was a good woman who practiced and went beyond her religion.

I did not react with prescribed answers, or worse, tell her that she should not think this way. Instead, I listened and encouraged her to share more. She said she felt guilty in that a woman of her age should not be questioning if heaven exists and if life on earth was the end.

I listened to this wonderful woman with awe and respect. I encouraged her to express and share her thoughts and feelings. After she finished her story, I told her that it was okay and good to wonder about heaven and such things. I also told her that I had similar questions, and I came to believe that there is a heaven and that it would be better than our best dreams. We sat still and silent, and smiled.

Like Margaret and Jake, to some degree and at some times we doubt what people have taught us to believe. With faith-and-doubt, we can eventually come to accept that our spiritual experiences of God and people are rhythms of light and darkness, faith and doubt, consolation and desolation. Faith without doubt and doubt without faith are static and inauthentic. Both are prescriptions for self-deception.

Doubt pressures us to maintain and grow in our faith, and faith helps us to keep perspective when we are in the darkness of doubt. On earth, we doubt God in order to believe, and our faith enables us to accept and benefit from our doubt. Doubt-and-faith is questioning and accepting in and with Love.

Thus, God draws closer and closer to and in us through the ongoing rhythm of faith-and-doubt. Religions tell us that eventually and ultimately, we will live in faith with no doubt. Meanwhile, we get glimpses of this heavenly bliss. We, too, can be still and silent, and smile.

Immanent Transcendence

Diana gives us another view of God experiences. "I would hesitate to tell a psychiatrist this, but let me give you some idea of what happens. One way to describe it is that I experience reality differently than I usually do.

I am intensely aware that I am a part of a greater whole. It is as if I am more than I am. I told you it might sound crazy.

"On the one hand, I feel very humble to be such a small part of this whole. It can be overwhelming, or simply calmly soothing. On the other hand, I feel greater than usual in that I feel that the whole is in me, or I am in it. It is almost as if I am the whole of reality. Philosophically, I suppose, it is as if my being is Being. From my Yoga, Hindu perspective, perhaps my ego loses and finds itself in the universal Self.

"Let me try to explain it another way. When I enter my class to teach, I don't see the students as separate from me or out there at a distance from me. Indeed, I can perceive them as them, people whom I lecture. I also experience the students and me as integral and interactive members of a common reality. Instead of distance, there is a kind of distant intimacy. I see myself as part of them, and they as a part of me. I find myself in this interactive whole.

"When I pause in class or in any situation, I can sense a presence that bonds us together. It is like an energy that is within and between us, and it connects us as one. I not only sense this power within me but also in others; it is a power that we share. When I am in tune with this experience, I feel a power that is greater than and yet a part of me. I experience that we are brothers and sisters, or variations of the same human kind. I feel a respectful intimacy with others.

"I also experience this sense of interrelatedness in solitude. When I am away from my everyday activities, and I sit in silence, I sense a reality that supports and empowers me. Although I am physically alone, I feel that I am not alone. There is something or someone present to and in me. Somehow, I feel, there is more to reality than just others and me. Thus, I know that I am never alone. In a very real way, this gives me more meaning or purpose. For lack of a better word, I call this reality, God.

"I experience this intimacy most intensely when my beloved and I are making love. When we are naked, not just physically, and we lose ourselves in each other, I sense a reality that makes us one. When we share ourselves, body and spirit, I feel that there is more to life than is ordinarily experienced. Our love gives us purpose and direction, and we feel most ourselves. As trite as it may sound, in love life makes sense, and, for me, this is what life is ultimately about."

We can say that Diana experienced transcendence as her most immanent way of being. She experienced a reality that is part of and beyond her and others, which we call reality's divine dimension, or God. She came to know a Presence who is part of and beyond her.

In chapter 2, we saw that transcendence does not mean that we go out of this world or repress problems, but rather we perceive a truer and healthier reality. Like Diana, we see "more than" the ordinary world of the body and ego. Our extraordinary perception uncovers a more fundamental unity underlying our differences and similarities, and our troubles and joys. This liminal experience involves a vision that goes beyond and yet inspires our body and ego functions.

Many people call the sustaining source of this "more than" reality, God (of their understanding). In this so-called divine transcendence, we experience God as more than us and as our most immanent and intimate dimension of being together and alone. Paradoxically, this is what and who we are—transcendent, immanent, and communal.

Listen to Mario. "It is very difficult to put into words, but I know that it makes all the difference in the world. Actually, it is like going into a different world, or I perceive reality differently. I feel a certain kinship with others, even when I simply walk pass people. Somehow, I sense that we are all threads of the same human fabric. Although I do not know these people, I feel a kind of intimacy with them.

"Sometimes when I am alone, I also sense a presence so that I am not alone. Especially when I am still and silent, it is as if there is a beckoning, a restless that invites me to rest. I experience an emptiness that calls for fulfillment. There is a subtle promise that there is more to life than this life on earth. It may sound like gobbledygook, but with or without people, I feel that I am more than I am.

"I do know that when I connect with this connectedness, I can cope better. It is as if I have a powerful resource within me so that, in a sense, I act as we, and not simply me. When up against a difficult situation or person, I would prefer a change, but I don't need it to change to be okay. Whatever happens, I maintain my serenity and freedom because they come from within me, and no one can mess with that."

We can say that Mario "goes beyond" the conventional (body and ego) to move deeper into (spiritual) reality. When his ego bonds with his spirit, he can cope more freely and effectively. Unlike a child, his well-being does not depend primarily on others or situations, but it comes from his inner bonding with his God.

Like Mario and Diana, we can draw on a resource that is part of and beyond us. We can experience our being together as well as its sustaining and empowering source. This "transcendent liminality" enables us to see the extraordinary in the ordinary, which helps us to cope more effectively. Indeed, this divine presence significantly affects our decisions and behaviors.

Since we know that we are interrelated with one another and with God, we know that what we do affects others, including our relationship with God. In our framework, when we draw on our Greater Power (Love/God), we are empowered to cope more efficiently and effectively. Our Spirit/Love strengthens our ego so that we are freer and stronger to promote peace and justice, if for no other reason that it works better.

Another advantage of divine and imminent transcendence is that we achieve a certain freedom from our limits. Being present to an Unlimited God helps us to accept, cope with, and learn from rather than reject, combat, or fixate on our limits and difficulties. Our Higher Power empowers us to accept and manage what we cannot change or control.

For example, our connection with God (Love, inner Spirit, Higher Power, etc.) can empower us to cope effectively and maintain our serenity in the midst of difficulties. When someone pushes our buttons, instead of reacting defensively, we can connect with Love and respond openly and effectively. Ultimately, drawing on our unlimited source of life helps us to accept and grow from our universal limits—dying and death.

It is important to emphasize that this divine presence not only is greater than and beyond us, but also among, within, and part of us. Thus, no one can take from us our divine power. In short, regardless of what is happening, we can connect with God who ensures our overall well-being.

This power of holy transcendence is not a function of ego control, but rather depends on a simple, spiritual presence with and for God. Thus, a person who is not very educated, rich, and successful and who has little social status and power may be healthier and holier (a better person) that a highly educated, esteemed, rich, and powerful person.

As with Diana and Mario, experiences of God also urge us to go deeper within ourselves, bringing us closer to ourselves and to one another. In Love, we are most intimately ourselves as well as integral members of a universal community with the same source and purpose. When we are intimate with God, we are close to others and ourselves as well. In short, divine transcendence is our preeminent immanent and communal experience.

Christians might say that they construe and experience God as three persons, all of whom manifest the same triune God in different and interrelated ways. They contend that these divine personas (from the Latin: persona, to sound through) offer us the paramount way, life, and truth. Our Sustaining Creator is the transcendent God. Jesus Christ is the incarnated God whom we see and hear in community, and the Holy Spirit is the imminent God who dwells within and among us.

In summary, we experience God as transcendent, communal, and immanent. All three manifestations or personas of God convey important lessons about God and about ourselves as well as enable us to be holy and healthy. Another woman, Terry, has this to say about her search for the Holy.

Holiness

"I guess you could say that I was addicted to 'more.' No matter what it was, it seems that it was never enough. After getting a couple of graduate degrees in business at top rated schools, I joined a large investment firm. As they say, I became a resident of Wall Street, and I forgot my Main Street background. I became one of those filthy rich people whom you may hate. Believe me; it was not easy for a woman to succeed in a man's world. However, I was not as fortunate as you may think.

"I made large piles of money. It seems that the richer I became, the more I wanted. It was like a contest of who could make the most. Of course, with extreme affluence comes extreme opulence and power. Everything I ever dreamed about or wanted as an adolescent and young adult, I could get, and I got it.

"Everything was first class and then some. The so-called best transportation, villas, meals, clothes, jewelry, cars, yachts, adult toys, wine, men, and on and on were obscenely costly. My mom and dad are probably turning over in their graves with shame. My dad had to work a year in the mills to earn what I could easily spend in a week. Most people would say that I came a long way, and they probably envied me. Actually, people should have pitied me.

"As time passed, I began to use cocaine and drink heavily, and consequently got increasingly weary running on this bipolar track. Eventually, I lost my edge in the business world, so that I was not making nearly as much money. People started to talk, and I got scared. Because my life was falling apart, and nothing seemed to be working, I had to do something different. I was losing my grip on life. Out of fear and shame, I secretly checked myself into a rehab. You could say that this was the turning point in my life.

"I came to admit the obvious—that the enormous amount of power and possessions that I had accrued did not make me feel and be better. I had no genuine friends, my two marriages ended in horrible divorces, and probably fortunately but sadly, I have no children. Now, I am a single and not so free woman. Moreover, I used and abused many people to achieve my so-called success. In middle age, I ended up a lonely, empty, and discontent woman without much dignity and integrity. Suicide was tempting.

"In my early adult years, I fell out of the religion that my parents taught me, and I no longer believed in God. Yet now, I found myself desiring more than what I pursued my entire adult life. I needed something to make sense out of my chaotic life, because power, possessions, and pleasure simply did not do it. My mom and dad had a very small fraction of my possessions, and yet they were infinitely happier. Maybe, I thought, they knew something that I did not know.

"Anyhow, I came to realize that my successes were illusions. I admitted that I followed false promises of fulfillment. There had to be more to life. It is humbling to say that what I learned in Sunday school was true— that I worshipped false gods, or believed in a lie. I came to realize that these outside pursuits did not fulfill my insides. After fifty plus years and with menopause, nothing worked. I had to do something differently, for the life I had lived simply did not work. I had everything I ever wanted, and ended with nothing.

"After my rehabilitation, I took a year off from work to find a better way, one that worked. In my sabbatical from the world, this so-called higher power kept emerging, albeit in various ways and with various names. Maybe, this God was worth giving a shot. Clearly, my other gods failed me.

"After listening to some people who took a radically different path than I, and after pausing to experience life's free treasures, I eventually came to follow a reality that was more inside than outside me. Instead of honoring the illusions of wealth, I came to honor a God of my understanding. Unbelievably, the path that I am on is working. I finally experience true serenity and freedom as well as lasting meaning and purpose. Indeed, happiness is an inside job. Now, I think, my mom and dad are smiling."

All of us operate according to a hierarchy of values, and each of us has a paramount concern—that standard, person, activity, or object which we value most, and consequently permeates all our behavior. For Terry, it was money, power, possessions, and pleasure. These pursuits (that many covet) were her central motives and values. Eventually, she turned to and centered her life on God, or Love, which worked much better.

In our context, holiness refers to our ultimate concern, or what or whom we most revere, respect, worship, love, and base our life on. A major tenet is that since God/Love, is our sustaining source, destiny, and reason for being, only Love/God, is (and must be) our paramount or holy concern. Only God and the manifestations of God are holy or sacred. As Terry testified, displacements of God do not work. However, when we live a life of Love, we are holy, and that works significantly better than anything else.

Like Terry, when we make the functions and fruits of the body and ego our ultimate concern, we pursue an illusion of happiness. When we value ego power and success and bodily pleasure and possessions at the expense of spiritual serenity and freedom, we will miss the paramount meaning of life—intimacy with self, others, and God. When we displace our spiritual activities with physical and functional ones, we become lost and empty.

Remember that since we have and are a desire for God (as well as to self and others), we must fulfill our divine desire with God. Only God is an adequate response to our desire for God. Thus, when our ultimate concern is not God, we displace God with some other reality. We can also argue that since God is our sustaining source and destiny, it follows that when we displace God, we displace ourselves. Thus, we are neither holy nor healthy.

Only God is ultimate, sacred, or holy, not pleasure, power, and possessions. In this way, holiness differentiates experiences not only from those of our body and ego but also from other spiritual experiences (such as philosophical wonder, transcendental meditation, and esthetic experiences). In other words, holiness comes from and is unique to our experiences of God.

When the center of our life is love for and from self, God, and others, a holy disposition will permeate all our activities. Our ideal is to manifest God's presence in all our activities—those of our body, ego, and spirit.

While maintaining our sphere of interest—work, study, play, etc.—our holy disposition is present.

Such a holy lifestyle is not unrealistic or unattainable. Think about it. Our paramount value and motivation influences whatever we think and do, no matter what this motivation may be. For instance, if we center our life on work accomplishments, our work ethic will more than less influence all facets of our life. If lust is our core value, lust will permeate our thoughts, feelings and behaviors. When God is the central motivation in our lives, holiness (God) permeates our lives.

Furthermore, our holy experiences of God are interpersonal. This simply means that God and we interact. As we have discussed, we desire God, and God beckons us. Know that God's response is seldom in the language of our ego, but rather in spiritual presence and absence. In our best moments, we go beyond the constrictions of words to a pure presence in Love. Indeed, we can be wonderfully mindless and speechless.

This is not so strange, for essentially the same process occurs with being in love. When a couple intimately and purely love each other, their presence goes beyond words. They rest peacefully in each other's love. They can abide naked in Love, or in the presence of God. Indeed, silence and stillness are more likely their language. In a similar and related way, God and we relate in liminal presence and beckoning absence.

Being uncreated and inexhaustible, God's love is also permanent and unconditional. God/Love is always there for us, without strings attached, like those of perfectionism. In fact, if we were perfect, we would not need love, for we would be in a state of perfect Love—in heaven. Love is for imperfect—lost, lonely, scared, depressed, broken, sinful—people. We can rely on and be grateful for God who embraces and heals our mistaken, bad, and sick selves.

Another consequence of living in, with, and through God, or of being holy, is that we engage others to be people of God. We not only manifest Love, but also evoke the Spirit who abides within others. We not only bring God to others, but more basically appeal to God who already dwells within them, whoever they are—atheists, agnostics, periodic believers, believers, sinners, sick, immature, weird—us. When we live in Love, we are inspired and inspire. We offer life/breath. Our charisma is to be people of God, or sanctuaries and ambassadors of Love.

We can also contact God intellectually. Although theology is primarily an indirect presence to God, it is a way (albeit terribly limited) of knowing God. However, if our theological reflections are not rooted in and in service of our pre-reflective experience, they become lifeless, abstract, and irrelevant.

In short, any "-logy," theory, or religion comes from and is in service of experience. Religion and theology are constructions of our minds that should help and not hinder us to experience God. In turn, religious homilies should not be words that appeal primarily to our minds, but rather to our hearts as well as help us to live better lives.

We can also be with God through spiritual experiences that do not incorporate God as clearly and directly as holy experiences. For instance, we can have an experience of philosophical wonder wherein we see and think in the light of Truth. Our experience of the mystery and transcendence of Truth can promote openness, growth, and fulfillment. However, since such involvement is primarily in Truth and not primarily in (but not exclusive of) God, sacred love or prayer is usually not an explicit issue.

Likewise, our experience of Beauty can involve transcendence, harmony, paradox, and mystery. Still, our aesthetic experiences (of nature and the fine and performing arts) may not be overtly holy because we do not focus on sacred love, worship, and grace. Nevertheless, our aesthetic and philosophical experiences are holy or include God at least implicitly if not explicitly. Moreover, beauty and wonder can lead us to or serve as springboards to God. Since they are to some degree spiritual experiences, they implicitly incorporate and can generate explicit experiences of God.

Truth and Beauty can serve to foster and embody holy experiences. For instance, it makes sense that places of worship usually have considerable artwork for its artistic and inspirational value. To that end, it may behoove us to experience fine and performing arts as well as natural beauty. They can be ways of connecting with and nurturing our relationship with God.

Although love is our most direct and intimate way to God, we can experience God anywhere and anytime—in and through nature, things, animals, dreams, thoughts, feelings, actions, etc. The intent is not to imply a pantheistic philosophy, but only to state that God is not limited to certain places and times.

In this sense, our approach is panentheistic in that God is present everywhere. Everyone and everything in the universe are reminders, symbols, and manifestations of God. Thus, let us give thanks and celebrate our truth and beauty in God.

A primary thesis is that love is our paramount and most personal way to encounter God. Being in Love, or in God, is holiness. In love, we respond with concern and care for the sake of God, others, and self. Paradoxically, coming from Love enables and encourages us to love. Our vocation is to Love. Let us journey, and consider some of the ways we love God, how we worship and pray, and what practical differences they make.

Worship and Prayer

"I remember when I was a little boy; my 'baba' would take me to church before Mass so she could join the other ladies to say the rosary. These ancient, at least to me, women with their babushkas and head and shoulders bowed in worship would repeat Hail Mary's and Our Father's in a mesmerizing, Slovak cadence. It was hypnotic and fascinating. I can still hear them.

"Later, in my 'enlightened,' college days and after earning a PhD in sociology, I pitied these women whom I judged to have naively indulged in superstition. They failed the tests of rational analysis and empirical measurement. I might add that these women and some men included my mother who followed the path of her mother. It is not easy, at any age, to criticize your mother, particularly in areas that were so important to her.

"Nevertheless, I agreed with Freud that if such mindless, rote behavior helped people feel secure and keep them out of trouble, well, good for them. However, such unenlightened nonsense was not for me. Please spare me rosaries, devotions, novenas, litanies, incense, candles, rote worship, superstitious liturgy, useless sermons, clericalism, opulent bishops, duplicitous and pedophile priests, etc. Open the windows and let that premodern, feudal stuff vacate my house.

"However, after many years of ageing and hopefully some wisdom, I revisited the practices of my baba and her friends. From a purely rational perspective, I could construe these religious practices as ritualistic behaviors that brought comfort, solidarity, and hope. Even if they were illusions and collusions, they were better than addictions and other dependent behaviors. At least, I was trying to be understanding and kind.

"I did not stop there. Perhaps, I wondered, there is more to what meets the empirical eye. There was something in me that would not let me settle peacefully with reason alone. I began to study the empirical research on spirituality and health, and I read many of the classic and contemporary works on spirituality and God. Among many things, I discovered that Christians and non-Christians practiced many of the ways of my baba.

"More importantly, maybe my mother and baba knew something that I did not. Could these uneducated, unsophisticated women teach this highly educated, sophisticated professor? Maybe they were not loving, kind, old fools. Maybe I could learn something from them. As crazy as it sounded, I thought I would take a leap in faith. To paraphrase 12-step parlance, I would fake it to see if I could make it. So I returned to my childhood with an adult's mind and a child's heart.

"With persistence and patience, I discovered that these repetitive behaviors became mantras that cleared my mind for deeper and lasting truths. Moreover, I integrated my prayers with my practices of Yoga and Tai Chi. I eventually came to realize and appreciate a reality that somehow was part of me and yet infinitely greater than I. I found myself freely bowing to and being grateful for this reality, that I eventually, for lack of a better word, came to call God.

"No longer did I feel that I was the center of the universe, or that I, learned Paul, was the paramount source of truth. Strangely enough, this insight was a tremendous relief that brought incredible strength and serenity. I actually began to live a life of worship in that I tried to give homage to a Reality that is greater than and related to me. I (including my mother and baba) am not a slave to superstition, a disciple of illusion, or a supporter of religious collusion. Life is simply freer and better with God. I now smile with gratitude for my mother's and grandmother's wise ways that went beyond mere reason."

It is not surprising that Paul took a circuitous route to find worship. It often seems that the more educated and enlightened we become, the less need we have for worship. It logically follows that if we assume that men and women are the primary sources of truth, we have no need for a greater truth, way, or light. We can heal, be healthy, make sense, and live on our own without a Higher Power. Thus, worship makes little logical sense.

However, if we follow the lead of Paul and go beyond our rational (and arrogant) minds we may experience a reality that calls for worship. We no longer see ourselves as the greatest form of being. Contrary to Freudian, Marxist, and other rationalistic approaches, we refuse to reduce life to what we can rationally grasp or explain. Such a leap in faith changes our lives.

Worship, another constituent of God experiences, points to the ways in which we respect, honor, revere, celebrate, receive, and give to God. Although indebtedness, anxiety, and guilt can move us to worship, our primary aim is not to pay our debt, to relieve our guilt, or to get rewards. Neither is our worship one of a lower subject looking up to a higher subject. Nor should we worship a judgmental or vindictive god, or compulsively submit our will to God. Rather, we freely choose to worship God because we are grateful to and love God.

Many books have been written about the many forms of worship, such as formal and informal, verbal and nonverbal, private and public, and reflective and pre-reflective worship. For instance, we can learn meaningful forms of public worship that have an advantage of incorporating a communal aspect. Indeed, religious worship sites should offer us various forms of individual and communal worship.

Our challenge is to foster a constant and conscious contact with God, to be mindful of God's presence always and everywhere. As we have shown, we can see God's presence in nature and art, hear God in words and music, touch God in a beloved, and respond to God in others. In sincere pursuit of the spiritual life, we can always bow to the Presence in you and me where we are one.

When we worship, we pray, and when we pray, we worship. In short, worship and prayer are two sides of the same reality. One needs, implies, and is related to the other. Worship affirms our radical dependence on God, and prayer deals with specific ways we choose to connect with our Higher Power.

Since our paramount connection with God (and anyone) is love, we construe prayer to be our love for and from God. Prayer involves listening and responding to our Holy Spirit's appeal to love. Prayer also involves our call to God to be with and for us. In short, prayer is being in and with Love, or God.

Perhaps the most important way to pray is to love. For instance, lovers experience, usually unconsciously, God in their love. Their love gives them a glimpse of and a feel for eternally being in Love, or in heaven. Their experience moves them to desire and deepen their love. If their love wanes, they feel empty, lost, or incomplete. Conversely, the more in Love they are, the more they become manifestations of God, of Love. They feel and are more alive, with evolving purpose and meaning.

We can also pray and worship God in a group. Our ideal is that we congregate and form a union with one another, and as a loving community, we present ourselves in, to, and for God. Liturgies, sacraments, communal prayers and interactions, and proclamations of God's word can be seen as public opportunities for grace—God's gift of love.

Moreover, we can and should pray in solitude. For instance, we may purposely withdraw from our everyday world to be alone with God. We may be in the woods, by the sea, in a house of worship, or anywhere. In solitude, we are in a mode of simplicity. Minimizing distractions, peace, quiet, and stillness enable us to be available to God. In the serene and simple situation of solitude, we intend to experience God.

Contemplation is the zenith of prayer. In contemplative prayer, we are purely present to, with, and in God. We transcend thinking (ego) and even words to simply being-with (spirit) God. Absent of (ego) mediations, we are immediately with God. In short, contemplation is being and seeing in Love.

Contemplation may not be as difficult or beyond us as we may think. Remember, for example, when you were simply one with your beloved (or with nature, music, art, truth, being). Thoughts and perhaps words were absent because they detracted from your experience. In fact, when you did begin to think, you began to lose the experience. In still silence, you were purely present to each other.

Such sacred times make a significant difference in your life. They endure so that you seldom forget them, and they remember you. Contemplation is to experience God in your beloved, to hear God in music, to see God in art and nature, and to do nothing but be with God. In short, contemplation of God and God's gifts are sacred times that influence and direct our lives in holy and healthy ways.

A caveat is that we can emphasize individual prayer at the expense of communal worship. Our culture of individualism can seduce us into thinking that we are self-sufficient or isolated egos. Remember, we are radically interrelated in the community of humankind. To pray and worship only and always by oneself is foolish, for it fails to benefit from our communal resources.

Psychologically, our love of God also depends on our personal and cultural state of development. For example, primitive people's dependent and simple involvement with nature will influence their love of God, and in this sense, it may be similar to a child's experience.

Likewise, our highly rational culture is likely to influence our understanding and experience of God so that we grasp, figure out, and even try to control God. Too often, religious ministers feel compelled to have all the answers or "to know it all," and fail to be humble enough to say, "I don't know." Clearly, our individual psychology as well as formal and informal education influences our views of and experiences of God.

In short, our prayer life takes many forms. Rather than fixating on one mode of expression, our challenge is to develop various forms of this divine connection so that we continue to grow in God. Some people know the fruit of prayer with others, and others pray more in solitude. Others see their whole life as a prayer when ultimately oriented to God. Still others sing and dance to God's silent music. A few try to do nothing but see and be with God. To be holy and healthy, all of us can and should honor and celebrate the God who dwells beyond, within, and among us.

Clearly, prayer and worship engender healthy consequences. They ground us in our inner and outer community of Love, giving us enduring purpose and meaning. We have and live our reason for being. These resources help us to cope better, to accept what we cannot control, and to live more serenely. As empirical studies indicate, we live better and longer than people who do not live a God-centered life in community.

Thus, it makes sound clinical sense to foster a spiritual relationship with God. When we root our lives in and in service of Love, we are empowered, and consequently can cope better. Such a spiritual life is not a cure for mental illness or a panacea for anything, but it significantly helps us to manage our problems, and improves the quality of our lives whether they are healthy or unhealthy. It pays to practice a holy life.

Unity

We are seeing that we can experience God in many ways so that we stand differently on the same ground. Listen to Mary's way to God. "If I were forced to describe, let alone explain, my experiences of God, I think I would focus on my experience of oneness. I feel one with myself in that there is no conflict, disharmony, or anything out of synch. I feel a quiet and serene stillness, as if everything is okay. It is somewhere I would like to be all the time.

"Let me be clear, my experience goes far beyond just me in that I feel that I am one with all that there is. Somehow, I not only connect with but am also part of the universe—and, beyond. Maybe that beyond is God; I do not know. I do know that I experience a personal presence that or who is in and beyond the world where I normally live. I know that this sounds clumsy. Still, it is real.

"Furthermore, along with peace and harmony, I feel clarity of vision and an inner strength. It is as if I know that everything will make sense and work out. Although I know that I am vulnerable, I feel fearless. I know that this absurd life ultimately makes sense, that eventually I will rest in peace, and that everything and everyone will come together in harmony. Maybe this is just wish fulfillment, and maybe it is true. I know that it is real for me, and that it makes a significant difference in my life.

"Sometimes I get moments of this kind of experience in church. I really experience community, that all of us are integral members of the same body. Along with experiencing everyone as my brothers and sisters, I am also aware of a Presence who is with us. It is as if this Presence is in each of us and holds us together. Again, there is a sense of safety, peace, and hope in being aware of this Presence. Call this Presence what you want; I call it God.

"I don't know of anything better or more important than being one with God, self, and others. When I can remember this experience, I am always better off. In other words, when I do not forget that others and I are parts of the same reality and that a God is our common source and security, life is infinitely better. In the best and worst of times, I can draw on this blessed unity, knowing that it makes all the difference in the world. It is consoling to know that no one can take this experience from me."

Perhaps you can resonate with or get a feel for Mary's words. She describes another quality of God experiences, namely: a sacred unity with God, self, others, and reality in general. As she points out, such experiences make all the difference in the world. Moreover, practically all mystical writers describe our desire for, journey toward, and experience of sacred Oneness, as well as the significance of such experiences.

In our best prayers or encounters with God, we experience a deep and intimate unity with God and others. We feel close to, in harmony with, and one with God and others. In this holy communion, we lose ourselves and yet we feel most ourselves. Indeed, it is true that we find our truest selves by giving ourselves to others and God. We have seen that it is good and enjoyable to be in this paradoxical and sacred Presence.

We also experience unity within ourselves, for when we encounter God, the various parts of ourselves move toward a harmonious whole. We grow in integrity—a sacred wholeness. Moreover, we feel more congruent with our experiences even when we are at odds with ourselves.

Our problems become more tolerable, and they have less of a negative impact on our lives. Even when our lives are fraught with problems, unfairness, or simply tough times, an inner peace and consolation resides within the core of our being.

We can see the relevance to mental health. For instance, living in the presence of Love gives us security to accept what we cannot change. Our well-being does not depend primarily on any one person, but primarily our inner community of love—love for and from God, self, and others who are in the core of our being. On this basis, we have the strength and freedom to cope with stress, achieve goals, and to nurture our interior lives.

Thus, it makes good sense that mental health providers and religious ministers encourage their clients and parishioners to foster God and other spiritual experiences. However, too often, health providers and pastors separate the spiritual and especially God and religion from health. As we have already stated, health providers respond to God issues when the client brings up the topic, but they rarely encourage spiritual-God practices in their therapy. Moreover, many religious ministers separate the psychological and God, as if God has no impact on one's mental health.

Once again, we are not saying that God practices are a panacea for personal problems, but simply that God should have an essential role in treatment. Health assessments, for instance, typically include valid topics like the client's affective status, cognitive sets, coping skills, interpersonal relationships, and healthy and unhealthy behaviors. Although religious affiliation may be included, one's relationship with God or spiritual practices is rarely included. Clearly, 12-step programs give evidence that God or a Higher Power has significant influence on mental health.

The world of uncreated and cocreating Love (God) is a world of intimate unity and serenity, not a world of painful alienation and disharmony. Remember, these energies of Love that are within (and beyond) us are available resources. They offer us a respite where we can rest, heal, and renew ourselves. In the midst of turmoil, we can connect with Love and find solace and serenity. Surely, this is relevant to mental health.

In our holy communion, we feel more at home with life. As Mary describes, we feel an intimate connection with people, experiencing them as our brothers and sisters. Like her, we can experience a Presence that dwells within and among us—rooted in and standing on a common ground that/who unities us. We find ourselves being one in our Spirit.

We come to experience ourselves as part of the original whole (the integer) of reality, where everyone and everything harmoniously interrelate. We are less likely to feel at odds with reality, and more likely to feel one with life. Rather than acting as if we are primarily individuals (ego) who separate from one another, our challenge is to listen to and act on our radical call to be together as one in Love (Spirit). To repeat, our divine connection strengthens us to cope effectively as well as give us enduring meaning.

However, when God is more absent than present, we may feel a disconnection or "holy tension." We may feel anxious rather than serene, depressed rather than joyful, disruption rather than harmony, and fear and trembling rather than the solace and serenity. Unity and oneness feel present in their absence. Still, their absence implies and seeks their presence.

We will show in the next chapter that this "holy tension" is a result of growth in divine Love rather than a result of unhealthy problems. We will see that absence, powerlessness, anxiety, and loneliness are desires for and can lead to a fuller presence, strength, serenity, and love. Instead of construing and treating such experiences as negative or unhealthy, we can see and respond to them as positive and in service of health.

To let go (of ego) and let God (Spirit) is more than a pious mantra, but is an efficacious practice that leads to consolation and empowerment—and, helps us with our mental health. To that end, let us reflect on the words of Saul who talks about the difference that God has made in his life.

Consequent Positive Changes

"I hesitate to say that I was born again, for, to me, that implies that I am some kind of a religious zealot. Understand, I have nothing against such born again people. In fact, I admire their commitment, but I am not one of them. Nevertheless, I have found new life since I have found God.

"Before my so-called conversion, I led a very active, successful, and full life, yet I was always restless. In college and graduate school, I had sex so often that I lost count, and I drank, but never quite crossed the alcoholic line. With the exception of some pot, I stayed away from hard drugs, thank God. I continued this lifestyle, while becoming successful and wealthy in my profession. In short, I had lots of fun, and probably people admired or envied me.

"Well, the ball game changed when I was in my early forties. Although I was in good physical shape, I had a heart attack, and I came close to dying. During my long recuperation, I began to look at my life differently. I was a single man with few obligations, was wealthy and successful, had frequent sex, travelled, and could do what I wanted. Some people would say that I had it made. I possessed more than I ever dreamed of, and yet I felt empty.

"I wondered if I wanted to live the second half of my life (if I were so fortunate) like the first half. No was my answer. I came to realize that on my deathbed, I wanted to make a significant difference in some people's lives. I wanted people to miss me for being a good person, not for what I had or accomplished. When you stripped me of my money, status, power, and sex, would I really matter?

"While in rehabilitation, I met an incredible attendant who was infinitely wiser, intelligent, and happier than I. She made a small fraction of the money that I made, and her job was humble, yet she was passionate and fulfilled. She was down to earth, streetwise, and full of life. Later, she told me that she was a recovering prostitute and drug addict. This loser, according to the world's standards, saved my life.

"This maverick of a woman introduced me to 12-step literature as well as various spiritual writers from the past and the present. In short, I began to explore my inner world. I began to pursue why I was here on earth. I know my successful life did not give me purpose and meaning to living. Slowly, I came out of my dark night to see in a more enlightened way.

"Eventually, I found a God of my understanding. Indeed, this was a radical change for me, for I seldom gave God a thought. I came out of my self-sufficiency to surrender to a power greater than I. If someone had told me in my thirties that I would find God, I would call them crazy.

"Yes, I go to church, often during the week. I attend church services, and I just sit in church, because it helps my spiritual life and my relationship with God and others. However, I am not dedicated to religion, but rather committed to God and the ways of God. I no longer depend on wealth, power, sex, status, or whatever exterior activities.

"Now I am more concerned with my interior life and interpersonal relationships. I know I am on a better road than I was. I am happier than I have ever been. I am at peace, have direction, am more secure and strong, and actually freer.

"I don't know if I'll ever get married; I do know that I am open to it. Thank God, I didn't get married in the past. Now, I think I am ready. Whatever happens, I know that I will be vigilant in running a good race, one that manifests virtue and centers on and in love. Now, when I die, I will be able to say yes to and thanks for life."

As Saul indicates, when we follow the way of God, we live an interior, interpersonal, and virtuous life. When we live a God-centered life, we live differently than when we do not center our life on God. A repeated theme has been that when we displace the spiritual life with relatively non-spiritual activities (pleasure, power, possessions, or whatever of the body and ego), we displace our Spirit and become displaced, or lack spirit. Our life and death are not very good, and people forget rather than remember us with fond gratitude.

How and why we live has consequences. If we center our lives on power, sex, possessions, or whatever, we will manifest a syndrome, that is, signs and symptoms of our lifestyle. Likewise, when we center our lives on the ways of our Spirit, we manifest a syndrome of holiness or of a good life. Clearly, there are consequences to how and why we live. In other words, our holy experiences do not remain in a vacuum; rather, they promote attitudinal and behavioral changes.

As we have seen, holy experiences influence all of our experiences in that they are good and virtuous, for they manifest God who is the sustaining source of goodness. For example, our work will incorporate holy meaning. Play becomes a dance in Love. Thinking is thoughtful and open to the inspiration of the Spirit. Feelings are gentle, respectful, and graceful. Day-to-day behavior manifests a spirit of holiness. Simply stated, our whole being is infinitely better when we live a life of our Spirit. Let us look more specifically at some of the qualities and consequences of living a life in and of Love/God.

The paramount mark of a holy person is Love. When we are holy, we manifest Love, so that people will see and hear the ways of God in us. We grow imperfectly in the perfection of Love, and consequently we see, hear, respond to, and manifest a God who beckons us to be one. Our core concern is to foster community—the unity of self-God-others.

Love centralizes and influences all our values. Since all our activities are in service of Love, we realize the importance of taking time to be with God, or to be in Love. We are careful not to forget or displace God;

we remember to foster our radical reason for living—Love. Indeed, we structure life so that we live our archetypical vocation—to live in and manifest Love.

If we are holy persons, people tend to feel at home with us. They can trust us, for we offer Love in terms of an invitation, not of a forceful demand. We accept, affirm, and appreciate who and what others are as well as who and what they can be. We respect people by giving them room to be and become. We avoid being self-righteous, judgmental, manipulative, or religiously arrogant (egoism). We shun playing god, and humbly try to manifest God.

Healthy people often cultivate an appreciation of beauty. Think of beauty as a harmony of the spirit, ego, and body with the spiritual being its main dynamic force. For example, from our perspective, when you enjoy a symphony, you experience a transcendent joy and sorrow (spirit) and intense and mild feelings (body) within the context of the musical technique and form (ego). From this perspective, beauty (whatever kind) manifests wholeness, or health. Thus, beauty affirms and invites us to enjoy health.

Likewise, our experience of beauty in nature and in the fine arts manifests the harmony of matter (body), form (ego), and meaning (spirit). In this light, it makes good sense that places of sacred worship usually include artwork, such as stained glass, paintings, and music. In short, certain places and events evoke the spiritual more than others do. Indeed, healthy people seek places and times to enjoy beauty, whether it is in the fine and performing arts, in nature, at home, in the woods, at the beach, in the city, in play, in love, in one another, etc.

Beauty in whatever form evokes, affirms, and celebrates our wholeness. For instance, along with the arts and nature, healthy people, regardless of their physicality, are beautiful because they manifest wholeness. Their spirit welcomes others in peace, invites them to be whole, and appeals to and evokes the beauty in others. With this vision, the wrinkled, seasoned hand of a ninety-year-old is probably more beautiful than a twenty-year-old person's smooth, youthful hand.

However, our mass media frequently present images and role models that are far from beautiful. The lack of civility and good manners, the overemphasis on functional success, the adulation of youth, sex without love, and cybersex are just a few examples of a fragmented or less than whole approach to life. Without knowing it, we can program ourselves to be less than beautiful, and consequently forget our spirit and health.

Play is another experience that can offer easy and safe access to the spiritual. Think about it. A significant factor in play is that it liberates and enables us to be at ease. We usually experience a freedom to be ourselves with a minimum risk of being hurt. Clearly, play differs from our customary activity. We take time out from our everyday and work worlds to re-create and play.

Furthermore, play is ordinarily an interpersonal relationship. (Even when we play by ourselves, another is usually present in our imagination.) In good play, we are usually equal. We put aside our differences, our inequalities, our superiorities, our inferiorities. We come together on a level playing field where we are all brothers and sisters. Play invites and enables us to have fun in community. In its relatively safe confines, play invites us to express and celebrate our being alive. Without knowing it, play proclaims our Spirit.

Thus, healthy people structure their lives so that they consistently engage in everyday love, beauty, and play. When we fail to see more than the physical and functional, we diminish ourselves so that we are less than whole or healthy. When we live a spirit-less life, we lack direction and meaning, and manifest symptoms, like boredom, depression, anxiety, and loneliness.

We also witness to qualities that manifest the presence of God, such as peace, justice, wisdom, understanding, counsel, acceptance, patience, respect, fortitude, compassion, mercy forgiveness, availability, kindness, integrity, gratitude, humility, etc. In short, holy people are virtuous, for virtues are the ways we manifest God.

As the etymology of virtue indicates, people of God are strong, serene, and secure. Although we never fully realize these virtues, we strive to realize them throughout life. Since virtues are spiritual and therefore inexhaustible, we perpetually and imperfectly perfect them. Consequently, as we grow older together in Love, life becomes better than ever.

We have seen that transcendence enables us to see life in terms of unity and integration (spirit), not separation and fragmentation (ego). Thus, we are unlikely to isolate individuals from the community, to form we-them dichotomies, or to subscribe to isms, like racism, sexism, or ageism that fracture community. We are more likely to keep others and ourselves in the perspective of Love that/who unites us. Our holy disposition seeks unity as well as its source and final resting place—Love.

Being in touch with God, we look for deeper and longer lasting values in both others and ourselves. We avoid our false selves and see through social masks to our true, inner self. Being compassionate, we enter with Love into humanity, and consequently have the ability to suffer with and help people. God empowers us to become loving warriors: seasoned and strong to face and deal with darkness as well as wise and loving to help and heal.

When we are truly holy, we are witnesses to the Holy. We manifest God in day-to-day living, so that our lifestyle reveals God. We strive to become sanctuaries and ambassadors of Love. We know that a culture that lacks a holy and transcendent perspective becomes fragmented and shallow, that a denial of God is cultural suicide. Instead of temporary satisfaction (body) and success (ego), we try to foster and manifest permanent life (spirit).

Too often, contemporary Western culture tends to repress or dissociate God from the current of life. Consequently, our culture can pressure us to displace God in favor of a life centered primarily on pleasure, power, and possessions. To combat this secular thrust, we need courageous and compassionate people of God; otherwise, our culture will dissipate into narcissistic egoism.

In this regard, it seems to me that our society of differing faiths can accept in Love other faiths and lack of faiths. For instance, good Taoists, Buddhists, Hindus, Jews, Muslims, Christians, and other spiritual people manifest common, spiritual characteristics. To be sure, there are individual and significant differences in teachings and ways of living, yet there is considerable common ground to live in peace, tolerance, and respect.

Our challenge is to stand on our common ground and embrace one another in Love. Then, we can proclaim and celebrate that we are integral members of God's community of love. One of the clearest and most significant impacts of holy living on mental health is that it gives us a healthy direction and purpose in life. With God, we are more likely to be holy and healthy.

When we psychiatrists, psychologists, social workers, counselors, or whatever providers of health focus exclusively on ego (cognitive restructuring, coping skills, self-esteem, etc.) and body (feelings, sexuality, pleasure/pain, etc.) functions, we reduce people to less than they are. Consequently, our treatment is inadequate. Definitely, body and ego weaknesses and strengths are very important to helping people become healthy. Without the spiritual, however, our care is terribly truncated and falls sadly short of health.

Through Love, we become persons who do good acts. (As its ety-mology indicates, the "good" seeks wholeness, unity, justice, peace, and overall a virtuous life.) Our morality is not a submission to a system of abstract rules, but the Spirit of the rules permeates our lives. Rather than being draconian, judgmental, or religiously arrogant, we accept and try to help and heal. From the perspectives of Kohlberg and Fowler, we think, decide, and live on the highest levels of morality and faith.

Although evil is incongruent with a holy life, we claim our sepa-rations from God and our potential for evil. We are well aware of the continual frequency of horrific realities that fracture the good. From a Jungian perspective, we counter the forces of evil when we face our de-monic forces and invest their energy in good behavior. We act on the truth that much virtue builds on its opposite vice. With the courage and compassion, we strive to heal brokenness, reconcile separation, and cel-ebrate togetherness.

Erik Erikson (1968) speaks of the virtue of hope that emerges from a healthy experience in the first stage of life: trust versus distrust. Al-though Erikson does not speak of God, he does imply the importance of the spiritual life when he discusses the importance of virtue. He contends that hope that emerges from trust is the foundation for all other virtues. If our hope is weak because of inadequate care, we will suffer dire conse-quences in later development. From our perspective, a redeeming feature is that trust in Love, or God and others, can help us to accept, heal, and cope with our lack of trust and hope.

In hope, we always look for more than is seen. Our horizon of pos-sibilities is inexhaustible. Indeed, we imagine the possibilities. Living in faith and hope, we trust that life will eventually get better. We do not rely simply on ourselves, but we also trust God. We are careful that our ego does not get in the way of God. Veterans of 12-step recovery will testify to such faith and hope that are rooted in a Power part of and greater than oneself.

Being people of faith and hope, we transcend the clear and distinct (ego). Avoiding the seduction of rationalism and scientism, we go be-yond what we can only rationally grasp and communicate. We refuse to reduce life to our purviews and paradigms (ego). Indeed, life in faith and in hope (spirit) becomes richer, wiser, and creative.

Holiness also engenders strength, security, and serenity. Rather than being suspicious of and uneasy with others, we feel at home with others. We transcend differences of race, culture, ethnicity, religion, gender, age, etc. We see and respond to our common ground, Love. We have little need to defend or argue because our security and strength come from our inner bonding with God and others. We do not need people to change, nor do we need to be right. Our need is to live in Love. Clearly, we benefit our health.

We have already said that holy persons are full of grace, or Love. They are charismatic in the sense that they inspire people to live the spiritual life. Knowing the folly of force, they invite people to Love. They see people as brothers and sisters, and desire their good. Indeed, people sense that holy people want what is best for them.

Sincerity is another virtue that emerges from living a holy life. Its etymology indicates that sincerity means to be transparent or without pretense—to be real. Sincerity is not a maudlin view of the world, but it is simply an honestly proud and humble stand toward life. As holy people, we are proud to affirm the privilege and joy of living, and we are humble in being grateful for this gift from God. In pride and humility, we appreciate being a part of the miracle of reality.

Mother Theresa of Calcutta is a contemporary and known example of such a holy person. Clearly, this woman chose to be an instrument of God's care for poor, suffering, and forgotten people. Along with her abiding faith in the midst of continual doubt, she humbly depended on God for her strength and enthusiasm. Moreover, out of her humility, she proudly proclaimed God as her source and reason for her ministry and life. Indeed, Mother Theresa made and is making a significant and positive difference.

When we are holy, we are always going beyond to new horizons. We do not necessarily speak out or draw crowds, though some do have the temperament and ability for such behavior. Even though we may be quiet, we are dynamic in that we constantly grow and experience new meaning.

Instead of living a mad life of mere maintenance, we discover purposeful and lasting meaning in life. We discover that life in Love makes ultimate sense as well as enabling us to cope effectively. Health providers can recognize and foster these qualities and behaviors as signs and symptoms of health.

From a Christian perspective, we can consider Jesus Christ as the paramount manifestation of God in a human being. He is an archetypical, iconic person who manifests God. You need not be a Christian to recognize that Christ shows us, through behavior and words, the way, truth, and life. Indeed, spiritual non-Christians also point the way to healthy living.

We can manifest, see, hear, and respond to God who dwells within and beyond us. Our universal vocation is to become daughters and sons of God, and we pray that we may be one with God, self, and others. To be holy and whole, therefore, means to be as close to God and others as we can. God calls us to be one in Love, to be like God.

5

EXPERIENCING NOTHINGNESS

W E STARTED OUR JOURNEY by listening to stories of God seekers. Then we presented a model that emphasized spiritual functions, and we followed with a discussion of God, religion, and psychology. We proceeded to describe the structure and dynamics of various God experiences. Our next task is to offer and analyze a model of how and why we can grow spiritually and experience God.

A major premise is that part of our growth incorporates discomfort. Although most of us know this maxim to be true, we find it difficult to accept that at times and to some extent, we must suffer. Progress includes both easy/enjoyable and difficult/uncomfortable times.

For example, losing weight and gaining muscle tone is painful. Achieving academic and professional goals takes work. Psychologically, to accept unacceptable truths and thereby change takes effort. To love is to risk being hurt. Likewise, spiritual conversions, breakthroughs, and overall health include suffering (as well as comfortable experiences). Unfortunately, we tend to misconstrue and avoid these realities, and thereby impede our health.

Various writers have described the necessary disruption of spiritual growth with such words as dark night, desolation, powerlessness, *apophasis*, *negativa via*, desert, breakdown, and disillusionment. We use the word "nothingness" because it includes the preceding words and highlights experiences of apparent nonsense that are challenging to those who seek (clients) and foster (providers) health . We will see that the concept and experiences of nothingness call into question many of our positivistic and professional assumptions of health.

Consider "no-thingness" as a spiritual experience wherein we desire more than we have—and, more than we are. In nothingness, we find ourselves restless and restive, dissatisfied and discontent, yearning for and seeking more. Our desire seems to be at the core of our being, reaching for something or someone that is just beyond our reach. Our desire seems unquenchable. No-thing seems adequate. No-thing seems enough.

From a theoretical perspective, no-thing-ness calls for "some-thing," more meaning, or being. Nothingness and being imply each other; they are dance partners. They are two sides of the same coin; one does not exist without the other. What does this theory of growth mean more concretely?

Think of when you experience the absence of your beloved, you probably yearn for her or his presence, and when your beloved is present, you feel the possibility of absence. Your joy of presence implies an impending sadness of absence, and your restless yearning in absence desires the serenity of presence. Indeed, absence seeks presence, and presence implies absence. One does not exist without the other.

Reflect on life and death. Life always implies the certainty of death, and death makes no sense without life. The practical relevance is that our impending death, or the uncertainty of life, can motivate us to grow and to live better. Death motivates us to live, and life answers our questions of death. Thus, to avoid death impedes and diminishes life. Once again, health providers can be open to and even encourage clients to take this spiritual journey.

Life and death, being and nothingness, presence and absence, fulfillment and emptiness are necessary polar opposites. From the perspective of dialectical behavioral therapy, we strive to integrate and learn from these polar opposites. However, when we perceive them in terms of either-or, or whatever dualism, we judge, feel, and act in ways that are less than healthy. Our failure to integrate these apparently opposite but actually related realities impedes our health and may develop serious problems.

In regards to God, if we want to grow in the presence of God, we will experience the absence of God. We must remember and accept that our disbelief yearns for more faith, and our disillusionment seeks more truth.

Instead of repression, displacement, or forgetfulness, we must remember that in the emptiness of our absence, we desire more fulfilling presence.

Our spiritual experiences of God involve these processes of absence and presence, desolation and consolation, separation and unity, negative and positive, darkness and enlightenment, and so on. It is wise to admit (and be grateful) that our coming closer to God involves distance, our divine empowerment necessitates powerlessness, our spiritual strength implies weakness, our healthy fulfillment calls for emptiness, our being demands nothingness.

In a certain sense, we go out of our ego mind (and may wonder about our sanity) and into the realm of mystery and paradox. Although our body intensely feels nothingness and our ego reflects on it, the accent is on our spirit—the most intimate expression of being. Thus, in nothingness we desire more than what the ordinary (body and ego) can give. Good counselors will help us not only to feel and cope better, but also to reach for the stars, the extraordinary, or what or who give us abiding purpose and meaning.

Nothingness intensely confirms that we are never completely certain and content, or that we are always restless and restive. What we have and are, including life itself, will change and eventually end. In other words, our lives are always evolving, and we are always in a quest for more meaning, for life to make more sense. According to the psychiatrist Viktor Frankl, our search for meaning is a matter of life and death. We will see how it is good and healthy that our being is to be in jeopardy.

In short, our experiences of nothingness are a necessary part of and prelude to becoming more intimate with the source and destiny of our life. We propose that our experience of nothingness is an essential dynamic of holy growth. Thus, when we avoid nothingness, we limit our experience of God and diminish our health.

To begin to understand these divine dances of being and nothingness, presence and absence, fulfillment and emptiness, joy and sadness, we will reflect on our experiences of nothingness, and its languages. We will then focus on the meaning of pain, the symptoms, dynamics, and significance of nothingness, and finally a discussion of the stages of nothingness. To repeat, our approach is neither solely psychological nor spiritual, but rather an integration of both of them.

Our Experiences of Nothingness

Listen to David's introduction to nothingness. "Life has been good to me. I am fortunate, and I am very grateful. Until recently, my life was going well, and I suppose it still is.

"Look, my kids have done very well, and more importantly, they are good kids. The oldest has an MBA, and will soon marry a wonderful woman. My youngest is in her senior year of college, and is preparing to go to medical school. My middle child is a delightful plumber who can fix almost anything. It is good to see my children successful and happy. This is not too shabby for a lost street kid who never graduated from high school.

"True, I eventually wised up, at least somewhat. Thank God, I managed to stay out of serious trouble. I got my GED, and I became a journeyman welder and inspector. I even learned to like reading, perhaps more than is good for me. I'm always questioning and searching. If reincarnation is true, maybe I'll come back as a philosopher. Sometimes I drive my kids and wife nuts with my incessant probing.

"I give most of the credit to my wife who was always there for our kids and me. It is also good to say that my wife is better than good; she is the best. Unlike so many marriages, we have grown closer, and we really like to be with each other. Furthermore, I have a good job, excellent pension, and some savings. My parents and siblings are still alive and we enjoy one another. As I said, I am very fortunate. So, what's the problem?

"In the midst of this good life, I find myself questioning the meaning of life. What else is new? It's stupid, for when I look at my life, I have more than I expected or have ever wanted, and I don't take this for granted. So, why am I questioning my life? I can only say that in the midst of this good stuff, something is missing. Clearly, life doesn't make sense the way it once did. Ultimately, I wonder if anything makes sense.

"What happened? Life was going so smoothly, and externally it still is. My wife and kids, Mom and Dad, brothers and sisters, relatives and friends love me and I love them. Nothing is more important. Internally, however, I wonder when all is said and done, if anything makes sense. Sometimes I feel that nothing makes sense.

"I wonder if this is all there is. Is this the last and only dance? Is heaven a mind game to ease our anxiety about death? When I look at the lives of many ministers of religion, I wonder if religion is a sincere ruse. Does God really exist? Indeed, religious services no longer do much for me. Sometimes, I look at people in church and see a community of fools. God, I never felt this way before.

"Life used to be meaningful and settled. I was active and liked being in church. There were answers; life made sense. I seldom doubted my religion, its clergy and members, and their God. Now, I wonder if such teachings and practices are valid, or if they make trustworthy sense. To say the least, life is unsettling. Nothing seems certain. Is this all there is?"

Our lives usually seem to make more sense than nonsense. Most things eventually work out, and life goes on without much reflection on the what, how, and why of life. Like David, however, there are times when our ordinary world of meaning changes. Like him, the meaning we once took for granted comes into question. "What's it all about?" and "Is this all there is?" are questions that demand answers. Does nothing make sense?

Nothingness is a rupture in everyday living. In nothingness, we find ourselves with David questioning what we once took for granted, or even on what we based our life. Our nothingness is an extraordinary experience that questions our ordinary life and demands extraordinary answers.

Another way of looking at this crisis of nothingness is as a desert experience. The word desert, coming from the Latin *serere* to join and *de* away from, refers to the experience when things, which are normally together, come apart. Instead of things making sense, now no-thing makes sense.

In our acute desert experiences, we feel abandoned—deserted. Something or someone is radically missing. In our most acute times, we feel anxious, powerless, and radically shaken. We feel our vulnerability, mortality, and ultimate dependency. Being stripped of our normal supports and feeling powerless in a dry and barren land, we seek answers and yearn for deliverance.

We feel that our world is turned upside down and inside out. We wonder what is happening. Often, the certainty of our death evokes uncertainty. Nothing may seem more real than something. We feel so different. People may ask us if something is wrong. Perhaps medication or therapy will bring us back to normal. We may find it difficult to accept that instead of medicating or purging our uneasiness, we should journey through these deserts to arrive at better lands.

In the desert of nothingness, God often seems to be absent when we feel we need God most. We may find ourselves questioning our past conceptions of God, or criticizing the gods of religions. Our religious practices and their ministers may no longer make much sense. We may become jaded toward our religion and its leaders. What may have been our bedrock becomes quicksand. Everything important seems to be an illusion. Where have the good old, secure days gone?

We will see that to follow God's way, especially when feeling abandoned, is our paramount test of faith. Competent and compassionate counselors will show us how in our dry and empty deserts, we are called to conversion, i.e., a turning away from the temporary satisfactions of our body and ego and a turning toward the unending fulfillments of our Spirit. Instead of purging or numbing our feelings, they will help us to grow in and through our nothingness.

Our experience of nothingness occurs when our world, others, and God recede into the background, leaving us with ourselves in the foreground. The therapeutic emphasis is on the interior, spiritual me. Although it may not feel to be so, this is a gift of self-confrontation because in nothingness we come face to face with our deeper selves.

In nothingness, we come to a crossroad where we move deeper into or farther away from authentic living. We can avoid, numb, or silence the radical questions that call for crucial responses. Our will to pleasure or power is not an adequate displacement for our will to meaning. Nothingness is a decisive time that results in fragmentation and fixation or integration and freedom.

Keep in mind that we neither create nor control nothingness. Rather, such deserts are spiritual times that are beyond mere rational control and call for spiritual faith. Our powerlessness (the limits of our ego) humbles us. We have nothing to grasp. Eventually, we must leap beyond our rational power and surrender to a greater power.

When we have nothing to control, nothing to hold on to, and nothing to look at, nothingness throws the meaning of our life into question. Nothingness throws us back on ourselves and demands responses to classical questions, like: Who am I? Where am I going? From where do I come? Why should I live? What is my heritage to be? What is the reason for my being? What happens to me when I die? Is this all there is?

In short, nothingness questions our most important values and experiences—life, death, work, play, sex, commitment, suffering, pleasure, faith, hope, love, and God. The paradox is that our world must come apart for it to come together in a better way. Surely, grappling with the essential meaning of life is an issue of major magnitude that deserves the attention of health providers.

When we are in the abyss of nothingness, however, we as well as health providers can construe these upsetting times as negative or even unhealthy. In the name of mental health, we can medicate or treat these spiritual experiences as unhealthy, and thereby risk impeding our health. We can look for some magical miracle to save us.

Desert demons will entice us to seek power, pleasure, and self-idolatry as ways to escape our powerlessness, pain, and divine dependence. Addictions, for example, lure us with illusions of painless contentment—heaven on earth. False promises of fulfillment can seduce us. Rather than trusting God, we depend solely on ourselves. We cling to things to avoid no-thing. In this way, the desert can provide the occasion of our undoing. Rather than journeying to freedom, we slip into slavery.

Our thesis is that nothingness empties and purifies us in order for God and others to fulfill us. Our powerlessness leads to empowerment, darkness to light, being lost to being found. In other words, a desert journey is necessary to reach the Promised Land. Only our Higher Power, or Love (God), not our individual egos, can give us true serenity, freedom, and fulfillment. Instead of medicating or purging these experiences, health providers should help clients grow from them.

The Language of Nothingness

Nothingness speaks many languages. Unlike conventional language, its communication is more affectively and spiritually adumbrated and ambiguous than cognitively clear and concise. We will now show how affective expressions of spiritual nothingness, like loneliness, anxiety, and depression, invite us to explore and progress to fuller communion with self, others, and God, and consequently health.

A serious mistake is to reduce all experiences to our Western models of health that explain and treat people only in terms of our body and ego functions. For example, when well-intentioned, Western-trained mental health professionals responded to the victims of the Sri Lanka tsunami, their treatment models were usually not helpful and sometimes harmful. Some clinicians eventually learned that most Sri Lankans deal with their death and devastations in ways much different than Western ways. Rather than stress debriefing, exposure therapies, cognitive, behavioral and grief therapies, and so on, the natives practiced very different and effective approaches, ones that are primarily spiritual.

To be sure, Western body/ego models have much value. However, to force all experiences (especially spiritual ones) into their treatment modalities is a serious mistake. Instead of subscribing to Cartesian, in-dividual/ego ideologies, the Sri Lankans followed Hindu and Buddhist visons that encouraged composure, acceptance, and grace in their suf-fering. Our goal is to integrate such Western and Eastern approaches. To that end, let us begin with Dana's experience of loneliness.

Loneliness

"I have been married for twenty-five years, and as marriages go, mine has been one of the better ones. I know my husband loves me, and I love him. We had a few rough times, particularly when our kids were having problems, but we got through them, and ended up stronger and closer. Now that the kids are becoming adults, we have more time to grow closer. So, why am I lonely?

"I know that Jim is always there for me, especially when I need him. Sure, sometimes it takes him time to come around, but he makes it. Even when Jim and I are in our most intimate moments, I still feel a lack, or a restless feeling of incompleteness. It is as if something or someone is missing. I am not blaming Jim, for I wonder if anyone could fill the hole in my soul.

"I wonder if I am seeking someone who does not exist. Even in my most complete moments of love, I feel a tad incomplete. It is as if my heart's desire is inexhaustible. The more I love, the lonelier I feel. Let me be clear, my loneliness is not for some other man. As I said, Jim and I have a good marriage and love life and each other. My lonely feelings are subtle; they are restless whispers. Something or someone is missing.

"The hole in my soul is not deep, but it is there. St. Augustine said, my heart is restless until it rests in Thee. Maybe that's it, but that sounds too mystical or holy for me. Maybe my loneliness seeks more than my husband can give. Will I ever be complete?

"I went to a counselor for a while. She thought that perhaps my self-esteem could improve, that I felt unworthy of my husband's love. Then she hypothesized that perhaps I was going through a mid-life crisis, and that I was regressing to my high school days of youthful romance. Then she proposed that I was still mourning the death of my father whom I dearly loved, and this was distorting my love for my husband. As a last resort, she suggest that I try some psychotropic medication to help me feel better. Although my counselor was a nice person, and I liked her, none of this rang true, nor was it helpful."

Like Dana, in nothingness we can feel deeply in love with another human being, yet still feel incomplete. It is as if our love seeks more love, or that our love desires Love. Like Dana, we may wonder if anyone will entirely fulfill our hearts. It seems that the more we connect in love, the more we feel a subtle but gnawing incompleteness, or a desire for more completeness.

We yearn for presence. We miss intimacy and want to be with some-one. We feel the tension between a striving to be with another and an inability to fulfill our desire. Even and perhaps especially when we are in love, we can feel lonely. In our acute times, we feel that our cry for love goes unheard, that no one, including God, hears our silent shouts.

Instead of seeing this as a problem to be solved, as in the case of Dana's counselor, we can see (like the Sri Lankans) her experiences as op-portunities for growth—troubling feelings that are positive, not negative. Not all discomfort is symptomatic of something wrong; it can indicate a desire for better health.

In our approach, we accept nothingness and its loneliness (as well as other spiritual feelings) as part of growing in holiness and healthiness. Rather than Dana's loneliness indicating something wrong, we are open to the possibility of something right and necessary. Her loneliness may be a symptom of health rather than unhealthiness. Indeed, her feeling the presence of others and God in their absence is not something to avoid or purge, but rather to pursue and foster. However, if we exclude, like her counselor, spiritual dynamics from health, we fail to help and may do harm.

Keep in mind that the loneliness of nothingness differs from clinical loneliness. Spiritual loneliness is necessary for spiritual and psychologi-cal growth, whereas unhealthy loneliness is due to such processes as dis-trust, low self-esteem, shame, unworthiness, and unhealthy dependency. Rather than engendering growth, unhealthy loneliness is a symptom of deprivation and fixation, and calls for treatment and recovery. With good intentions, Dana's counselor was probably taking such an approach.

In contrast, healthy loneliness is the partner of love, for it motivates us to love more and better. For example, think of a woman who separates from her beloved. She misses and yearns for him. In such an instance, his absence can serve as an opportunity to appreciate and deepen her love. Nevertheless, it is not easy, and she may be tempted to repress or numb her feelings, and thereby impede her love. Ideally, she embraces her loneliness.

Thus, we can distinguish between psychological loneliness (and other feelings) and spiritual loneliness. Our psychological feelings are unique to us, and can be healthy (when you miss a loved one), or unhealthy (neurotic neediness, poor self-esteem). Spiritual loneliness is a natural or archetypical motivation to deepen our love. These should be pursued, not purged.

Our yearning in nothingness pressures us to renew our love for God as well as for others. In other words, spiritual loneliness helps us to seek love. The paradoxical process is that in the incompletion of loneliness, we desire completion in Love.

Beware; many seductions can lure us away from our loneliness. The pleasure of casual sex (body) can sooth the sting of loneliness, and gratify us. Sometimes anything or anybody feels better than nothing or nobody. Hyperactivity or workaholism (ego) can also enable us to escape the empty yearning of loneliness, and give us some measure of satisfaction. We can try to live out of our mind in a futile attempt to escape the yearning of our lonely heart. However, such fruits of the body and ego are always inadequate for our spiritual desires.

We must remember that no substance, activity, or person can appropriately take the place of Love. Indeed, even religion can displace God in our desperate attempt to escape nothingness. Conversely, religion (and the health professions) should help us embrace our loneliness so that we can deepen our connection with God, self, and others.

Like loneliness, aloneness can be healthy or unhealthy, as well as psychological or spiritual. Aloneness, for example, may be unhealthy when we feel compelled to be alone because we are afraid to face others. In contrast, healthy aloneness is a choice that is in service of growth.

For instance, we can withdraw from others to be in solitude, to reflect on life, to contemplate, or simply to rest. In contemplative solitude, we can come closer to others because we come to the source of being together—God/Love. In service of health, we can encourage others and ourselves to practice solitude, for it helps us to be in touch with self, others, and God. Let us continue to reflect on another language of nothingness—depression.

Depression

"What is happening to me? What is wrong with me? Last year, I felt good, or at least relatively good. Although I did not love my work, I still went to work with some purpose. More importantly, I enjoyed my kids, and my wife and I had a good love life. Now, I hate going to work; it seems so endless and boring. My kids are no different, but I no longer enjoy them. Yes, you guessed it; my wife and I seldom get close. In short, I just feel out of it—out of life.

"It is as if life has left me. I really don't like living, although I would like to like life. I don't want to die. I want to live, but with some enthusiasm. I feel empty, like life has drained out of me, that I've lost interest in life. Too often it is tough to get out of bed. I try to be kind and love; sex: forget it. I walk around with a smile on my face, but with a void in my soul.

"My wife and friends say that I should see a psychiatrist because they believe I suffer from depression. I am reluctant to follow their advice, for I know what will happen. The doctor will listen to me and tell me that I have clinical depression. Then he will treat my disease with medication and perhaps with some talk therapy. Somehow, I feel that more significant than a sickness is going on.

"Moreover, I know from reading and friends that drugs only take the edge off your feelings so that you may manage better. It is as if they lighten the weight on your shoulders. However, the effects soon wane and you return where you were. Granted, the drugs may gave you needed relief. Anyway, that is what people tell me.

"I also know that drugs will not teach me coping skills; granted counseling may help. Still, I don't think that these approaches will help me find what is most missing—purpose, meaning, enthusiasm, reason for being. In short, I don't think I have a disease. I simply want life to make sense again so that I can savor and enjoy life."

This man, Jacob, is depressed. Does he have the disease of clinical depression? Should it be treated with medication and counseling as something to purge. Or is something else going on, like a spiritual depression? Could Jacob's depression be a good and necessary experience for spiritual growth? Maybe his "dis-ease" calls for a different approach.

We can differentiate spiritual and psychological depression, and both usually involve significant loss and powerlessness. For instance, in unhealthy depression we may be depressed because of a biochemical imbalance, very low self-esteem, pent up anger, or an environmental loss over which we feel helpless. Such clinical depression may warrant treatment, such as medication and counseling. Movement, physical, psychosocial, and spiritual, usually helps significantly.

However, to diagnose all depression as a clinical disease or an untoward problem to treat and solve may be a serious error. Like Jacob, we can feel lost and powerless in our nothingness. Life's nothingness can throw us back on ourselves, and our life can be "de-pressed"—as if our air/spirit has dissipated. Instead of being wrong or sick, such depression can be right and healthy.

In spiritual depression, we lose the familiar sense of things around us: others are different, values change, and our past world may be suddenly outdated. We are distant from the world of things, and we are "pressed in" on ourselves. Our once familiar world seems foreign, leaving us with no-thing to grasp. Our interest wanes, energy dissipates, vision darkens, and movement stagnates. We feel stuck in a deep, dark hole.

Unlike clinical depression, our spiritual depression is healthy and necessary for growth. Spiritual de-pression pressures us to slow down and reflect on our life. It invites us to be still and silent, to listen to what is unheard in our loud and busy life. Our spiritual depression is an invitation to journey in our inner world, to find more meaning, perhaps to discover more of the kingdom of Love on earth. Paradoxically, spiritual depression is ultimately in service of joy.

Like Jacob, our emptiness seeks more than the temporary fulfillment of our body satisfactions and ego successes. We feel deeply within ourselves that there must be more than the ordinary, that there is more to life. Our emptiness seeks fulfillment, our listlessness wants joy, and our weariness desires enthusiasm.

Possessions, power, and sex—such ordinary signs of success—fall terribly short of fulfilling our deepest desires. Moreover, physical (drugs) and functional (ordinary counseling) approaches are inadequate responses to the questions of spiritual depression. They do not fulfill our restless emptiness, energize our powerlessness, and give us direction and meaning for living.

Well-intentioned health providers who treat our spiritual depression only with drugs and coping skills could make matters worse. We must accept (not reject or purge) and grow from our spiritual depression, for it beckons us to renew our lives. Spiritual depression and all the manifestations of nothingness are opportune parts of life, not diseases.

Spiritual depression can motivate us to seek more than the ordinary ways to gain so-called success, esteem, and happiness. Although we probably feel tired, gloomy, and stuck, our depression invites us to move in a different direction. In our spiritual depression, we seek enthusiasm (*en*=in, *Theos*=God), or purpose, meaning, and Love.

In short, our spiritual nothingness calls us to seek new ways or to rekindle old ones that give more than the ordinary. The bottom line is that we must courageously pursue the love of God, self, and others that give new energy to our weary spirit. Once again, only love for and from self, God, and others can fill the hole in our souls.

Guilt and Shame

Maybe you resonate with Shelia's feelings of guilt and shame. "I don't know why I feel guilty, or even if I am guilty. I can only say that it feels like guilt, but I did not do anything terribly wrong. In fact, when I have done something wrong or sinned, I have always tried to be responsible, make amends, and improve myself. Maybe the issue is not what I have done wrong. Maybe I am not doing enough right.

"When I listen to and reflect on my feelings, I wonder if I could do better or should make some important changes. For instance, I have had tremendous parents who gave me so many opportunities to become successful. Imagine that I was the first woman in our extended family to graduate from college and be a professional woman.

"Do I take my blessings for granted? Am I grateful? Have I given to my parents a fraction of what they gave to me? Too often, I think I take my children and husband for granted. What would I do if my kids were drug addicts, criminals, or incorrigible? What would I do if they were retarded or autistic? What if my husband was self-centered and did not cherish me? I feel small when I feel and think this way. Sometimes I feel like I just want to disappear.

"Moreover, I can so easily get caught in my own little world. As I have indicated, my life is one that some may envy. There is very little wrong or troubling. I see neighbors who live in financial debt, whose kids are failing in school, are sick, and have a bleak future. I have none of these problems.

"It's simply not good to forget my many blessings. I know better, and I have taught my children to remember to count their blessings every night before they go to sleep. Indeed, there is considerable room for improvement. To be sure, I cannot nor do I want to be perfect, but I can remember to become better and better."

One way to describe guilt is that it is anxiety that results from doing something contrary to our values. Simply stated, we feel guilty when we do something that we think or feel we should not do. In everyday guilt, we act in ways that violate our behavioral standards. Like Shelia, if you value gratitude and forget to be grateful, you will feel guilty. Such guilt is good, for it helps us to take stock of and improve ourselves.

Not all guilt is healthy. Unhealthy guilt arises from unrealistic standards, and therefore impedes rather than fosters improvement. For example, if you think that angry feelings are bad and unacceptable, then when you feel angry, even though you have not done anything wrong, you will feel guilty.

Whether healthy or unhealthy, guilt pressures us to improve ourselves. With unhealthy guilt, we usually have to modify our standards for thoughts, feelings, and behavior. In our example, we must accept that angry feelings in themselves are not bad. With healthy guilt, we have to modify our behavior so that it is in harmony with our values. The importance of guilt is to improve ourselves and to make amends to those whom we have harmed, both others and ourselves.

The guilt of nothingness motivates us to reflect on our values and to question the quality of our lives. For instance, we may question what makes something good or bad, and what difference does it make. Is it worthwhile to be good, regardless of the consequences? Does it pay to be good? What is bad? What makes behavior bad? What is evil? Am I good, and if so, how and why?

Similar to Shelia in our vignette, our spiritual guilt can move us to remember to be grateful. Guilt may arise when we forget the gifts that people as well as life have given us. When we forget to be grateful, we should be guilty, for it can help us to remember.

Another form of spiritual guilt is to feel corporate guilt for our inhumanity to humanity. This means that our guilt enables us to be more aware of the plight of our brothers and sisters, and to be ever mindful that we are never completely content as long as there are oppressed human beings. Our guilt can move us to be more compassionate, act justly, and help others. Indeed, we can be grateful for our guilt and shame, for they remind us to care.

We may feel guilty because we are not becoming what and who we can realistically become. Our guilt may mean that we are not giving back nearly as much as we have been given, or that we are not nearly as grateful as we should be. Whatever types of guilt, psychological or spiritual, our guilt can help us become better persons.

In contrast to the action-centeredness of guilt, shame centers more on being. Guilt arises from what we do, and shame more from who we are. In guilt, we feel conflicted and out of sorts. In shame, we feel worthless and often want to disappear. Guilt irritates and disrupts, and shame wounds and kills. In shame, we feel painfully diminished and want to be unseen.

In the shame of nothingness, we may question or lose our bearings, feel lost or not our old self. We may wonder if we have been on the wrong track, and therefore deceived ourselves. We may feel less worthwhile than we thought we were. We may even wonder if we are worth much at all. In stark nothingness, we hesitate to look at ourselves. In light of what can be, we feel darkly diminished.

If we have centered our life primarily on the fruits of our body and ego, we are candidates for shame. However, "shame on us" can be a redeeming feature, for such shame challenges us to find and affirm our true worth. Ultimately and pragmatically, our true and sustaining worth centers and draws on the Source of our lives—God. This simply means that Love is the basis and nourishment of our worth, and therefore only Love can free us from the chains of shame.

We must avoid or heal from unhealthy shame, a shame that is undeserved and thrust upon us. For example, unhealthy shame can arise in childhood when authorities (parents, relatives, siblings, teachers, et al.) shame us. They may tell us that there is something wrong with us, as if we are a mistake or less than others are. Perhaps (with good or bad) intentions, people lie to us and about us.

Victims, especially of sexual abuse, usually feel shame. They feel stained for life. A predator (parent, relative, neighbor, minister, etc.) has violated their trust in what and whom they need and hold most sacred. Understandably, distrust can significantly impede interpersonal relationships as well as hope. Heinous acts undermine their spirit so that they are left on shaky ground with seemingly no exit. Even when their wounds heal, irritating scars remain.

Love wants us to listen to our guilt and shame in order to increase our worth—to realize that we are people of Love. God wants us to heal and increase in worth rather than diminish. Love is our healing, strength-ening, and liberating force. Indeed, this road is not easy to travel, and frustration and anger can impede, challenge, and motivate our progress. Listen to Steve.

Frustration and Anger

"I'm so frustrated and angry that I could scream, but I don't know at what or whom I would scream. Work is going well. The kids are doing fine. My wife has few complaints. We pay the bills and are out of debt. Everything seems all right. So why am I frustrated and angry?

"It seems like I am upset with nothing in particular and everything in general. If you ask me what I am angry at, I couldn't nail it down. Furthermore, I am edgy and irritable, and not a pleasant person to be with. Understand, I am not always like this, but it is always smoldering beneath the surface. So, I make it a project to avoid dumping on people, particularly on those I love.

"When I sit still and listen to my feelings, I get some understanding. In some respects, I get mad at how unjust, dishonest, and crooked people are with one another. When I read about how so many rich and powerful people exploit people, how politicians live in a different world from their constituents, or how people are out for themselves regardless of how their actions harm others, I get disheartened and angry. In my church, it is just as bad, for they preach one thing and do another. Most of the bishops live more like the rich and famous than the ordinary folks. They certainly don't live and smell like the sheep they are supposed to shepherd.

"I wonder if it pays to live a good life. I see so many people who manipulate others for their own satisfaction. When push comes to shove, it seems that people are out for themselves. People do get away with mur-der. Crime does pay. What goes around comes around is a cruel illusion. You better get what you can before the other gets it. I feel like a naive chump. Does it pay to care about the common good and to care for oth-ers? Is it stupid to be fair, honest, and loving?

"The promise of a reward in heaven seems so lame. Should I sub-scribe to the law of the survival of the fittest? Is heaven an illusion? Is there justice? Is being a good person a better way? Where is the so-called kingdom on earth? Is the promise of eternal life a lie that people use to control people? Do religious leaders tell us that we must suffer for a reward after death in order to control us? Where is justice and happiness on earth? Are God and his justice a hoax?

"It seems that those who do not believe in God do just as well or even better than those who believe in God. In fact, it seems that those who believe in God seem to suffer more and are often less successful. You can live a good life without God—and, save a lot of time and energy. It seems that you can be a bad person and live a good life. Where does God fit into this picture?

"Is it best to live a God-centered life? I could be angry with God, but that would be stupid if God does not exist. If there were a God, it would be foolish to be mad at an all-merciful and loving God. I guess I am mad that life is not what I thought it would be or is supposed to be.

"Nevertheless, I am not going to give up on God and his teachings. My spiritual living centers and grounds me which helps me manage living in a scary and chaotic world. It seems to me that any other way does not work as well. Without God, this messy world would be totally absurd. Clearly, there is much to improve in our approaches towards God and religion, but for me, it is the best imperfect way."

Before we respond to Steve's frustration and anger, let us reflect on the nature of these emotions. Frustration usually means that we feel blocked or inadequate in attaining what we want or need, which, like most experiences, can be healthy or unhealthy.

Psychological frustration occurs when we cannot satisfy needs (body) or achieve goals (ego). Examples of unhealthy frustration are perfectionists who often feel frustrated because they seldom reach their goal of perfection. Likewise, people who repress emotions feel frustrated because they are not being what they can be—affectively expressive.

Frustration can also be necessary and healthy. For example, learning and growth often include healthy frustration because it demands discipline and a delay of immediate gratification. Suppression of immediate, short-term gratification (sex, food, anger) can be in service of long-term gains. When we can accept frustration as a necessary part of life, we can say "no" (frustration) in service of a "yes" (satisfaction, success, and fulfillment).

These types of frustration and possible anger are relatively clear as contrasted to the ones the man in our example is experiencing. This man is frustrated and angry with many of the most basic tenets and religious teachings of life. Actually, he is questioning his beliefs and what he thought was the way to live. Although he criticizes the state and church, he still feels that a God-centered life is the best imperfect way.

As we have previously indicated, we should perpetually perfect ourselves, and therefore we are always somewhat frustrated. When we yearn to love better or want to learn more, our life can be frustrating. When we question our basic assumptions for living, we will experience frustration and can get angry. Spiritual frustration means that since we are pilgrim people, we will question, and answers are not immediately forthcoming. Moreover, when questions do get answers, more questions emerge.

When nothing is closer to us than anything is, we can be frustrated. When we want to make sense of things, and no-thing makes the most sense, we may feel immersed in frustration. When we question religion, we can feel duped and become angry.

Although it may be scary and unsettling, it is good to question our assumptions, religion, and faith, for our frustration and anger can lead to more contentment and serenity. Rather than avoiding and repressing such disruption, we can welcome the challenge to deepen our faith. Moreover, with reason and faith, we can accept that spiritual life works this way, and therefore be patient until more sense emerges. Remember, nothing and its turbulence lead to God and serenity.

When we are angry, we want or need reality to differ from what it is. We want our standards, expectations, or needs to be met. When angry, we do not like what is happening, and we seek change. Mental health professionals often construe anger as a secondary feeling that conceals or expresses primary feelings, like frustration, hurt, insult, injustice, and fear. In this light, anger can energize us to improve matters.

Our anger can help or harm, be healthy or unhealthy. Our challenge is to listen to our underlying feelings so that we can make healthy changes. For example, a common cause of unhealthy anger is to need someone (other than oneself) to change to feel better. When our needs or expectations are unmet, we get angry and try to do the impossible—to change the other. Such anger invariably makes matters worse, and we become even more frustrated and angry. We must come to accept that we cannot control and change others, but we can change ourselves.

Healthy psychological anger can be a protest and protection against unfair treatment. For instance, if someone exploits, demeans, or betrays you, you should get angry. Your anger clearly states that you do not deserve such treatment, and it moves you to protect yourself.

Of course, what you do with your anger is critical. If you demand justice, try to make the offender apologize or make amends, or simply try to stop his behavior, you will probably make matters worse. A key is to attend to your underlying pain yourself so that you do not need but certainly want and deserve justice.

Spiritual frustration and fear of being stuck in nothingness can lead to anger. Like the man in our example, what once made sense loses sense. We may feel that religion has let us down, or that God has abandoned us. Perhaps after living decades of a good life, we may wonder if we were deceived, if God is an illusion. We can become sick and tired of nothing. In addition, we may blame God, or like Steve, try to make more sense of religion and God.

We may question assumptions about life and God, such as the idea that a good life will bring happiness, that our good acts will evoke good acts in return, that bad people will get their just punishment, or that good conquers evil. We may wonder if religion is a way to control people, if religious leaders are really just and good, or if in practice do they favor the rich over the poor.

It behooves us to remember that, like Job, fighting with God (and religion) can be a holy act, a passionate way to become closer to God. Anger can help us cut through life's illusions, and to shed light on darkness. Anger can help us to see the blindness of leaders, and to help them to see more accurately and to act more justly. Anger can help us to be strong and proactive in seeking justice and truth. Anger can help us improve our spiritual lives and manifest Love.

Rather than exercising blatant expression or closed repression, we ought to claim, name, and listen to what our anger is protecting, protesting, and proclaiming. It behooves us when we pause and listen to and learn from our underlying feelings, connect with our inner power of Love, think, and take appropriate action. Spiritual frustration and anger can help us seek truth, justice, and Love.

Let us continue to listen to and reflect on more daunting companions on our journey to health and God. Chris talks about the unsettling and challenging feelings of anxiety and dread.

Anxiety, Dread and Fear

"I have always been a religious person. I never miss Sunday liturgy, and I often go to church during the week. Lately, however, I find myself questioning what I used to base my life on. I did not plan to undermine myself; it just happened. It seems unfair that in middle age I am critical of my religion. I assume that life and my reason for being would become more certain, not less certain. What is going on? Do I live in darkness? Do I pretend to live in light?

"My religious leaders are not much help. They seem to reduce my questions, and me, to their framework so that I am left wanting and frustrated. It seems they put me into their box of ready-made answers. Well, one size does not fit me. Moreover, when they cannot answer a question, they tell you it is a mystery or that you must have faith or pray more. Something is not right about such mental gymnastics. I feel dismissed and patronized.

"I wonder not only about religion, but also about God. I know that you can be spiritual without religion, and that you can be spiritual without God. Still, I wonder. What is God? Who is God? Must there be a God? It seems that some people are happy and live good lives without believing in a God.

"What do I really think about God and religion? My religion tells me things about God and about how I should live, but it does little to help me experience God. Nor does it field my questions, doubts, and criticisms. The next time someone tells me that I lack faith or that the matter is too complex, I think I will vomit.

"I used to feel secure and certain. I felt I knew myself, where I stood, and where I was going. I felt relatively solid and strong. Now, I am shaky, uncertain, and lost. I feel like I am walking on the edge of quicksand with no solid ground in sight. In my most intense times, I feel like I am suspended in the middle of nowhere and nothing to hold. Although I feel more honest, I also feel lost. But, damn it, I am not going to give up. I will keep my legs moving and my mind active until I find a better way."

Chris probably verbalizes the feelings of many people. She feels like someone pulled the proverbial rug from under her. She also feels that she gets little help with her religious doubts. She wonders if she subscribed to a religion that has constricted her life. Besides feeling frustrated and angry, she feels anxious and dreads a life of uncertainty.

However, Chris is not dropping out of religion or putting her God aside. Because she sees herself as part of her church and religion, she not only rejects insipid responses to her questions, but she also pursues truth on her own. Because of her nagging questions and desires, she is hanging in. Let us reflect on the nature of anxiety.

Think of anxiety as a change or threat to our identity. In anxiety, we are in a state of not-yetness—no longer back there where we were and not yet where we are coming to be. For example, we may experience psychological anxiety when we begin a new job. We cannot know exactly how to or if we can meet the employer's expectations, or if the new job will significantly change our life.

Unhealthy anxiety is the price we pay for not being ourselves. It usually means that we refuse or cannot admit to certain thoughts and feelings. In contrast, healthy anxiety is a symptom and harbinger of growth. In short, the healthiness or unhealthiness of anxiety depends primarily on whether our anxiety mobilizes effective behavior, or whether it impedes us or is the result of negative coping, like denial, repression, or rationalization.

Spiritual anxiety results from a crucial change that seems to have no purpose. Like our middle-aged woman, we may feel that the ground of our being is undermined. We may feel thrown into a bottom-less pit. Our anchorage found in things gives way, and we may dread losing ourselves in the vortex of nothingness. There is no-thing to grasp and manage, and seemingly no-where to go. We feel primordially uneasy and powerless in the throes of our nothingness.

We may dread that there may be nothing more than there is right now. Is there really a God? Does heaven exist? Is God an illusion that we use to ameliorate our dread? Do we squeeze life into a box of religion, and worship an illusion called God in order to ameliorate our dread of death?

Dread challenges us to have the courage to pursue these ultimate questions of life and death. In short, spiritual anxiety and dread motivate us to broaden and deepen our identity primarily by grounding ourselves deeper in love with God, others, and self. As we have seen with Chris and others, sometimes religion and its people hinder and harm our spiritual odyssey, and sometimes they help. Clearly, it behooves us to find people who help.

In contrast to anxiety, fear is more specific and goal-directed. Physically and psychologically, there is often good reason to be afraid, for it can be a signal to defend ourselves, to set boundaries, to avoid unnecessary pain, and to care for ourselves. Instead of avoiding, repressing, or numbing our fears, we can listen to them and let them help us.

Unhealthy fears diminish and paralyze us, and are often unrealistic and unnecessary. For example, unrealistic fear, like phobias and obsessive-compulsive ones, motivate us to avoid situations or futilely try to undo them. Moreover, fears that were necessary in childhood can be inappropriate in adulthood. What or who could harm us in the past need no longer injure or frighten us as much. Our challenge is to unlearn these past coping skills.

Spiritually, we can be afraid that we can be lost and stuck in nothingness. We can fear that there is no God, that there is no heaven, and that what we based our life on is a lie. We can fear facing our dark, shadow sides. We may be afraid that if we avail ourselves to the good, light, and joy of living, the bad, dark, and sadness may also appear. It is rare to have no fear of death, for death is beyond our control. Such fears are at the core of our being. They are essential parts of our unfinished symphony.

Indeed, perfect love casts out all fear. The rub is that there is no perfect love on earth. Thank God, we get glimpses and moments of perfect love. Such love wets our appetite and moves us to want more, but there is never enough, nor does it last. Still, love connects us with Love who helps us manage and ameliorate our fears. Actually, courage is love-facing-fear so that in this sense, our fears can strengthen us.

In short, healthy fears mobilize our defenses. They move us to stop, think, protect ourselves, and defend against destructive behavior. Unhealthy fears immobilize and diminish us. Whatever our fears, they call for psychological management as well as using our spiritual resources.

Life guarantees that our life will end. We know that no one, including ourselves, escapes dying and death. Conception is a prescription for death. Let listen to Margaret's words of death and dying—and, life and living.

Death and Dying

"I may be a little afraid of dying or the way I will die. I don't want to suffer, but if I have to suffer, I will accept it. I am not afraid of death; in fact, I welcome death. After all, I have lived 99 years. I wonder why I have lived this long. Moreover, I wonder just what is on the other side.

"Do you think there is a heaven? Will I meet my husband, my mom and dad, brothers and sister, friends? Will God be there? I hope so. Even if none of my hopes comes true, I can still say that life has been good to me. Although I made mistakes, I have no serious regrets. I have always tried to be a good person, to be kind and help others.

"Even if I found that God is a hoax, I would not have lived any differently. God's way is the best way. However, somewhere deep within me, I feel that God and heaven are true. There is something or someone in me that says yes. I rest easily with that yes. Thank God for that yes.

"Whatever happens, I am grateful for what life has given me. God blessed me with a loving husband, son, parents, friends, and wonderful experiences. Indeed, I was very poor in the first 25 years of my life; nevertheless, life was still good. Actually, my so-called poor life later helped me to appreciate the simple things and never to take life for granted. I can look back on life with a smile, and say: thank you."

Margaret can be a role model of how to face life and death. Instead of avoiding death and dying, she faces them. Instead of avoiding or rationalizing ultimate questions, she responds to them. Instead of being negative, she is positive. Instead of trying to control, she accepts and appreciates. Instead of taking life for granted, she is grateful. Her dying words will probably be "thank you."

Death and its dance partner (life) are the clearest manifestations of nothingness. Our certainty of death evokes our radical uncertainty of nothingness—our anxiety, dread, powerlessness, mortality. Death affirms that we cannot control nothing. Unfortunately, we often avoid, deny, or forget nothingness, and therefore impede a better life. Paradoxically and ironically, our denial of death leads to an impoverishment of life.

In the throes of nothingness, death embraces us. Especially as we grow older, nothingness speaks the language of dying. Nothingness proclaims that we will die, that the longer we live, the closer we are to death. Death invites us to realize that we are beings moving toward death. We can follow Margaret's way, and embrace death. Any other way is foolish. Instead of denying or avoiding its inevitability, we can be hospitable with death.

As we did with the beginning of a new life, we can be good hosts. We can prepare for death the same way that we prepared for birth. We make room for dying persons. We invite them into our hearts so that they are not alone. With reverence and respect, we care for them. From the beginning to the end, we strive to be present with and in Love. Likewise, we should also care for our own coming to death. (Actually, we cannot care well for others in dying unless we accept and respond to our own mortality.)

In nothingness, death comes to the foreground of our existence, and demands that we look at and listen to the truth of death. Death evokes the radical and ultimate questions. How and why am I going to live? What is my reason for being? What difference do I make? Will my death/life mean anything? Will people remember or forget me?

Death, particularly in nothingness, relentlessly pursues and questions us. What is the good life? Does it really matter if we are good or bad? Why do we suffer? Why are some people more fortunate than others are? Why do some people suffer more than others do? What happens when we die? Is death really a passing over to eternal life? When we die, is there simply nothing? Is there a heaven, and if so, what is it?

We emphasize that we progress because we die. This means that when we listen and respond to death's questions about life, they help us to live better lives. Actually, death and its articulation in dying are essential to living a healthy and holy life. Death moves us to live. Moreover, when we listen to our mortality, we can hear the voice of immortality. In this way, death seeks eternal life.

Our thesis is that nothingness is the harbinger of death, and therefore of life. Life and death, and living and dying are inseparable and necessary to live a good life. In short, spiritual loneliness, solitude, withdrawal, depression, emptiness, apathy, guilt, shame, frustration, anger, fear, anxiety, and dread in nothingness are necessary for healthy growth.

Thus, when we fail to accept death and nothingness, we diminish life and being alive. We can be grateful for the gift of coming-to-death, for it motivates us to live life fully as well as proclaims our reason for living. Health providers must speak of death not only as something to accept, but also as a motivator to live. Death is more important to life than any experience except love.

Our call and challenge is to accept that nothingness engenders growth in loneliness-and-love, depression-and-joy, apathy-and-enthusiasm, guilt-and-reconciliation, shame-and-worth, fear-and-courage, frustration-and-freedom, anger-and-peace, anxiety-and-serenity, dread-and-trust, emptiness-and-fulfillment, despair-and-hope, dying-and-living, death-and-life.

Impediments to Nothingness

We have proposed that nothingness is a spiritual desert where we re-evaluate our values in service of being a better and healthier person. In a seemingly barren land that bears fruit, we ask questions: What is a good and healthy life for me? Can I live it? What is the purpose of my life? Is there a heaven? Is there a God? Although this desert is a crisis of our identity and destiny, it is not easy to journey through and benefit from it.

Too often, we take negative attitudes toward nothingness. We falsely assume that since our experience is disruptive, it is symptomatic of something wrong or unhealthy. Sometimes in the service of mad models of mental health, we repress, deny, medicate, and escape from our uncomfortable feelings. As health providers, we seldom see nothingness as good and necessary to mental health. Worse yet, we can construe nothingness as unhealthy—an experience to purge rather than to explore.

A common mistake is to fall into "double feel," and consequently impede our growth. We can become depressed about being depressed, anxious about being anxious, and guilty about being guilty. In addition, we can refuse the gift of nothingness with defense mechanisms, like escapism, displacement, and repression. Along with wasting time and energy, we hurt ourselves and impede our health.

Other factors, like immaturity, mental illness, and addiction may delay or hinder our experience of nothingness. Clearly, when we are healthy and open to nothingness, we are likely to learn and grow from being in nothingness. Regardless of our situation, our challenge is to live through the experience and benefit from it. Indeed, the experience can be painful and scary. Nothing is upsetting.

Compounding matters, our Western society often conditions us to reject nothingness. We falsely assume that its discomfort is senseless and something to purge as quickly and easily as possible. And there are plenty of health providers ready to help us achieve these goals. When we live according to this pleasure principle, we find it difficult to accept that nothingness liberates and strengthens us.

Furthermore, the experience of nothingness is contrary to many of our values. An overly pragmatic society makes no room for nothing; the worst sin is to do nothing. People feel guilty if they cannot justify what they are doing, for we measure our worth in terms of what we produce, not according to what and who we are. Clearly, our pragmatic milieu makes it more difficult to cope with and learn from nothingness.

Spiritual growth simply is not congruent with many cultural norms. Since we expect ourselves to be vital and "happy"—without a care in the world, we are prone to avoid the necessary and positive sense of nothingness. With sincere and naive intentions, we are the cause of our own undoing.

Thus, we seldom embrace loneliness as a prelude to deeper love. We seldom accept depression in service of fulfillment. We seldom see anxiety in service of serenity. We are more likely to construe loneliness, depression, anxiety, and other similar feelings as negative and something to get rid of. Indeed, often with good intentions, we hinder healthy and holy growth.

Moreover, we may be alone without help, or we seek help that hinders. Pressure to take drugs, legal or illegal, with false promises of happiness or health can actually militate against true health and happiness. Although drugs may ameliorate severe symptoms and enable us to cope better, they do not teach how to cope effectively, nor do they give us meaning and purpose.

Instead of trying to purge, numb, or repress our nothingness, we ought to accept our experiences. Indeed, when we fail to face our nothingness, we risk getting lost in nothingness. When we accept our nothingness, we free ourselves from wasting time and energy in fighting who we are, and we free ourselves for becoming our true selves.

The Redemptive Power of Pain

Growth and happiness involve both pleasurable and painful experiences. Love, play, and celebration usually exclude pain and include comfort and exhilaration. We welcome such enjoyable experiences, for they are more pleasant than and just as necessary as the unpleasant ones. The painful ones, however, are usually more difficult and daunting, but just as necessary as the enjoyable ones. Clearly, we invariably have more trouble with the painful times of growth. Thus, let us reflect on the meaning and value of pain.

One way to look at pain is as a function of change, specifically of existing structures. Pain can certainly indicate change that is neither congruent with nor supportive of growth and integration. Physically, the pain of cancer points to pathological processes that can destroy our body. Psychologically, when we deny important experiences, we pay a painful price. Spiritually to live without purpose and meaning is hell. Pain—physical, psychological, or spiritual—conveys that something is awry and that we need care.

Pain can also be symptomatic of healthiness. For example, proper exercise and diet can be uncomfortable but healthy. Psychologically, becoming aware of repressed feelings can be a painful movement toward learning effective coping. Spiritually, a dark night of the soul can be a daunting road to enlightenment.

The importance of pain is that it summons us to listen to and look at what is happening, and to attend to others and ourselves. Pain keeps us honest. When we heed pain, we seek care. Without pain, we might forget to care—a prescription for a miserable life. Pain relentlessly pursues us to seek an adequate response from self, others, and God. Nevertheless, too often we avoid or numb our pain, or respond with inadequate care.

Pain is also a force that unites us. We all stand on the common ground of pain. Indeed, pain is the universal equalizer that binds us together. Still, we blunt the magnet of pain that draws us together. For instance, we are prone to avoid or silence the dying and poor because their pleas of pain evoke our own mortality and poverty. Someone said that if you want help, go to the poor, for they understand our need for one another.

Suffering calls for competent and compassionate care. Sometimes our competent skills can "fix" what causes pain. Often we can do nothing but help others (and ourselves) bear, ease, and lighten their discomfort, simply by being compassionately present to them. Clearly, when we are with people who genuinely care, we become closer, and this makes all the difference in the world.

Indeed, our pain reminds us of our need for care, and it draws us together to help and become closer. Pain strips us of our pretense and humbles us; it pressures us to depend on and trust one another. In this way, pain engenders intimacy, mercy, and care. This call to care includes everyone as caregivers and receivers.

We can see people in pain, disabled, with special needs, and in general sub-functional people as gifts, for they constantly remind us of our primary reason for being—to care for and love one another. Perhaps the less fortunate (in terms of ability and opportunity) help the more fortunate. For example, in spite of the heavy burdens of caring for a special needs child, many parents will say their disabled child challenges and evokes the best in them. Read the book *Far from the Tree* by Andrew

Solomon (2011), for an insightful and compassionate account of this phenomenon.

Actually, our own faults can be our assets. For example, it is common to hear old timers in Alcoholic Anonymous say that they are grateful for their alcoholism. They came to admit that they could not control their drinking, and that only a reality greater than they could restore them to sanity. Consequently, they turned their will and life over to the care of this Higher Power that most call God. Indeed, Oh *felix culpa*—Oh happy fault.

Although no one lives without any pain, life is not fair in its distribution of pain. Clearly, some people suffer much more than others do. Most of us, however, are fortunate not to suffer chronic pain, and we should be grateful. We should never take for granted a life of relative comfort, or forget to be grateful. Perhaps our relatively painless life calls us to care for the less fortunate. Perhaps comfort calls for care of the uncomfortable. Perhaps care is incomplete without pain. Perhaps pain with care is redemptive.

A common paradox of pain is that when we are in pain, we also want to be alone. For example, when sick, we want to be treated and cared for, but we also want privacy. In nothingness, sometimes we want to share, and at other times, we prefer to be alone. Thus, pain desires both the caring presence of another as well as solitude.

We have seen that spiritual pain is seldom a message for prevention or treatment, but it is an invitation to accept and grow. However, most models of mental health exclude nothingness and God. Within such frameworks, the pain of spiritual development may make no sense, or be judged as symptomatic of something wrong or unhealthy, and thus be something to treat and purge.

Spiritually, sometimes we must suffer disintegration that leads to reintegration. Metaphorically, we must descend into hell to ascend into heaven. Sometimes we must undergo a breakdown (of ego function) to experience a breakthrough (of spirituality). The bottom line is that we must journey through deserts of nothingness to experience self, others, and God more intimately. Then, heaven makes experiential sense. From this perspective, health providers can help their clients avoid counterfeits of heaven (addictions) and achieve more true heaven (love) on earth.

When we suffer in and with Love, we can manage and care more effectively, and suffer less. Although love and competent care do not purge pain, they do mitigate and heal. Instead of heaven merely being a future reward, our suffering with and in service of Love helps us have times of heaven on earth. In faith, we desire with hope that ultimately we will be in Love without any pain, or perpetually in heaven.

In short, growth in holy experiences involves being in and out of nothingness. From Judeo-Christian perspectives, nothingness is the desert that leads to the promised land, the Lent that leads to Easter, death that engenders life.

From therapeutic perspectives, health providers can address the spiritual dynamics and avoidances of nothingness. Instead of medicating or misconstruing the symptoms of nothingness, they can help their patients learn and grow from their spiritual feelings. Health professionals can see and foster spirituality and even God as essential to health.

6

JOURNEYS FROM
NOTHINGNESS TO GOD

VIRTUALLY ALL PSYCHOLOGISTS WOULD contend that aging is a significant factor in growth and development, but few would include God in their theories. We have proposed that God (or a similar conception) is necessary for health, and that the experience of nothingness is a necessary prelude for deeper experiences of self, others, and God. Our thesis is that no-thing leads us to the Source and Destiny of being holy and healthy.

We can experience nothingness for many reasons, like one's life experience, age, personality, fortuitous factors, and so on. Indeed, whatever generalizations we make, people do not follow the exact same pattern. As with grieving, we experience nothingness in our unique way and according to our time, and we usually share many similarities with others in our individual way.

Moreover, we can encounter nothingness at virtually any time. For instance, stressful experiences may manifest its adumbrated presence. A national catastrophe such as war, a personal crisis, or psychotherapy may evoke nothingness. A common way is to experience it at certain stages in life. We will show how such crises of nothingness are important because they pressure us to grow.

We have seen that nothingness involves a deflation of ego in that we experience the limits of our ego's power to manage and make sense of life. For instance, the many languages of nothingness demand answers that include and go beyond our ego. Moreover, in and out of nothingness, death, dire illness, catastrophes, life-changing crises, falling in and out of love, victimization, betrayal, despair, violence, solitude, and so forth can also bring us to our knees. In this humbling position, we admit that mere rationality cannot adequately answer the ultimate questions.

Most spiritual writers contend that we must go through times of desolation and darkness to come to consolation and enlightenment. En-lightenment includes dark nights, consolation embraces desolation, faith needs doubt, promised lands include deserts, and life is the meaning of death.

Our proposal is that we can experience nothingness at certain times throughout life. Although there are no exact ages when everyone enters the desert, there are general periods when many of us are more likely to experience a developmental crisis. The proposed stages of development are flexible and have a wide range with regard to age. Clearly, the older we get, the more variables there are, so it is foolish to predict with certainty. Thus, our framework is more of a guideline to and concretizations of what often occurs.

Most of us experience at least one significant transition in our lifetime. In addition, such crises may be due to idiosyncratic events or existential dynamics, or both. Furthermore, crises can vary in intensity from very mild to severe.

For instance, although "midlife crisis" is probably an overused and perhaps a trite phrase, many people do experience a transitional time in their early forties. Many mid-lifers do reflect on their limits and mortal-ity, their past dreams and future goals, their relationships, androgyny, and themselves. Many mid-lifers, because of age and situational events, begin an inner journey that differs from their previous outer journey.

We give age ranges or stages to concretize our theory as well as to enable us to compare ourselves with one another and to prepare for our own experiences of nothingness, whether or not they fall within a specific time period. Even though epigenetic transitions do not follow a strict chronological schedule, many people do experience significant changes within or close to the age parameters.

Such spiritual deserts are important if for no other reason than that they tend to keep us honest. If we are running away from ourselves, living inauthentic lives, or simply misguided, nothingness pressures us to reevaluate and renew ourselves. No-thing can lead us to a better appreciation of everything. In this way, no-thing is a harbinger of being healthier.

In the following sections, we will describe periods of holiness (being God-centered) and healthiness (being whole) and how they relate to stages of nothingness. We present succinct descriptions and analyses of developmental, spiritual transitions.

Adolescence

Let us begin with exploring the world of a young adolescent who is beginning to experience nothingness. "Why are they always on my case? Why are they always questioning me? Why are they always checking up on me? Why don't they trust me? Why don't they understand? Why don't they give me more freedom? They say that I have to show them that I am responsible. How can I show them when they prevent me from doing what I want to do?

"They ask me what I want. Just leave me alone. Let me do what I want. In six months, I'll be sixteen. I'll be old enough to drive, and then I can go where I want. I can't wait. However, my all-knowing parents say that if I don't shape up, I will not get my license. Look, I am not sexually active in contrast to more than half of my class. Nor do I use drugs. Give me some credit. Why did God make parents?

"To be honest, I don't know what I really want. Sometimes, I am so bored I could jump out of my skin. Nothing makes sense. When I was a kid, life was simpler and easier. There was not so much going on. I didn't care about my weight and looks, boys, sex, dates, parents, teachers, and so many things. Ah yes, teachers are another example of people who think they know it all.

"When will life make sense again? Will I ever know the answers? Will I ever be able to live my life the way I want? What am I going to do? What college do I want to attend? What will be my major? Who cares? Do I care? Do I want to go to college? I feel stuck, and nowhere to go. I feel like I am drowning in a sea of questions with no answers."

This teenager shares some of the features of the first explicit experience of nothingness, which usually occurs in early to mid-adolescence. *The Catcher in the Rye* and *The Diary of Anne Frank* are literary examples of this adolescent nothingness. Let us look at how in early adolescence nothingness lurks in the background and comes to the foreground of our lives.

A common symptom is boredom, when we feel we have nothing to do or be. Although we have boundless energy, we are often tired. Feeling stuck in a meaningless situation, our behavior seems to be aimless and nonintegrated, and it is, for nothing appeals to us. We have lived scarcely a decade and a half, and we are sick and tired of life. We feel that no one understands. We are isolated and alone. No-body and no-thing make sense. Our world is a cosmos of opposition, ambivalence, and nonsense. Yet, our apparent disorder is necessary for new order.

We suspect almost everyone—"the whole damn world is phony." We see the imperfections and mistakes of elders—especially those in authority, like parents and teachers—and, we can criticize them with ruthless discernment, often to our elders' frustration and irritation. People who seem to have their life in "perfect" order, have all the answers, or are authoritarian, especially irritate us because we feel much the opposite. Since we feel a lack of order and sense, such orderly know it all people turn us off.

Since structure is a painful reminder of our nothingness, we want little part of it. In fact, we may take keen delight in criticizing parents or breaking the rules (ego); obedience is an ambivalent burden. Indeed, parents are often at their wits' end to know what to do with this new edition of daughter or son.

Spiritually, we experience our Spirit in its absence. What this means is that since we have not yet come to an explicit spiritual experience, our nothingness feels decidedly negative. To be sure, children are spiritual beings, but more in an implicit or subtle way. Part of leaving childhood is to come face to face with the spiritual in a new way.

Paradoxically, our negativity is positive because it leads to a new and more direct experience of the spiritual. Like the blossoming of Anne Frank, most of us eventually emerge more overtly as spiritual persons. Out of nothingness, we come to a fuller mode of being.

This developmental stage, particularly in its negative phase, can easily frustrate parents, teachers, and other authorities, as well as adolescents themselves. In reaction to our stress, we as parents too often try with good intentions to purge their adolescent's negativity. We may falsely assume that their experience is a problem to solve and purge rather than to accept, manage, and grow from it. We should realize that this kind of spiritual negativity and ambiguity is uncomfortable but healthy. As parents and adolescents, we live through this stage in order to develop spiritually.

If we are patient and keep the future in perspective, we will come to more sense. However, if parents try to force adolescents to become mature adults before their time (in Erikson's framework, foreclosure), adolescents will only suffer needlessly and risk unhealthy development. With good intentions, we (parents, teachers, counselors, et al.) can impede their development.

As parents, we can help by understanding and accepting our children's experience and give them the needed structure and freedom to grow. We can be healthy role models as well as being available when our teenagers call on us. We can understand, support, console, and guide them so that their experiences are more likely to be meaningful and fruitful. Indeed, we give them consequences and alternatives when they behave inappropriately. They do not have to understand or like the rules in order to keep them.

Out of this seemingly negative nothingness, most adolescents, eventually and directly come to actualize and express their spirit. Again, they appear to change suddenly. No longer are they bored of living in nonsense. Often just the opposite, they are enchanted and romantically in love with everything. They perceive reality in a radically new way. Pessimism changes to optimism.

They may still criticize (ego) but not from boredom but from a sense of idealism (spirit). Before nothing was possible; now everything is possible, or at least should be possible. Being idealistic, these adolescents tend to take an "all or nothing" approach. Although reality curbs their idealism and their future is uncertain, basic enthusiasm persists.

Reality may now serve as a catalyst for romanticism, beauty, wonder, introspection, or spiritual reflection. Teachers may no longer be an object of criticism, but they may now become a source of emulation and inspiration. Mid-teenagers also begin to think of life commitment. "Where am I going?" becomes a lived question from within, not an irritating question asked by someone else from without.

Love also changes, for it begins to incorporate such factors as responsibility, respect, and commitment. For some adolescents, love may also include the sacred more personally in that they try to experience God and others as well as themselves more dearly. They may even begin to have a vague sense of kinship with humankind and even its Source. Indeed, they are novices of spirituality; nevertheless, they are on their way.

In the past, adolescents experienced an implicit presence to the sacred, but now they begin to have more opportunities for direct holy encounters. Although holy experiences are not of the same intensity and quality as mature adults, their experience differs from and is more mature than that of a child's.

They may begin to experience some mystery and paradox, a sense of divine dependency and indebtedness, and deeper love, faith, and doubt. Their initiation into this new life promises significant changes. Moreover, since their cognitive skills have also developed (formal operations), they are able to reflect on, make more sense of, and integrate their new experiences.

In adolescence, we begin to personalize rules. Morality, for instance, has new meaning. In Kohlberg's framework, boys can begin to take a post-conventional approach toward morality in following principles of justice. According to Gilligan, girls are more likely to cultivate an ethic of care.

This experience of nothingness can be relatively easy because there is less danger of repression, distortion, fixation, and pathological decisions. Adolescent resiliency and inexperience decrease the possibility of unhealthy coping. Youth is often a redeeming feature.

On the other hand, some adolescents may undergo unhealthy experiences of nothingness. Because of one's premorbid personality and the stress of nothingness as well as other adolescent pressures, latent pathology may emerge. Another possibility is an adolescent may be too immature or weak to experience nothingness. Drug addiction and sex are common and futile responses to such problems.

In reaction to the threat of nothingness, some adolescents regress to an earlier level of development or become fixated in nothingness. For example, some regress to preadolescence where life is simpler, while others are stuck in nothingness well into their thirties. For various reasons, we can fail to grow up.

In short, most adolescents eventually cope adequately with their problems and possibilities. Their spiritual functions begin to emerge more personally and overtly. Although they are neophytes, adolescents do begin such life-projects as mature love, responsibility, commitment, morality, freedom, and spiritual experiences of God, others, and self.

We should not take adolescence lightly or carelessly. There are so many significant physical, sexual, emotional, cognitive, social, and spiritual changes. Although there are volumes about adolescent development, relatively few address the spiritual let alone God aspects of adolescent growth.

Keep in mind that the values we form in adolescence tend to guide us throughout life. Nevertheless, we seldom teach and witness to the importance of spirituality and God in living a healthy life. To forget, deny, or exclude God from development and growth is a serious mistake.

Young Adulthood

From adolescence to young adulthood, we continue our journey through the desert of nothingness. Listen to this college sophomore. "Sometimes I feel like I am trapped in a sound proof box made of one way windows. I can see people, but they cannot see me, and they cannot hear me. No one understands. No one listens to me. No one knows me. I cannot get out of my invisible, lonely prison. Sex does not work. Drugs ease the pain, but I always return to the same place. Nothing works.

"Things used to make sense. In my first year of college, fear, challenge, and enthusiasm moved me. Perhaps I was naive and idealistic, but I liked university life. I found the teachers and classes interesting. I wanted to learn more and more. Now, I feel stuck. If I leave, where would I go? What would I do? Would life be any better? I may as well stay here.

"It seems like I question everything. The same and similar teachers that inspired me, now irritate me. I look at life with cynical eyes. For example, I used to go to daily religious services and pray; now these practices seem like meaningless rituals. Maybe Marx and Freud were right, that religion and its God are illusions that soothe and control the masses.

"Moreover, I feel alone and lonely. No one seems to care or understand. My fraternity brothers offer me alcohol, sex, parties, inane advice, or to do something, not nothing. But I feel like doing nothing, not something. Anyway, who knows what is best? What makes something good or bad? What makes behavior healthy or unhealthy? Is what is right for me also right for you?

"One good thing, I think, is that I question everything and I am learning in a new way. Although there are few satisfying answers, I no longer take life for granted. I look at life and at what others say with critical eyes and ears. I especially like writers and philosophers who question assumptions and offer different paradigms. I certainly think, feel, and act differently."

This bright, young man speaks of our next crisis of nothingness, which usually begins in our late teens or early twenties. Experiences of teachers and students along with research have shown that the sophomore year is often conspicuously different from other college years. The lonely, withdrawn, bored, and angry sophomore is well known. The energetic and naive freshman often turns into a confused and complicated sophomore.

Instead of going to college, many late adolescents and young adults take a different path. Some go to school to learn a trade, while others join the military, and others get married. Such young men and women are likely to have less time and environmental opportunity (as in college) to explore themselves in nothingness.

In many respects, these young adults may mature earlier in practical matters than their university peers. In a sense, they cannot afford the luxury of studying life, for they must live life. A caveat, however, is that these young people may be so involved with environmental demands, they find little time or opportunity to question themselves and life. They may postpone their crisis, act more mature (foreclosure) than they really are, or avoid or numb their feelings via activities (work, play, sex, drugs). Nevertheless, many face their nothingness, but in ways that may differ than their university peers.

Whether or not one is in school, a "sophomore moratorium" is a daunting prelude to a more mature life. As a student once said, "It's as if I had to be disenchanted before I could became enchanted with life." (The etymology of a sophomore is "wise fool.")

In this nothingness, we often perceive the relativity of reality, so that objective absolutes seem untenable. To that end, we avoid being judgmental, and are apt to accept almost any behavior. Many of us think that perception is reality. We assume that if one perceives something as good, then it is good for that person, but not necessarily good for another. That is, our individual (ego) cognition and perception highly influence our meaning and ethics. What is truth for "me" becomes a serious question.

Another issue of the twenties is commitment, both personal and professional. Will I be married, single, or a vowed celibate? Do I want to be a parent? When will I decide? Is marriage or any personal commitment relevant? What do I want to do? How will I make money? How do I want to live? Why do I want to live? Clearly, our responses to such questions will significantly influence our future.

It is also common to discern our inherited "shoulds"—what we received and learned from authorities. Our young adult crisis pressures us to focus on the limits and imperfections of our inheritance, and we may criticize what we did and did not learn and experience. We can become angry with people who formed and informed us, like parents, siblings, teachers, and civic and religious leaders.

A common danger is that as young adults we can become fixated in this stage and refuse to grow until we receive what we think we had the right to receive. To speak of ideals and to engage in protest demonstrations are not unusual. The realization that life is imperfect and unfair may seem obvious to older, mature adults, but not so to many young adults.

It may be frightening to realize that we must develop freedom and autonomy primarily within ourselves (spirit) and not acquire them from external agents (ego). A caveat is to look outside ourselves for the source of freedom and happiness, and demand that people and situations satisfy our needs. Especially if significant people seriously deprived us in childhood, we can act like children in seeking and demanding others to satisfy our needs.

Demands take many forms. "It's the teacher's fault that I'm not learning." "I'm not free because of sexism, ageism, and racism." "It's your fault that I'm unhappy." "If you don't love me, I'll go crazy." "It's society's fault that I'm so miserable." "I'm entitled to be given what I did not have."

Some people fixate and never resolve such feelings, and consequently expect others to change so they (themselves) can feel better. Indeed, external and societal changes can enable us to be free and happy. Nevertheless, adults cannot afford to place their well-being in the hands of others. Such dependency is appropriate for children, but not for adults.

Another common and key dynamic is loneliness. In the uneasy and quiet nights of young adulthood, we may hear, deep within ourselves, questions: Can I give to and receive from another? Am I worthy? Will I ever be genuinely intimate with another person? We reach out but our touch falls short. We speak but no one hears. We listen but we hear nothing.

For various untoward experiences, some of us may be frightened of what we want most—intimacy. We may simply feel helpless or ignorant about how to be genuinely intimate. We may have feelings of unworthiness, and feel ashamed to offer ourselves. We may feel afraid of rejection, not measuring up, or making a fool of ourselves. In contrast, we may have inflated self-esteem or be narcissistic so that we are prone to manipulate and use others for our satisfaction. Clearly, when a person with an inflated ego hooks up with a person who has a deflated ego, their dance is toxic.

Frequently, our yearning for love goes unrequited. We sense that casual sex falls terribly short of fulfilling our lonely desire for love. We desire the healing love of another person, but the other is not there for us. Although we may feel alone, afraid, or unworthy, we want to reach out, to touch, and be touched. Indeed, this can be a very vulnerable time, or an opportune time.

We must accept that healthy loneliness, like in nothingness, is essential to coming to love, that it purifies us for the gifts of Love. In and through loneliness, we can become aware of ourselves as well as discern what impedes us from loving. Spiritually, we may begin to be aware of a Higher Power who resides within us and who can give us the courage to love. In the silence of our loneliness, some of us begin to hear whispers of divine help.

In the nothingness of young adulthood (or at any time), we can realize that self-confrontation in loneliness is a crisis of loving and ultimately of being loved. Our loneliness is not the opposite of love, but rather it inextricably relates to love. In this advent of love, we ask: Can I love myself? Can I love another? Can I live the true spirit of life—love? Am I worthy of love? Will someone ever love me unconditionally? Does love exist for me? Will someone answer me?

Without such questions, without lonely nights, it is difficult and perhaps impossible to live an authentic life of love. Remember that love without loneliness is an illusion. Remember that loneliness desires, motivates, and nourishes love. Remember that life without love becomes bland and listless, lacking enthusiasm and lasting meaning.

The paradox is that as young adults we must travel the deserts of loneliness to enjoy the lands of love. The dangers are to commit to immature love or to numb the pain of self-discovery. To surrender ourselves before we discover ourselves is a common prescription for failure. Marriage, for example, is a common escape from nothingness. Other escapes, like sex, work, and drugs (body and ego), are available, numerous, and tempting, but are inadequate responses to the desires of our spirit.

Another danger is that a person's loneliness may become unhealthy. For instance, if a woman has had past experiences of severe neglect or dependency, she may feel that her life depends totally on the love of others, and that her happiness is out of her hands. She needs the panacea of another's affection in her futile attempt to make up for her past deficits.

Indeed, such deprivation makes her especially vulnerable to exploitive and abusive men.

In the midst of this personal pursuit of love, it is common to question and challenge conventional morality, even more deeply than in adolescence. Rather than conforming to rules and expectations of society just because they are conventional, as young adults we may become acutely aware of individual rights and values.

This period of questioning is often part of the process that leads to a "post-conventional" stand toward morality. Unfortunately, too many young adults remain conventional, following or simply criticizing the law rather than listening to its spirit. On the other hand, some develop a morality of justice, or even better: a morality of love.

Along with morality, most young desert travelers question religion. Some become quite critical of religious institutions, their practices, and their members. In young adulthood and later as well, we are especially critical of phoniness, irrelevance, double standards, sexism, manipulation, abuse, and ready-made solutions. In reaction, many young adults drop out of formal religion (ego), or try new ones.

While some criticize and reject religion, some pursue it. Instead of focusing on its limits, they subscribe to its possibilities. Becoming passionately involved, they may engage in extraordinary service, such as helping the poor and oppressed. Indeed, some may use their religious activity to avoid nothingness, while others journey through nothingness and commit to a life of Godly service. Whatever path we take, most of us want religion (ego) to be experiential and helpful (spirit) rather than just cognitive and abstract.

Other young adults grapple with their God. For instance, some take a humanistic position, stating that life can be meaningful without a transcendent God. Others regard religion as a dead issue, and become indifferent to God. Perhaps most simply drift away and get stuck in a secular rut. Still others seriously discern conceptions of God, doggedly question, and persistently pursue a meaningful relationship with God.

We have seen that we can fail to accept our feelings of nothingness because we mistakenly assume that they are unhealthy. To our detriment, we can become anxious about and try to escape from our nothingness. We can use reason to purge rather than to promote faith. We forget that nothing increases our being in Love.

With or without family and friends, a mentor usually plays a significant role in adult development before mid-life. Ideally, parents are primary mentors; however, they often fall out of favor during this time. Other mentors, such as a teacher, supervisor, counselor, 12-step sponsor, older friend, or relative, can be crucially influential in the way we develop at this or any time.

A good mentor is primarily a person who witnesses to holy and healthy attitudes, who lives a wholesome life, and who encourages, supports, and inspires us to become our best selves. As mentors, we avoid imposing God or anything on people, but rather we evoke God who dwells within and among us.

Our challenge is to choose and cultivate mentors of the heart as well as of the mind. Academic and career mentors can guide our intellectual and functional pursuits and successes. The spiritual mentor, however, is crucial in the ongoing formation of the spiritual life. With the help of a mentor, novices of adulthood can learn to be their true selves. Good mentors accept and encourage us to question our assumptions and teachings as well as offer us ways to make spiritual sense of life.

Should health providers be spiritual mentors as well as psychological ones? Indeed, 12-step sponsors are both psychological and spiritual mentors, and they play a significant role in recovery. If spirituality and a God are essential components of health, then it follows that psychiatrists, psychologists, social workers, and counselors should be mentors who help clients grow in their spiritual relationships with themselves, God, and others. Clearly, how you construe health highly influences the way you try to help others and yourself.

Solitude, as in any life passage, can help us take time and space to discover and be ourselves. A personal journal may also help us to pause to clarify the confusion and darkness of self-emergence. However, the energy of young adulthood coupled with the cultural pressure for immediate gratification can make it difficult to slow down and take time. Like any significant change, this advent of adulthood calls for a prudent and patient journey. Mentoring and counseling should facilitate this development.

Life can be so busy with personal and professional tasks along with opportunities to explore and have fun that we can easily forget what is most important. We can find ourselves in the position of having little or no time to respond to our desire for God. We must take time to be still and listen to what and whom our heart desires most. We must remember the message of nothingness—to find and cultivate experiences that last and matter.

Established Adulthood

However we deal with our youthful years of adulthood, most of us get older and come to our next desert passage. Listen to Olivia. "I have this vague but strong sense of anger. I am not sure if my anger is just or reasonable. My husband asks me if something is wrong, and I tell him nothing. I don't want to hurt him, and besides, I'm not sure. We love and support each other, and we are parents to two wonderful children. We are blessed. So why am I uneasy?

"I have my degree in accounting, and worked for a few years until my husband finished medical school. When he started his residency, I quit my job to bear and raise our children. Indeed, we are financially affluent so that I have almost anything I want. So why am I a malcontent?

"Let me be candid. What about me? I am a bit resentful that I helped put my husband through medical school, and have taken most of the parental responsibilities. Inside me is a voice that asks when is it going to be my turn? Sometimes I feel like I got the short end of the deal. I would like to get my CPA, and return to my professional work. Bur who will take care of the children? I almost feel guilty for feeling this way. It feels so selfish.

"When is it my turn? Everyone, except me, seems to be doing his or her thing. More importantly, I wonder if I want or can live the next 15 or 20 years like the last 7. I know I love my husband and kids, but I question my willingness and ability to keep my commitments. It seems like I am missing the boat.

"Maybe I can make some changes. They seem so radical. What would happen to my children? Still, both will soon be in school. Can I go back to school? Can I reenter the work force. Will I make it? I am tired of feeling the way I do. I must try to do it; otherwise, regrets will haunt me. I don't want to grow older as an angry woman."

The third desert of nothingness usually occurs in our early thirties. Emerging from the "last year of youth"—twenty-nine, like Olivia—most of us are becoming established in our personal and professional commitments. The experimenting twenties are ending, and a new desert is on the horizon.

As seasoned adults, we may expect life to be settled and predictable. Moreover, our busy lives afford little time for personal reflection. Thus, critical changes can be a disturbing experience. Nevertheless, once again, nothingness throws us back on ourselves, and we are likely to experience loneliness, anxiety, and anger as well as issues of identity and commitment.

As in earlier transitions, there are new expectations. For instance, people expect us to "act adult"—to be sober, settled, and sane. Unlike young adulthood, it is more difficult to be silly, unsettled, and different. Striving to be responsible and successful can engender a fast and pressured pace. Yet, just when life is becoming orderly, seemingly nothing unsettles it.

We again question life—or, life questions us. Who have I become? Do I want the next ten years to be like the past ten years? Who really loves me? What are my goals? Do I want to stay in my job? Do I want to stay in my marriage? Will I ever get married? Do I want to stay single? Why am I so restless? Why am I so angry? What is happening to me? Is this all there is? In short: The focus is on "me."

We can call this crisis of nothingness the desert of self-concern. It is a time when we are concerned about our own welfare. Instead of egotism or excessive self-centeredness, this time can engender respect and care for oneself. This need not be self-serving or narcissistic. Rather, we should feel guilty if we neglect ourselves.

The desert of established adulthood invites us to claim our freedom—freedom from impediments and freedom for success and health. Paradoxically, we focus on what life can give us as well as what we can freely give in return. For example, a woman may become acutely aware of how some people treat her mainly as a function—mother, wife, provider, servant, and perhaps "second-class citizen." In her discontent, she may strive for and demand more freedom.

In this nothingness, it is common to feel angry at injustice, oppression, and disrespect, feel a lack of appreciation, or simply feel taken for granted. Although most people have difficulty in learning and growing from anger, it is important in achieving self-respect, protection, assertion, strength, and freedom. Anger can motivate us to make productive changes in self as well as to improve our affairs.

As we have seen in the last chapter, it may be difficult to listen to the truth of our anger especially if we have learned that anger is wrong, or that it is expressed thoughtlessly. Instead of accepting and listening to our angry feelings, we may get mad at ourselves for being mad, or feel guilty, and build up a slush fund of anger, or express anger without concern for the welfare of anyone. When we cope in such negative ways, we are prone to express our pent-up anger inappropriately, or become depressed.

Listen to this woman: "I am tired of being a servant, of giving, giving, and giving. I've worked for ten years without pay or recognition. My family simply expects me to wait on them. To say the least, I am tired of people taking me for granted. Except for my service, it is as if I am invisible. Who acknowledges me as valuable? Who gives to me? I want more. I want to do more. I want to be more."

Rather than being selfish, this woman seeks appreciation and freedom. Her angry "no" can be in service of freedom—a "yes" to a better life for herself and others as well. She can listen and respond to its challenge. She wants to be a free person and not a functional servant. Her nothingness calls her to being. For various reasons, women often experience this crisis more acutely than men do.

Concern about personal (spiritual) commitments is another common issue. We may ask if our marriage is good as we initially thought it would be. Too often, we find that it has digressed rather than progressed. We may also question past motives: Why did I get married? Do I live a life of love? Do I still really love him (or her)? What has happened to my love?

If single, people may pressure us to get married, or they patronize, pity, or isolate us. If we are members of a religious community or celibate cleric, we may feel that this is the time to leave, or to renew our vows. Whatever our situation, we may think of changing our commitment, or of ways to renew and promote it.

Nothingness also questions the relevance of our functional (ego) life. If I am a paid or unpaid worker, I may wonder about the worth of my work as well as if my work and values are in harmony. Does my work impede or facilitate healthy living? Is my functional life more important than my spiritual life? Is my life primarily one of service, so that personal intimacy, sharing, and support are secondary or forgotten?

Is my life so busy that I have little time for loved ones? Am I so busy being useful that I am too tired to be "uselessly" present to more permanent and life-giving experiences? Too tired to play, too preoccupied to relax, too busy to keep the Sabbath holy, or just a general feeling of being on a treadmill are symptoms of maximizing functionality and minimizing spirituality.

With good intentions, we can forget our spiritual lives and lose our bearings and purpose for living. When we forget and fail to draw on our energies of Love, we can lose our enthusiasm for life. To help us not to forget, nothingness pressures us to take stock of how our functional and spiritual lives can work together. The voice of nothingness calls us to remember our Source of living a balanced life.

Because of our hectic lives, we can easily forget the essentials for healthy and holy living. We can be actively involved in religion and still forget to work on spiritual growth. A well-intentioned life of social service can displace or impede a direct and active spiritual life. This seductive trap does not bypass disciples of religion. We can use religion to avoid nothingness, and therefore impede our experience of God.

As we grow older, we can mistakenly think that our present adult struggles are entirely different or have no connection to previous ones. We may take foolish steps to resolve our plight, like getting out of a relationship, finding a new job, moving to a different location, or accumulating things. We look outside rather than within ourselves so that we avoid and conceal the main issues that are not only psychological but also spiritual as well.

We can neglect or withdraw from such experiences as solitude, creative pauses, and prayer as well as interpersonal caring and sharing. Consequently, we can feel that the spirit of our life is distant or lost. Nothingness is an invitation to slow down in a busy life, to be patient in an impatient world, to discover our lost Love, and to rekindle our reason for being.

Nothingness intensifies the pain of loneliness and isolation. For instance, single people may acutely feel the problems of loneliness. Although they may have more freedom from external restraints, their freedom for genuine intimacy is often restricted. Being celibate and being intimate are possible but difficult to integrate in a society that gives little support and opportunity for healthy celibate intimacy. Whether married or single, sexuality compounds the issue of intimacy. As one nun stated, "These are the thirsty thirties. Sometimes it seems that my hormones have a life of their own."

Indeed, most women are reaching their sexual/genital peak. Their physical urges ardently desire pleasurable union in love. Parenthetically, a woman's urgent longings for sexual love may threaten a man who has already passed his genital peak and may not know how to love. Sex seeks love, and without love, sexual satisfaction falls short of abiding contentment, and can lead to more loneliness, frustration, and anger. To be sure, sex can never adequately replace Love.

For most of us, established adulthood inundates us with demands and responsibilities, and leaves little room for nothing. Understandably, we can mistakenly think that we can circumvent nothingness or fill it with things to do. Our restlessness is a living reminder that we are primarily and ultimately dependent on one another and on God. Without Love, we futilely try to satisfy ourselves. With God, we can help ourselves and one another grow older together in Love.

Our lonely and vulnerable absence in nothingness seeks a more permanent presence. In nothingness, we come to realize that loneliness is a gift that presents God-to-be-discovered—that in absence, God is present. When we remember that in nothingness we desire God-and-others, we are apt to slow down, pause, and be mindful of our interpersonal lives.

When our life lacks enthusiasm, vitality, and spirit, we can question and restructure our lives in ways that foster a life of love. We can be silent and still, and hear renewing questions. Where and how can I find healthy intimacy? Can I love? Whom can I love? Am I loveable? Who really loves me? Can I love? If not, why not? We can come to realize that love, the core of spirituality and health, is the paramount response to our nothingness.

Rather than whispering its message as in young adulthood, death speaks its message more clearly: Live! Even though death is the most poignant and persistent articulation of nothingness, we try to escape death and dying, and consequently nothingness and its benefits. We can forget to allow room for death in our lives. Indeed, death without Love can lead to absurdity.

This is tragic because the ability to accept death, our own and that of others, is necessary for health. An acceptance of death leads to more life, fulfillment, and peace. When we ask the question: Is this all there is? We can answer: No—there is infinitely more! Our desires in nothingness call for hope that engenders a vision of infinite possibilities.

In summary, we have seen that a common way to escape nothingness is hyper-activism. The demons of hyper-activity can easily seduce us at any age, for the expectations to succeed are strong. It is imperative to take (ego) time and make space (body) to love (spirit). Too often, we try to find the meaning of life in what we do rather than in who we are. Consequently, we seldom take time simply to be, to celebrate the mystery of being alive.

When we do have time, we become anxious or anesthetize ourselves. Without much awareness, our lives become matters of adjusting to and coping with an unending series of demands (ego). Reactively, we may use substances, including food and alcohol, to slow down or to numb ourselves. Although we probably have many years to live, we already feel weary and discouraged. True enjoyment and enthusiasm have been crowded out.

To tame desert demons, whatever they may be, Anne Morrow Lindbergh in *Gift from the Sea* (1955) encourages us to take creative pauses to listen to and reflect on our lives. It helps to take stock of our interpersonal spirituality. How is our life of love really being lived? How can we improve it? Reflective reading, listening in solitude, and consistently involving ourselves in love are ways to promote spiritual growth.

Perhaps somewhat facetiously, St. Francis de Sales once said that all of us should take a half an hour per day to be with God. However, the exception is that when we are very busy, we should take an hour. Indeed, our busyness can serve as a warning to slow down and take time to rekindle and nurture our love and be more intimate in Love.

Rather than becoming hyperactive and taking the ultimate meaning of life for granted, we could learn to appreciate, help, and enjoy one another. Realizing that love does not grow automatically, we can set structures to practice the daily art of loving (spirit). We can structure (ego) time and space (body) for genuine play, enjoyment, and love—for life of the Spirit.

Unfortunately, too many of us have learned to adjust to a life with minimal love. The thriving thirties and thereafter can result in a mad adjustment to a spiritless life. Nothingness beckons us to stay in Love. Trusting in nothingness, we can come to fuller being and being-with, to Love, or to God. As a psychologist, I think it is my responsibility to help people with such psychospiritual issues.

Mid-Life

Mid-life ushers in another desert, one that is familiar and different than the previous deserts. Listen to Bart who shares some of his thoughts and feelings about approaching mid-life. "Tell me about it. I have to tell you that I really know the meaning of the saying that the spirit is willing, but the flesh is weak.

"For example, when I play basketball, I have become a heady player. What I used to do automatically, I have to think about it and push myself. I try to be a good defense player to compensate for my lack of offense. The young whom I used to run over are running over me. I have lost a half step, a split second, and that makes all the difference.

"More importantly, I better make my professional moves now, for soon I will hit the ceiling for advancement. Moreover, I feel the stress of working the extra hours. When I was in my twenties and thirties, I could easily work overtime and on weekends, take care of household chores, and spend time with my kids and wife. Now, I feel tired more quickly, and yet I have even more responsibility. I wonder if I can handle it or if I want to handle it. Sometimes I feel like taking a leave of absence.

"Too often, I feel stuck in a rat race of work, paying bills, taking care of children, going to meetings, and trying to get some relaxation. Even our vacation gets to be a chore. I wonder who I am, and what has become of me. Somehow, I think that life should be better than it is. Most people probably think that I have it made or that I am a good husband and father as well as successful at my job. However, I feel lost and that life is passing me by. Look, I am not old; I am 44 years old. Nevertheless, I feel old.

"I hear the ticks of the clock. When I was younger, I never gave time much thought. I guess I felt I had all the time in the world. There were always tomorrows. Now it seems that there may be more yesterdays than tomorrows. I feel that time is running out. What am I going to do with the time that I have left? How am I going to live the rest of my life? Better yet, why am I going to live?

"Have I been my true and real self? Have I played the roles of husband and father? Have I sold out my values in exchange for professional success? Where have my dreams gone? Do I want to live the rest of my life the way I have been living? With good intentions, have I been travelling on the wrong road? What is the right road? Have I been a naive fool?

"No longer do religion and Sunday services give me the direction and solace that they used to give me. I just see the hypocrisy and hear the inane sermons. It all seems to be so much cognitive crap. I am trying to make sense of my life, but nothing makes sense anymore. It is as if an endless supply of questions inundates and imprisons me. I look for answers, but all of them seem so inadequate.

"I am around the half-way point in my life. God willing, I may have another 44 years to live. How do I want to live those years? How can I? When I am on my deathbed, can I say that I have lived fully? What is a full life? Will I be able to give a good account of myself when I die? Will I be ready when death knocks on my door?"

In our schema, mid-life is the time between adulthood and middle age, or for most people between ages thirty-nine and forty-nine. Although we are not yet middle-aged, most of us are nearing the halfway point of life. Like Bart, our mid-life man, our focus is no longer on growing up, for time is running out. Nothingness emerges again, and we reevaluate our life.

In mid-life nothingness, we are likely to experience our limits and the limits of life. For example, most of us begin to experience the limitations of our body. Our flesh (body) is weaker than in our youthful past. Indeed, the axiom "The spirit is willing but the flesh is weak" takes on new meaning. Moreover, more personal and financial responsibilities (ego) face us; in addition, there may be a relative paucity of enjoyment and fun.

We can meet our limits in many ways. For instance, we may question our past. Have past dreams, goals, and ideals been fulfilled or unfulfilled? Have we reached our personal and professional goals? Have we been true to our values and ideals? Have we made a significant contribution to life? Have we stopped dreaming?

We may wonder what is happening. Fatigue, weakness, tension, and depression are indications that something has happened and is happening. Such body language speaks to us. Weariness may mean that we have been overactive. Tension and anxiety may be telling us that we are overextended and fragmented. Depression may be saying that we have lost our health in our frenetic pursuit to "make it." The limits of our physical selves may be telling us to take better care of ourselves as well as to seek more than the limited.

A particularly painful but redeeming experience occurs when we confront our deceptive and foolish selves. Mid-life nothingness unveils, de-masks, and exposes us. Nothingness invites us to face the ways we have deceived others and ourselves. It is time to realize how we have failed to live according to the values we have professed—how we said one thing and did another, how we convinced ourselves to believe illusions. We can fool ourselves in many ways, often with sincere and good intentions.

For example, couples may pretend to be happily married while they deny their misery. Religious and ministers may sincerely exhibit one lifestyle in public and quite another in private. Successful and powerful people may avoid their feelings of powerlessness. Instead of responding to the Spirit of the Unlimited, some seek escape in work, alcohol, sex, or power (body and ego). Do we face our foolish selves and become wise, or do we prepare to die as fools?

We may assume that our past is gone forever. The truth is that both positive and negative experiences from the past continue to have an impact upon us. For instance, we can be startled with old or "seemingly new" feelings that are reminiscent of the distant past. Not infrequently, latent and unresolved adolescent and childhood problems can emerge, confuse, and scare us. Instead of facing and processing these feelings, we might regress by trying to look and act much younger than we really are.

Repressed feelings often emerge in mid-life. For example, a married couple may find their marriage rapidly dissipating because they deceived each other as well as themselves, albeit with good intentions. Often because they were unable or afraid to share their feelings, they treated each other decently, but they failed to grow in passionate love. What they thought was being happy was really a counterfeit. Now, they pay the price of their collusion. Rather than running from or numbing their embarrassment, they will fare far better to face their crisis and grow from it.

In short, nothingness decimates our illusions and demands honesty. Especially in mid-life, nothingness brings to clear relief the temporary and precarious security of the limited—that success, pleasure, status, and power are inadequate in responding to the questions of nothingness, or life.

In our most dreadful and redeeming times, we see nothing. We hear nothing. We feel nothing. Rather than succumbing to depression, regression, or escapism, our challenge is to accept our limits as an opportunity to improve and strengthen our life. Our experience of limits can lead us to a deeper experience of the Unlimited. We can come to know that the finitude of time calls for the timeless, that the ultimate limit—death—evokes eternal life.

In a radical way, in nothingness, we seek Being, and paradoxically we find Being in nothingness. In absence, we discover an enduring and life giving Presence. We come to believe that only God, or Love who dwells within, among, and beyond us, can give us a permanent and sane reason for living.

A new experience of time also pressures us to reevaluate life particularly in light of mortality and immortality. The shortening of chronological (*chronos*) time makes us more aware of the importance of intimate, sacred (*kairos*) time. For instance, enjoying personal time with family and friends can take precedence over functional and work time. We can seriously consider restructuring our lives to give priority to more spiritual times like love, prayer, beauty, the fine and performing arts, joy, and gratitude.

In mid-life nothingness and throughout life, we realize that there is a time for all seasons: a time for unrest and a time for peace, a time to mourn and a time to rejoice, a time to be foolish and a time to be wise, a time to cry and a time to laugh, a time to be blind and a time to see, a time to question God and a time to thank God, a time to withdraw and a time to love, a time to die and a time to live.

A recurring theme is that as we age, no-thingness urges us to go beyond the immediate to the "more than." In our loss of meaning, we seek meaning. In our emptiness, we desire fulfillment. In our sense of being lost, we want to find our way. In arid absence, we thirst for refreshing presence.

If we are scared, wounded, or lost, it behooves us to embrace our broken selves and to reach out to others. In time, we come to realize that in and through despair, we come to hope, that in and through doubt, we come to faith, that in and through brokenness, we can heal, and that in and through death, we live.

However, it is tempting to try to escape or numb the redeeming discomfort of nothingness. The anxiety and stress of change are seldom easy or welcomed. In the short run, it is easier to stay in our comfort zone, but in the end, we create more debilitating stress as well as miss enjoying the ultimate meaning of life.

For instance, if we have given priority to our work or have based our personal commitments only on convenience, our relationships have seriously dissipated by now. Our Spirit cries out for "more than" what we have pursued (ego). However, nothingness will not let us be content. Nothingness pressures us to reconsider and restructure our lives for the better. This recovery takes time (body), courage (spirit) and consistent work (ego). Be assured: It is worth the struggle.

Another caveat is that our feeling of feeling older can lead us to make immature choices to recapture our youth. For example, a man may regress to try to look and behave half his age. His talk, walk, dress, and activities are more like his children than age appropriate. He may even have or think of having an affair with a woman who is as young as his daughter is. Such regression may be exciting, invigorating, and give the illusion of youth, but it is self-deceptive and militates against health.

A woman who is at her sexual peak and lacks intimacy may begin to play with the possibility of an affair. She feels the power to seduce a man as well as the advantage to escape from her nothingness. Soon she may be culturally less attractive; so if she is going to fulfill her fantasy, now is the time. Again, such behavior may take the edge off nothingness, but it fails to work in regards to health.

Our challenge is to avoid the many ways to escape the unsettling and scary experiences of nothingness. It is common, for example, to numb unsettling feelings with prescription drugs, and thereby abort opportunities for growth. Drugs may initially take the edge off your tension so that you feel better. However, the long-term effects are usually detrimental in that they impede health and even engender unhealthiness.

Instead, we must accept our feelings of feeling nothingness, mourn our losses, and learn and benefit from growing older. For example, we can come to realize that our desire for meaning is boundless and therefore lead to an abundance of life. We can accept and listen to our restless spirit, and respond to its challenge to improve our lives. We can face our limits as an opportunity to seek more than the limited.

Indeed, intimacy is a critical issue. Nothingness moves mid-lifers to love and to be loved. A common caveat is to expect others—parents, spouse, friends, relatives, community to be our primary source of love. For children, such expectations are valid and necessary; however, for adults they are understandable but futile. We may need counseling to heal from and cope with our spiritual deficiencies of love, trust, and worthiness. Ultimately, however, only God can fulfill our restless spirit for Love.

God in, with, and through others and ourselves is our paramount resource for living a good and healthy life. It is foolish to depend on God and isolate from others, and it is equally foolish to rely on people without God. The nothingness of mid-life intensifies that we must love and be loved by others-God-and-self.

We come to realize that our love of others opens us to the source of love and life—God, and our love of God engenders a love for others and self. Practically, this divine providence as well as the supportive love from others helps us to gain the courage to grow in Love. God's love, or the Love of loves, gives us the strength to live a life of Love.

In mid-life, death speaks clearly and loudly. Rather than knocking on our door, death opens our door and greets us. Death questions us, and demands that we listen: Can you cope with and transcend a culture that denies death? Can you really face and listen to me? Can you admit, that I, Death, affirm your ultimate powerlessness? Can you transcend me, the ultimate limit, by surrendering to God, the ultimate Unlimited? Do you believe that you live forever, that Love is the final answer?

The death and impending death of others such as grandparents and perhaps parents also throw us back on ourselves, asking us to reevaluate life. Accepting our own being-toward-death and recognizing our powerlessness can lead us to transcend death—to embrace the ultimate Unlimited that conquers the ultimate limit. Paradoxically, to accept our radical powerlessness and to surrender to a greater Power empowers us.

It is wise to seek support that helps us to listen to the call of the desert. For instance, to share with a trustworthy and competent person or group, to read spiritual books, and to pray may benefit us. Instead of identifying with or avoiding our limits, we can meet their challenge, grow from them, and continue to seek ways to satisfy our thirst for our unlimited God.

From our perspective of health, it is imperative that we nourish our spiritual lives. This means that we concretely and consistently structure our time and space to love not only with words or intentions but also with behavior. It is not easy to make other activities, like work, secondary. However, if we love—family, friends, community—only when convenient, we pay the horrible price of becoming less than we can be.

Mid-life can be a time for hell or heaven. It can be an exercise in frantic futility or growth in enthusiastic living. It can be a time to dissipate physically (tired and in bad shape), to weaken psychologically (anxious and depressed), and to forget the spiritual life (unsettled and aimless). We can become lost, depressed, and spiritless. However, if we are still and silent in this stagnant, dark pit, we will hear our pleas and feel our desires for a Love who gives us enduring purpose and fulfillment. To reaffirm, providers of health should help us to listen and respond to these spiritual issues.

Health providers can assist us to face and respond to our mid-life demands, perhaps to get in better physical condition and learn from our affective self (body), to cope effectively and succeed (ego), and to renew and practice our love of God, self, and others (spirit). Counseling should take this "wholistic" approach.

The spiritual message of mid-life is to accept our limits in order to connect more consistently with the unlimited powers of Love. Our limits affirm the truth that in Love we are ultimately unlimited.

Middle Age

Middle age broadcasts the signs and symptoms of aging. Listen to Louise. "Menopause has not been the big, bad bugaboo that some people have said it would be. However, a challenging issue has been whether or not to take hormone replacements and what kind. On the easier side, I feel more than ever my being a woman. Actually, my sexual desires are greater than ever. Although there have been losses, overall menopause has been a liberation.

"One of my problems is that my husband has less sexual desire than I have. It seems that he has gone backwards, and I have gone forward. When we were in our twenties, it seemed that he always wanted sex, and now he seldom wants it. Moreover, he often fails to get an erection, and this seems to mortify him. I tell him that we do not need to have sexual intercourse to make love, but he looks at me as if I am speaking a foreign language.

"Perhaps more importantly, I have to admit that I am likely to be past the half point in my life. I have lived more years than I have left. Our children are building their own lives, and one of them is already married. I guess that means that one of these days I will be a grandmother. That sounds old, but I do not feel old.

"I look at my husband, whom I have been living with the last 28 years, and I wonder who he really is. It is as if we have grown to be friendly strangers. We have a civil relationship without passion. Our lives seem so insipid. I want life to be better than it has ever been. After all, I have fewer responsibilities, am financially in good shape, am more perceptive than I was, and I should have more opportunities to do what I want. So why am I not jumping for joy?

"I feel restlessly and restively lacking and empty. It seems that there should be more to life than what is. What used to make sense has changed, or it does not make sense anymore. I feel down, but I do not want to be or stay down. Life should not be so dark. Where is the light? Am I depressed?

"What am I going to do with the rest of my life? My husband seems to be content in being a workaholic and watching sporting events. That is not enough for me. I am not preparing to retire or to slow down. Indeed, my life has changed in that I need not be so child-centered or even work-centered. I want more being and less doing. I want more life.

"Although I do not feel old, I know that I am closer to death than to birth. When I look at my aging parents, I think about death, and I wonder about many things. Should I stay in my marriage? Jack is a decent person, but he is such a lump, so predictable, so constricted. Still, I could have done a lot worse. Can I or should I do better? Starting over is not easy.

"What does God want me to do? Better yet, who is God? Is there a God? Religion was always a stabilizing factor in my life, and I felt it important for the children to have a religious education. We were actively involved with our church. Now, instead of seeing the possibilities of the church, I see its limits, hypocrisies, and scandals. I realize that not all clergy are out of touch with the real world, but I wonder how many are mature adults?

"I try to accept, understand, and even be compassionate with the dark side of my church. I remind myself that I can have a spiritual life without religion, or within the confines of my religion. Still, is it worth my time and energy? Should I leave religion as so many people have done? It seems that people can be successful and happy without religion and even without God. Is God necessary to live a good life? Does God exist?"

A crisis of middle age begins around our early fifties and may periodically emerge into our sixties, and like other ones, it can be futile or fruitful. If we have successfully resolved our previous transitions, then experiences like spiritual depression and coming-to-death will be more familiar and less threatening. Although it also has its challenges, middle age can be less daunting and certainly beneficial.

Depression is a frequent symptom of middle-aged nothingness. As we have seen in chapter five, psychological and physical depression usually indicates specific causes. For instance, our depression may be due to significant loss (of a loved one, valuable possession, and work), a hormonal imbalance, repressed anger, low self-esteem, chronic shame, etc.

In contrast, we can be spiritually depressed about nothing in particular and everything in general. Like Louise in our vignette, we may feel at a loss to say what is going on except that again nothing makes much sense. Even though we may have lived a meaningful and worthwhile life, we may feel that our reasons for being have deserted us. We can find ourselves trying to dig ourselves out of a deep, dark pit of depression and guilt.

In this spiritual depression, we experience a fundamental loss of meaning. Life may seem to make more nonsense than sense; everyone and everything may seem distant and not worth attaining. Compounding matters, we may feel lonely and alone in our meaninglessness. For instance, we may see our spouse more as a stranger than as an intimate companion, and we may experience an empty nest syndrome (children leaving the house). Consequently, we may feel forsaken, gloomy, empty, and at a loss.

Some of us may wonder if we will ever love again, or if we have ever really loved. We may feel that we have lost a good portion of life, or that we can never relive or regain our life. In the throes of nothingness, we may feel melancholic, lethargic, guilty, inadequate, and restless. Our mood baffles people, including ourselves. Once again, it can be a dire mistake to medicate ourselves into stagnate contentment.

We may question the values on which we based our life, and religion and God may be prime targets of our critical eyes. Religion may not make the sense that it once did, or be very helpful. Moreover, God does not seem to fill our empty soul. We may even doubt the validity and relevance of God. We may wonder if religion and its God have been mental machinations to relieve anxieties rather than necessary and healthy realities.

Remember that our usual medical and psychosocial approaches to treat clinical depressions are inadequate for and may harm spiritual experiences. We can construe our spiritual depression (as well as anxiety, loneliness, etc.) as a disease and treat "it" as if it is unhealthy. Thus, with good intentions to achieve health, we impede our health.

Instead of mistreating ourselves, we can accept and learn from our gift of nothingness. Instead of purging our depression, we can journey through it. We can see our depression as an opportunity to grow especially in our spirituality. We can come out of this desert of depression as better persons.

Once again, we have to accept our experience with understanding and compassion. With patience and trust in self and others, we eventually discover that God and God's people can lighten our heaviness, vitalize our listlessness, fulfill our emptiness, and bring joy to our lives. These promises are not pietistic wish fulfillments or foolish reactions, but as 12-steppers would say, it works if you work it.

Along with depression, we may feel guilty. Like in mid-life, forgotten experiences may reemerge and plague our conscience. For instance, we may feel guilty for something we did decades ago and never made amends. We may feel responsible for another's sad condition especially when we have done little to help that person.

As with other transitional and transformative disturbances, we can react in understandable but less than healthy ways. For instance, it is common to "double feel," that is, to become depressed about being depressed, guilty about being guilty, and anxious about being anxious. When we fight ourselves in this way, spiritual experiences can too easily turn into clinical problems. For example, we may become clinically depressed in reaction to our spiritual depression.

Rather than rejecting, numbing, or escaping from middle age nothingness, we can listen to these sources of truth. For instance, depression can be an invitation to slow down, to reflect, and to recollect life. Guilt can motivate us to make amends for past commissions and omissions. Questioning can lead to relevant truth.

Spiritually, our nothingness invites us to accept our radical poverty. We can come to admit that we are ultimately powerless, and that only a greater power can fulfill our nothingness. Indeed, we must let go of our ego control, and take a spiritual leap of faith. With faith and hope, we move beyond all things—into no-thing, and we come closer to the ground out of which all beings emerge and live.

Most middle agers have lived a half century, have experienced and achieved much, and are very seasoned adults. Thus, it can be daunting and humbling to admit that we are powerless, that on our own we can ultimately do little. It is not easy to give up trying to control our destiny.

Nothingness pressures us to change what we can and accept what we cannot change, and more than ever, to know the difference. We come to believe that with a reality that is greater than our individual ego, wisdom and serenity are possible to attain. From radical poverty, we can come to infinite richness.

Physical changes are usually prominent. For instance, most men experience a decline in strength and endurance. Indeed, if we have centered our identity on such so-called masculine qualities, we may become even more despondent. Instead of fostering the enthusiasm of our Spirit, we fight the loss of youth and its physical vigor. Like the husband in our example, we may fixate on the loss of genital vigor and lose the vigor of spiritual love (which invigorates sex).

A woman's climacteric changes are usually more overt and acute than a man's are. Menopause along with other bodily and emotional changes can compound the stress that many women feel during this time of nothingness. For instance, hormonal changes bring a generalized atrophy of the reproductive system, and secondary sex characteristics often change. Some women may feel and act neuter, while others feel more sexual than ever.

In general, women often adjust and enjoy life better than men do, partly because women are more inter-independent, take better care of themselves, and are more actively spiritual than men are. Adjusting to and learning from personal and interpersonal changes, women build a strong foundation for the second half of their adult lives.

Once again, we question our personal and professional commitments. Have we succeeded in our work? It may be too late to change careers. Women (more than men) are likely to question their marriage. For instance, although in the past they tried to improve their marriage, they watched it dissipate into mediocrity. Divorce, which was once relatively rare in middle age, is becoming more frequent and accepted. A woman or a man may decide to venture into a new life.

Our challenge is to allow the force of nothingness to renew and improve our lives. When we successfully grow from our experience of our nothingness, our strength, freedom, and security come from within ourselves. We come to appreciate the reality that underlies and goes infinitely beyond our differences and problems. We can come to honor the Presence in all of us where we are one. New freedom and light can emerge out of middle-aged stagnation and darkness.

Although we are not yet "old," we are getting farther away from being young. As we have seen, this can be good news, for getting older and changing our pace can engender new experiences that evoke more fulfillment and satisfaction. Out of nothingness, we can seek and come to a fuller appreciation of our reason for being alive. This is not magical musing, sentimental self-deception, or spiritual nonsense. It is concrete, practical, and smart.

Compassion is truly broadened and deepened. More than ever, we help one another bear the burdens of living. As wounded warriors, we face life's dark side, lessen the pain, and heal brokenness. Rather than avoidance or not caring, we act in ways that improve our being together in Love.

Rather than being stuck in darkness, the light of wisdom can give us a glimpse of eternity. Rather than being blind, we can see with our inner eye that nothingness is a way to health and its source: God. Rather than being isolated and lonely, we can learn to live with and in Love.

Indeed, there are more yesterdays than tomorrows. Death and dying become clearly critical. The death of a loved one—parent, spouse, sibling, or friend—is likely to thrust a mirror on our own mortality. If we have run from death and dying, they often catch us at this time. Though some of us still escape death's grasp, we know that death will catch us. The tragedy of trying to escape dying and death is that we impede the best of living and life. Our frantic and futile attempt to escape our mortality muffles the voice of God and blurs our vision of eternity.

No longer does death whisper, silently open our door, or walk in our room. Death comes up to us, shakes our hand, and speaks. Death looks at us, touches us, and talks to us. Death holds us and asks us how and why we have been living. Death demands life.

Death pressures us to seek ultimate sense, or a God or Truth of our understanding. Life without an eternal vision is an inadequate response to death. Without eternal life, death wins, and nothingness is permanent. With the Truth of Love, we conquer death, and Love fills our nothingness. Death loses; life triumphs.

Elderly Adulthood

Finally, we come closer to our finality. Listen to the elderly. "Honestly, I don't feel old, but I know that I am 92 years old. I hate when people treat me as if I am senile and incompetent. They condescend and patronize me. Their sweet and cute treatment sickens me. I've forgotten more than they know. Rarely do they listen to me. Too bad, I could share many interesting stories, and maybe teach them a thing or two. I think I have something to give, but there is seldom someone willing to receive.

"When I look back on my life, I can smile with gratitude. I have outlived my three husbands and one of my children. Yes, I have been married three times, and I emphasize that all three of them were good, passionate, and committed—and, I loved all of them. I was 22 and pregnant when my first husband was killed in the war. Our marriage was short, but so young and sweet. I wonder what kind of a life we would have had if he had lived, but I will never know. They were short but fond years. It seems like only yesterday.

"After the war, I married another soldier who made it through the Pacific jungles. He too was a good man who provided for my boy, and we had three more children. We had our difficulties, but overall, we had a good marriage. Just when three of the kids were out of the house, Mike got pancreatic cancer and died. It was and still is very sad. Poor Mike, he deserved a better fate. Every day, I think of my two soldier boys.

"I thought two marriages and two dead husbands were more than enough. I resigned myself to living the rest of my life as a single woman. Actually, I returned to school and earned a nursing degree. I worked well into my seventies as a nurse and retired to live a leisurely life. Life, however, had more surprises for me, ones that were beyond my wildest dreams.

"I met Jim on an AARP trip, and we fell in love. I might add that Jim was a very wealthy man. I will never know why he went on an AARP trip. Perhaps there is divine intervention. Anyhow, we travelled, danced, dined, walked and talked, and made passionate love. Then last year, Jim died. Cancer robbed me again.

"I mourn for all of my men, but more so I am grateful for the gift of life that they have given me. I do not know why I continue to out-live almost everyone. However, as long as I live, I will sing and dance. Maybe my mother was right when she told me that I will never get old, that I would be young forever. Mom, Thank you.

"I know that death will eventually catch me. He is waiting for me. I have faced too much of death to be afraid of death. I am ready to die. Until then, I will live to the fullest. My answer to death is life. If it comes in the irony of cancer, I hope to die gracefully and gratefully. Will my men, children, parents, sisters, brothers, and friends be waiting for me? Will there be a God to embrace me? Will there be a heaven where we celebrate being in love? I do not know. I hope so."

Our challenge is to emulate this wonderful woman, to sing and dance with life until we die. With the exception of death, the last critical stage of nothingness occurs in the elderly years. Our body and ego continue to change and evolve. Some of their functions weaken, while others strengthen. Clearly, there are considerable individual differences.

As the saying goes, there are go goes, slow goes, and no goes. Our thrice-widowed woman was a go-go. Contrary to popular opinion, research indicates that many elderly are go goes. Regardless of our situation, our body and ego become less significant in contrast to the functions and values of our Spirit. Our Spirit takes over more than ever. It is pathetic that too many health providers respond to the physical and functional needs of their clients, and fail to honor and help them with their spiritual life.

A main thesis is that instead of being the worst of times, the elderly years can be the best of times. If you exclude the spiritual, this is an absurd statement. However, from our perspective, although youth is long gone and our body is diminishing, like our vibrant 92 year-old nurse, we can feel and be young in Spirit. More than ever, we can become people of enthusiasm (*en*=in, *theos*=God).

On the one hand, our body weakens, is more vulnerable, and less resilient, and on the other hand, our body is more expressive, touching, and loving. Actually, our body can manifest more Spirit than ever before. Old bodies tell stories filled with joy and sadness, laughter and tears, strength and brokenness, courage and fear, love and loneliness, life and death. Surely, we can honor, learn from, and foster the lives of the elderly.

Indeed, with aging, there are quantitative decrements to body and ego functions; nevertheless, they increase in quality when they are instruments and manifestation of Love. For instance, in spite of our ego functions, like fluid intelligence and short-term memory, falling short of past performance, we can still live a better life. Our Spirit can permeate our attitudes, thinking, decisions, and behavior. In a sense, our life becomes a ministry of our Spirit.

In the elderly years, life usually changes radically. As retired workers, we must learn a new way of living. We may suddenly find that we have time on our hands, or we may find to our surprise that we are busier than ever. If we are full time married homemakers, we also make new adjustments, for we have more and new time with our spouse. We find that our situation has changed due to the frequent presence of our spouse.

If we are single, we may have to face our nothingness alone. We may have no particular one who cares for us and for whom we care. There is no one waiting for us when we get home. Our house is silent. Loneliness can envelope us, and we can wonder if we really mattered to anyone. Even if we live in a religious community, we find that many of our friends have died or have moved to a different location, and that the future of our community is in jeopardy.

If widowed, he and more often she finds herself alone. Our beloved is present in absence. This person must find new friends or old friends in new ways. No longer can she expect the companionship of her husband; no longer can he depend on his wife. Regardless of our particular situation, as elderly people, we undergo many significant changes that challenge us to go out into the world anew.

It would be cruelly remiss to exclude the elderly who suffer from dementia. It is harrowing to watch a loved one fade away. (Who really knows what it means or feels like to lose your cognitive and physical functions?) Their brain damage impairs memory, abstract thinking, judgment, emotions, and behavior. Living with and caring for such a parent or spouse is very stressful, and can evoke uneasy and ambivalent feelings.

If we exclude the spiritual and identify our impaired loved ones with their inadequacies, then our lives (and theirs as well) become a living nightmare or meaningless. However, if we focus on their spiritual dimension, then their disabilities, like impaired communication, may take on a different meaning. Even though rational (ego) functions are disordered, our loved ones' spirits are still present. We can be with and for them as well as appreciate and enjoy them as human, spiritual beings.

We can sit and be still with them. We can listen to and learn from their stories. Their repeated stories are never quite the same. Indeed, if we simply focus on information (ego), then their communication becomes irritating. However, when we focus on being-with (spirit), then our being together becomes paramount. Remember, brain damaged persons are like you and me—persons of infinite worth. They invite us to enjoy the infinite possibilities of the now.

If we lack a spiritual life, we are apt to slip into a life of quiet depression, or at best live a less than enthusiastic life. We can become "old" before our time. Conversely, with the higher power of God, or indwelling Love, we are more likely to manage effectively, accept with serenity, and live a life of purpose and ultimate meaning. Regardless of our circumstances, we reason that it is good to live in Love.

Death is practically impossible to deny. Many friends and relatives may have already died, and youth is a constant reminder of our age. We feel the harbingers of death increasingly more in the limits of our body and ego. Life is nearing its end, and we reflect on our impending death.

Death embraces us, and if we return the embrace, we experience an enormous sense of power and vision that no one can take from us. When we accept death, nothing else can ultimately harm us. In dying, we really destroy death and restore life.

In our early or late elderly years, we commonly raise questions about integrity. Am I a truthful person in touch with myself and honest with others? Have I merely lived a cerebral existence? Have I placed too much emphasis on what I have rather than on who and how I am with others? Have I lived a life of love? Will my death matter? Can I say yes to my life? Does my life story make for good reading? Will I sing and dance until I die?

If we have listened to death throughout our life, it will hold less ter-
ror for us. Death will be more of a companion who helps us to live life to
its fullest. However, the desert of death can look overwhelming if we have
denied or run from death. Rather than reaching its zenith, life becomes
meaningless and inert. Nevertheless, nothingness persists in encouraging
us to face death, and therefore life. We can admit to our powerlessness (of
our ego and body), and surrender to our Higher Power (of our Spirit).

If we had journeyed successfully through our deserts, our life in-
ventory can bring a sense of integrity and dignity. If we have run from
the demons of death, death will more than likely catch us at this time.
Remember, however, death brings life.

In the practical faith of hope, our desert of death will lead us to the
land of life. Seeing life in the light of death makes our life more acceptable and manageable. Nevertheless, life experiences will challenge our
acceptance and well-being.

As senior citizens, we must encounter demons that are peculiar to
us. A common one is ageism, the prejudgment that the elderly are worthless and burdensome. People who judge themselves and others on their
ability to function productively and autonomously are prone to see many
elderly as burdens to remove from the main stream of life.

A sign of ageism is that too many people seldom listen to and show
delight with elderly people. Too often, they simply tolerate or treat them,
or pay their respects. Some elderly even feel that they get in the way and
are not valued. In reaction, they may learn to act dependent, dumb, and
docile.

"We" perpetuate ageism by assuring that "they"—the elderly—are
powerless, weak, dependent, and perhaps worthless. Medically, economi-
cally, and functionally, many old elderly may approximate this syndrome.
However, in other ways, and especially spiritually, they can be powerful,
strong, and full of worth. In fact, research has shown that the elderly are
the happiest of all adults.

Another problem is that the elderly may intimidate us by evoking
unresolved issues. For example, being closer to death, the elderly may
evoke our denial or forgetfulness of death. Being on the threshold of
death, the elderly are apt to avoid game playing and cut through pretense.
Moreover, their relative lack of productivity may question our reason for
being.

Rather than listening to and learning from the elderly, too often we
react defensively, try to control, and oppress them. Rather than caring

for them, we treat them. Rather than embracing them, we avoid them. Rather than honoring and thanking the elderly, we take them for granted, or simply forget them.

This time can be an opportunity to reconcile submerged resentments or familial conflicts. To be sure, the elderly may harbor resentments as well, and their coming closer to death can motivate them to seek reconciliation. In short, we should take this opportunity to come closer together.

We have seen that death summons us to question our values and behavior. Too often, we assume that we can live without death. We delude ourselves into thinking that death will someday happen, rather than accepting that death is always happening to all of us. We stand on the common ground of life-and-death. Since we are all beings-toward-death, we share our coming to death. We would be wise to listen to and embrace our dying/living and death/life.

Standing in the shadow of death, we can question our lives. Do we visit the elderly only on holidays, as if we are doing a duty? Do we honor and show delight with the elderly? How often do we have fun with them? Do we learn from and thank them? Our challenge is to face and heal the "we-them" dichotomy. Can we see that we are different threads, of various ages, of the same enduring tapestry? Can we sing the songs and dance to the music of our common Spirit?

We must rediscover, rekindle, and celebrate our being members of the same humankind. Whether or not we admit it, we partake of the same origin and destiny of Life. We can be glad and grateful for our common Spirit who binds us together. We can rejoice in growing older together in Love.

We have stated that most elderly do not fit our ageist stereotypes and are source of immense worth. Although they are physically weaker and functionally less active, their spiritual and personal worth are greater than ever. Our shame is that we value the physical and functional over the spiritual, and consequently we alienate, minimize, or forget the elderly. Remember: when we violate them, we diminish ourselves.

Due to many factors such as death and ageism, loneliness is common. The elderly cannot love someone who is absent in the same way as when he or she was physically present. This is painful. Nevertheless and paradoxically, we can love the presence of others in their absence, and in some ways, even more intimately. Though still lonely, we can love our dead beloved.

How elderly people accept and live through their nothingness depends largely on how they have responded to their previous experiences of nothingness. If we have made healthy options, this time can be relatively easy, though somewhat uncomfortable. If we have not or do not renew ourselves in nothingness, we can fall into a depressive stagnation and bitter despair. We can become tired of living and afraid of dying.

It is normal to question beliefs in the elderly years. As this ninety-seven-year-old woman said, "God forgive me, but I wonder if there really is a God, or who God is. Although I have always believed in heaven, I wonder if there really is an after-life. When we die, do we just disappear?"

Rather than circumventing or silencing such questions, we should accept and pursue them, for they can lead to a deeper faith, consolation, and serenity. At any age, our disconnection with the God of our understanding can lead to a deeper understanding and connection with God.

Becoming relatively disengaged from previous roles and functional responsibilities can liberate us to deepen our lives. Now we finally have more time and space to pursue our reason for being. Indeed, such pursuits can at times be unsettling, but they eventually lead to deeper and abiding consolation. Being relatively detached from conventional living can enable us to appreciate and enjoy life more than the average person.

Love of life and particularly of people become paramount. We enjoy loved ones and simply people in general with a compassionate and zestful heart. There is too little time to waste on less fulfilling activities. (Clearly, we can learn so much from the elderly.) We accept, enjoy, and are grateful for life as it presents itself. Mature adults of any age seize and savor each day as if it were their last one.

The inevitable fact is that the elderly years call forth the spiritual more than ever. In these final years, which may be short or quite long, we more than ever experience the need to know and experience the Truth. Our redemption lies in coming to the Truth of becoming companions with Love. We can learn to sit with God, converse, give thanks, break bread, and be consoled.

We conquer death with life in Love. No matter what illness, deprivation, loneliness, or rejection, we appreciate the truth that we are people of permanent and infinite worth. When we affirm this divine reality that pervades us, comfort and consolation abide within us. Moreover, this Love nourished by faith gives us hope in a future and better life.

In spite of ageism, illness, or economic oppression, we can be happier than ever. We can look back with a compassionate smile at our attempts to be satisfied (body) and successful (ego) as being impossible and ultimately inconsequential. Rather than succumbing to a premature death or identifying life with physical satisfaction or functional success, we can spiritually dance and smile.

We can say that we have run the good race. Rather than empty desolation, life is fulfilling and consoling. Out there beyond our reach yet within us, we still touch and are touched. Wherever and whenever we look, we see the Spirit of life. We know that God protects, comforts, and cares for us. We realize that life has been a search for home, that on earth we journey to heaven.

Do health providers encourage or invite the elderly to share such issues and experiences? Do they listen to and honor what the elderly can teach them? Are they quiet more than they speak? Do they intend to learn? Do they avoid solving or medicating unsettling feelings, but instead listen to them? Do they journey with the elderly to death?

Do health providers address the elderly's spiritual issues of feelings like loneliness and depression, coming to death, God, and after-life as positive and healthy? Or do they treat them as problems to treat and purge? Do they offer ways to accept and nurture such issues of life and death? Do they help them make their final times the most meaningful?

Do we abdicate our responsibility, and give it to the clergy? Unfortunately, many clergy avoid descending into hell, and leave the elderly with heavenly answers. They too can fail to face and grow from nothingness. However, most clergy and hospice workers more or less try to be compassionate care givers.

Of course, we are all (non-professional) health providers and ministers. All of us can help or hinder the elderly with their physical and psychosocial, and especially spiritual issues. Moreover, we can listen to, enjoy, and learn from them. What do we do?

Final Nothingness

Death is our last encounter with nothingness. For the last time, death and its nothingness beckon us to live. Finally, we let go of the illusion of self-sufficiency and surrender to God. We depend on God and not primarily on ourselves. We can take the final leap in Love.

We need not be on our deathbed to know that life is a rhythm of nothingness and being, fasting and feasting, truth and error, deserts and promised lands, dying and living. We can reasonably conclude that when we finally stop dying, we live.

We come to know that death is the springboard for eternal life, that death offers heaven—no more nothing, uncertainty, suffering, and pain, but rather being together in permanent and serene Love. With Spirit, we pass over to eternal life. We know the Truth; it is Love.

7

DISPLACEMENTS OF GOD

WE HAVE SEEN HOW nothingness is crucial in achieving healthier and holier living. Our thesis has been that we must accept and journey through deserts to arrive at and enjoy promised lands. However, for various reasons, we can fail to accept, cope with, and learn and grow from nothingness, and therefore impede our health and holiness.

Remember that our attempts to escape from nothingness not only militate against health but also cause more problems. Since nothingness is part of our being, it relentlessly remains and demands an adequate response. We have emphasized that our only healthy response to our desire for more than our body and ego is the Love/Truth of spirituality, or love for and from self, others, and God. Thus, to treat nothingness as a symptom of unhealthiness is a serious mistake.

In this chapter, we explain how we try to replace God with objects and activities of our body and ego in order to fulfill or escape from nothingness. Instead of keeping Love (God) in the center of our lives, we displace God, and consequently ourselves. Instead of seeking and following the Truth of Love, we err, and thereby impede our health. Before analyzing some specific displacements, let us begin with a general explanation of displacing God.

Displacement

From a psychological perspective, displacement is an ego defense mechanism by which we transfer energy from a true but inaccessible or threatening "object" (someone or something) to a substitute object that is more accessible and less threatening. In other words, we rechannel thoughts, desires, or feelings to something other than what they naturally seek.

Consider, for example, a man who for various reasons cannot directly express his anger toward his boss, who originally evoked the anger. Arriving home, he becomes angry with his unsuspecting wife. In this case, his wife acts as a substitute object (person) that replaces the true but inaccessible goal of his anger—his boss.

Instead of recognizing and dealing with the true object of his anger (his boss), he "lets out" his "angry affect" on his wife. Although this man gets some relief from displacing his anger, he not only mistreats his spouse but he also prevents himself from understanding and learning from his feelings. Moreover, he is probably still angry with his boss.

Another example is a married couple who harbor resentment toward each other, while they cannot admit it to each other or even to themselves. These people could easily displace their anger on innocent people, like on their children. Although they may feel guilty about their inappropriate expression of anger, they are afraid to look at the real source of their anger. Thus, their covert anger persists, and problems escalate.

Similarly, we can displace our spiritual energy toward God (and others as well) by replacing God with a substitute person, object, or activity. In this case, we do not direct our spiritual desire toward its proper object—God; rather, we displace God with a substitute object. We invest our spiritual energy of and for God/Love in body and ego objects and activities.

Keep in mind that our displacements of God are responses to our spiritual desires, but with inadequate behavior. Although our God displacements give us some satisfaction, they are temporary and inappropriate. Simply stated, anything other than Love will not adequately fulfill our nothingness, or our desire for Love. When we do not follow the Truth of Love, we fall into error, and thereby live mistaken and displaced lives.

It is important to realize that a displacement implies its original object. In error, there is truth. In our psychological example, the man who displaced his anger on his spouse implies the goal of his angry motive—his boss. In addition, his feelings of anxiety and guilt indicate his inappropriate behavior. He can resolve his anger toward his wife when he admits and copes with its true object—his boss.

Likewise, spiritual displacements implicitly refer to God because our displacements are attempts to respond to our desire for God. From therapeutic and pastoral perspectives, our futile attempts to displace God are indications of God. As counselors or anyone who seeks health, we must honor, listen, and respond to the only reality that adequately fulfills our spiritual desires—Love.

Our challenge is to discover our hidden God in the thoughts, feelings, and behaviors of our displacements. As counselors, we seek and see the truth in errors. We show how our erroneous ways of coping are less than healthy. Along with the psychological, we can help people to discover the hidden God in their displacements as well as more effective ways to respond to their desires for God.

Consider, for example, a sexually promiscuous person. She (or he) literally bares herself with another to have fun, pleasure, and perhaps power. Her satisfaction, however, is temporary, and she soon finds herself with terribly less than what she truly desires. Her lonely spirit seeks infinitely more than her bodily pursuits can deliver. Thus, her sexual exploits do not engender virtue, foster healthy intimacy, or evoke enduring purpose and fulfillment. Sex simply falls short of Love. A counselor can hear and respond to her spiritual self who seeks the strength and serenity of a spiritual union.

To be sure, counselors should help clients deal with their psychological displacements as well as other negative defense mechanisms. However, when they avoid spiritual displacements and only attend to (or treat) physical needs or functional coping, their attempts to help are inadequate. For instance, people can learn to satisfy basic needs and to cope effectively, but remain without enduring meaning, purpose, and fulfillment. Though satisfied (body) and successful (ego), they lack the true serenity and freedom (spirit) of Love.

Think of alcoholics. They symbolically and literally ingest spirits instead of Spirit. In, with, and through alcohol, they try to ameliorate and forget their problems. Some alcoholics use alcohol to fade away to some semblance of comfort and peace. Others drink to find courage to assert or aggress. Still others imbibe to feel mellow and to be pleasant with others. However, alcohol only gives them counterfeits of what they really seek—enduring serenity, courage, and connection. Alcoholic spirits cannot do the job of Spirit.

In the alcoholic's emptiness, futility, and pain, we can hear his or her true Spirit seeking health. The negative consequences (powerlessness, unmanageability, pain) of alcoholism (or any displacement) clearly proclaim that the alcoholic must pursue a different course. Alcoholism or any "ism" never engenders health. Alcoholics must admit that their drinking offers an illusion, a lie, a false promise.

A.A. members would say that only a Higher Power (than ego, alcohol) works, or can restore them to sanity. Their recovery usually begins with hitting bottom, for it reveals the need for their Higher Power. To accept that alcohol (or any substance or process) does not adequately fulfill our desire for God (the Higher Power of Love) is the gateway to true health.

Thus, a main task of pastoral counseling and wholistic therapy is to evoke and nourish our desire for God in nothingness as well as to discover and to rekindle the adumbrated God in displacements. To do this, we do not bring God to others as if God is not already present in them. We do not "put" God in people.

What we can do is evoke the God who always resides in everyone, albeit displaced, hidden, lost, or underdeveloped. We see our unseen God, hear our silent God, respond to our forgotten God, and manifest our hidden God.

A life of displacement becomes a constant contradiction. Our striving for enduring purpose, fulfillment, and serenity eventually leaves us lost, empty, and disconnected, or Loveless. We lose our primary way and proper place in life—to be in love with self, others, and God. Since we respond inappropriately to our spiritual needs, our restless spirit yearns for more than our displacements can give. We find ourselves less than whole, or fragmented, and consequently ill at ease.

Nevertheless, most of us who displace God are "normal." We satisfy our basic needs and have sufficient ego strength to cope and prevent psychopathology. We are not mentally ill, nor do we cause overt disruption. However, our absence of psychopathology does not equal healthiness. In fact, we delude ourselves when we assume that normality equals healthiness. It only means that we are normal.

If we are merely normal, we may maintain peripheral contact with God. We may attend religious services, routinely pray, and appeal to God in times of want. Instead of God being our paramount motivating force, God is more like an activity among other activities that we use when needed. In this way, religion can be a displacement for a true spiritual experience of God.

In short, when we respond to our desire for God via displacements, we live a normal and mad life. We are normal insofar as our displacements of God are acceptable and often rewarded—and, we are not mentally ill, criminal, or abnormal in any obvious way. Nevertheless, when we repress, displace, or forget our spiritual dimension and its desire for God, we are mad in that we are less than holy and healthy.

In short, attempts to fulfill our spiritual selves without God are normal modes of madness. Instead of minimizing, circumventing, or denying such madness, we can honor and process it. Instead of avoiding such hidden desires for the Divine, we can help people and ourselves to listen to and learn from them. Surely, this can be an essential part of good counseling.

Practically anything can become a displacement of God. For instance, we can understand the spiritual dimension of addictions as displacements of God. In this sense, for example, alcoholics displace their Holy Spirit with "spirits." They try to make alcohol their Higher Power, and consequently become powerless. Instead of love, they opt for alcohol, or alcohol becomes their lover.

Alcoholism or any addiction offers the seduction of immediate pleasure and the temporary illusion of well-being. While under the influence of a drug, we do not have to worry about the demands of nothingness, and of course, other issues as well. Drugs purge pain and give us the illusion that everything is all right. Drugs help us to forget our need to face and deal with ourselves, including our powerlessness and need for God. Clearly, addictions and/or displacements always fail to give us what we need—freedom, serenity, strength, security, dignity, integrity, love, etc.

As professional or lay health providers, we can help people to process the sense in the nonsense of their displacements, to accept their nothingness and powerlessness, to seek the Truth of Love and not ego self-efficiency, and to surrender to their Higher Power of Love. Let us look at some examples of God displacements.

Individualism

A common form of God displacement, particularly in Western societies like the United States, is individualism. Before analyzing the dynamics of individualism, listen to Rex who well describes this common madness.

"Most people would say that I have done exceedingly well. They would desire and even envy my professional success, social accessibility, material possessions, recreational options, and of course: my multi millions of dollars. Most would gladly trade places with me. And they would agree with my philosophy that you get as much as you can. If you can make five, ten, or twenty times the money for the same amount of work, you would be crazy not to get it.

"There are few exceptions to this view of life. Personally, I know only two such persons whom I befriended in college. One is a CEO like me, but his vision of success is radically different. He demands that his salary be a maximum of ten times his lowest paid employee. Thus, he reasons, if he wants to make more money, he must pay others more as well. Currently, his cleaning women make $27,000, which means that he draws a salary of $270,000.

"He states that he has more than enough money to live a good life. He simply thinks that it is stupid and selfish to get all that he can get. Unlike many and perhaps most of his CEO colleagues, greed and power do not rule his life, nor does he have any need to compete with other CEOs who make many millions. In short, he values the common good more than his individual success.

"Most of his friends and colleagues, including his board of trustees, thinks he is nuts, and besides, they say that he makes them look bad. As I said, his response is that his salary is more than enough money, and he argues that his lower level employees need money more than he does. Moreover, Frank seems happier as well as more content and at peace with himself than the rest of us. Although I am a bit more successful than he is and much wealthier, I secretly envy him.

"The other person is a brilliant and beautiful woman, who could have done practically anything. She was at the top of our class of very bright and talented people. Men drooled over her. Well, she quickly got her MBA and PhD, and rapidly advanced up the corporate ladder. She was ahead of the best and brightest. Nearing the top and in her thirties, she did something that sent shock waves throughout the corporate world. She joined a religious community.

"When I asked her why on earth she would do such a thing, she said there were many reasons. One was that it was painful for her to watch how people used others for personal gain. She thought the games people played, the arrogance, power, and exploitation were obscene and obnoxious. Moreover, she said, she felt called to a life that would witness to radically different values and lifestyle. She was a multi-millionaire, powerful leader, and beautiful woman who vowed to practice poverty, obedience, and celibate chastity.

"Most people judged my friends at best to be odd and foolish. What most people do not say is that these two mavericks seem more secure and serene than most of us. Somehow, they came to dance to different music. They are just as concerned for the welfare of others as they are for their own. Individual success particularly in terms of money, possessions, and power is not very important. They have and follow a different vision.

"What happened to me? I am filthy rich and miserable, divorced twice, and my kids are strangers. I am busy but lonely, and few people genuinely like me. I admire my past college friends. Nancy lives the vow of poverty and is far richer than I am. Frank is happily married and enjoys his kids. In college, I talked with them about business ethics, philosophy, theology, and in general making sense of life. They continue to live their ideals, and I have forgotten mine."

Probably most people covet the public life of this miserable man, and are apt to criticize or dismiss his friends. More often than not, they want to get as much as they can, regardless of its impact on others. In short, it is normal to assume that individual success is more important than communal success.

Nevertheless, there are people, like our two meaningful mavericks, who live contrary to our cultural benchmarks of success. They affirm that individuality and its ego functions are essential to mental health, but secondary to the primacy of community and its spiritual functions. They would agree with our proposal that health tilts toward community.

To reiterate, community is the basis and purpose of individuality. When we march to the beat of individualism, we separate ourselves from one another and act primarily in service of self rather than communal welfare. Like Rex, when we make our individual ego paramount, like most successful do, we distance ourselves from one another as well as risk using others for self-gratification. We falsely assume that individual success is primary so that the cost to others is irrelevant or secondary. We delude ourselves in acting as if we are independent of and have no responsibility to one another. Indeed, such a life militates against healthiness and holiness.

Unfortunately, our Western society favors and promotes individualism. Consequently, it is easy to forget rather than remember and follow a life of communal Love. Indeed, although love is often present, it is secondary to our individual satisfaction and success. Our aforementioned nun and the married CEO are countercultural as well as being odd and even foolish according to many of their peers.

Many of us would say that if we can get more money, we would take it. From the viewpoint of individualism, it would be stupid to do otherwise. From a spiritual perspective, we might limit or reject a pay raise if it harms or is at the expense of others. Occasionally, we read about a professional, like an athlete, who rejects a substantial pay increase or who requests a pay decrease for the good of the franchise, company, or community.

Individualism refers to a lifestyle wherein we invest our desire for spirituality in ego functions. We displace our will-to-Love (spirit) with a will-to-power (ego). Indeed, individuality and power are important, but when we make them our central motivating forces in life, we displace and forget God. Egoistic individualism replaces spiritual community.

As disciples of individualism, we devalue paradox and mystery, reject faith and doubt, avoid surrender and powerlessness, and withdraw from Love and its oneness. Since we are prone to see interpersonal relationships in terms of "conquest," we thrive on competition, dominance, and winning. We refuse to admit that we are dependent on a spiritual Power that is part of and beyond us. We falsely assume that our ego power is sufficient and that there is no healthy need for God. Actually, we assume more power than we have, and thereby delude ourselves.

Clearly, our society, mass media, and education foster individualism. Thus, there is pressure to be an individualist, to be normal. We are taught to assume that we have more power and control than we do actually have. We strive to have mastery over the world and others. Our willful intent to control everything protects us from facing our fear of nothingness. For example, instead of honoring God as no-thing, we make a God a thing or concept that we can control. Indeed, nothing scares us to death, rather than bringing us to life.

Some of us may even preach community and God, but practice individualism and religious narcissism. For example, some religious leaders use God to foster their power, control, and individual satisfaction.

They choose to go along to get along rather than confront and convert. They choose expediency over justice.

Actually, our will-to-power is often a reaction formation against our feeling of powerlessness. We try to control life, including others, because we are anxious about nothingness. Since our lifestyle is a constant compensation for basic powerlessness and anxiety, we strive to be certain of and in control of everything, including God. Thus, we diminish our spiritual life and become weaker.

In time, particularly in midlife, our self-sufficiency often shows signs of dissipating, and we begin to feel impotent. While young, our ego strength was often sufficient to escape from nothingness, but in midlife and thereafter, nothingness comes closer and threatens to overpower us. The great leveler—death—lurks in our shadows. We get tired of running from this hound of heaven.

Particularly if we are manipulative and self-centered, people withdraw from us. Consequently, we become lonely, bored, and anxious. Our displacement of Spirit with ego has left us inaccessible as well as unable to live meaningfully. Desolation stalks us. Ironically, the feelings from which we tried to escape are the ones we experience. We end up as a pure individual—an isolated unit.

To break through individualism, our ego must break down, accept its relative powerlessness, and surrender to a Higher Power. Similar to recovery from addictions, we may have to hit bottom to go up. Our ego must deflate in order to inflate with Love. Our egocentrism must surrender to theocentrism.

As health providers, we can help and even encourage people to let go of their willfulness (ego) and accept that they are dependent on a Higher (Spirit) Power. Being more dependent on a Reality that is greater than but related to who we are engenders a humble and reverent experience that dissipates our proud and arrogant individualism and leads to an empowered interdependency.

Workaholism

Jeff gives a good description of his workaholism. "I plead guilty. I am a workaholic. Maybe I should start a 12-step group, like A.A., for workaholics. I can picture it: Hi, my name is Jeff, and I'm a workaholic. I am powerless over work, and my life has become unmanageable. I have come to realize that only a Higher Power can restore me to sanity. Therefore, I turn my life and will over to the care of my God.

"Seriously, I doubt if my work is an addiction, but it could be. I do know that work is too important, and that it is harming my life. Indeed, I work too much, but it's not all my fault. To meet my quotas, I often have to work 60 to 70 hours a week. Moreover, I travel about once a month for a few to ten days. This is what my job entails. I admit that I spend more time at work than at home. Yes, I wonder if this is what life should be?

"Indeed, I make a lot of money that enables my children to get a good education and my wife to buy almost anything that she wants. We live in a large house, and have expensive cars, televisions, computers, appliances, sauna, or whatever adult toys we want. However, my children are practically orphans, and my wife is almost a widow. They see me passing by, or when I do settle in our house, I often fall asleep.

"Even when we go on vacation, I am far less than purely present. I bring my technological gadgets to keep in contact with the firm. Reading spiritual books or even novels is rare. Even when I am not at work, I often find myself thinking about work. Nevertheless, I can and do have some fun, but it is too infrequent and often scheduled or rushed. For instance, it is almost a moral task to make love with my wife, which is not often enough. Theoretically, I know that love is more important than work, but experientially, this is not the case. Actually, it is pathetic.

"Look, I don't think I'm a bad guy. I take the family to breakfast after Sunday services. I try to make it to some parent-teacher meetings, and I make sure I am home for the holidays. In short, I do what good fathers and husbands should do. Most people probably think that we are a model family. Again, all this is too much like work. Seldom do I simply let go and relax, stop thinking about a project, and just be with my loved ones.

"Where is God in my life? Like everything else, I put God on my list of things to do. By that, I mean that I go to church on Sundays, say a night prayer, and pray at meals. However, I seldom if ever give God a thought beyond these times. If I gave a tenth as much time to my spiritual life as I do to my work, I, my loved ones, and my life would be much better off. I admit that I live to work, and I hate it. How do I get out of this trap?"

This good and successful workaholic describes well some of the factors of one of our most common, well-intentioned, and rewarded displacements of God. "Workaholism" occurs when task-oriented behavior is our paramount value. As Jeff relates, work and its rewards are primary, and everything else is secondary or in service of work. When our lives are primarily in service of work rather than of Love, work becomes a displacement of God.

Even more important than the amount of work is the general attitude of the workaholic: being "project" oriented. This means that we are always thinking about what to do, so that even when we are not overtly working, we are working. We always have a job to do, a task to accomplish. When we complete one task, there are always more on our horizon.

It is as if work, instead of Love, justifies our existence. Thus, when we are not working, we more or less feel uneasy or guilty. We feel as if something is wrong, incomplete, or less than it could or should be. In this way, workaholism is an attitudinal and affective as well as a behavioral problem. Work, not Love, is the primary source of our worth.

Like proponents of perfectionism and individualism, workaholics operate primarily according to ego processes, not those of our Spirit. They, too, try to escape nothingness and inadvertently impede their relationships with God and others. Like Jeff, we invest too much of ourselves in work, and too little in and for others and God. Instead of being primary, Love takes second place.

We forget that the spiritual life affirms uselessness as the ground of usefulness. Instead of experiencing being and being-with as primary, we make useful doing paramount. Thus, we burn ourselves out, and we fail to nourish and enjoy our lives as much as we can and should. We fail to remember God in all our activities, including work. Our challenge is to integrate the biblical ways of both Martha and Mary.

As we have seen, although we may have good intentions, we can neglect our spouse, children, and other loved ones. Since our primary concern is work, our loved ones are secondary at best. For instance, children have phantom fathers (or mothers). Even when we are physically with our children, we may be texting, mentally preoccupied with a project, or half watching a TV program, and therefore not fully present to our children.

Such preoccupation and multitasking impedes rather than fosters interpersonal presence. Although as workaholics we may be successful at work and can give our loved ones (children, spouse, friends, parents) presents, they really want and need interpersonal presence more than material presents.

Our society can easily push us into the trap of workaholism. For instance, our society praises functionality at the expense of spirituality, and it measures our worth according to what we do rather than according to who we are. To do something, to be fast and efficient, to have control, to achieve success, and to perform well are fostered and sanctioned. To do nothing, to be patient, to let go, to be useless, and just be are seldom encouraged.

With good intentions and hard work, we can live a life that impedes true spiritual living. This normal mode of madness occurs when being work-oriented is paramount, while being spiritual is secondary. We are too busy and too tired to take time for God, especially in a communal setting. Often with good intentions, we forget and neglect our most important experiences—those of our Spirit.

As workaholics, we are prone to judge others and ourselves on the kind and amount of our skill, talent, education, personality—generally, on our functional (ego) impact. We measure our worth according to our possessions—the kind of house and car, how many children, how much money, education, etc. Having is more important than being. Something is more important than nothing. Work is more important than Love.

Indeed, if we identify our life with our work, retirement can precipitate a crisis. Retiring from work can mean retiring from life, or a frantic search for something to do. Women in contrast to men often adjust better in the elderly years because of their interpersonal skills and different work ethic. However, as women adopt a male model of worth and success, they too may experience the same discomforts of workaholism as men.

As workaholics, we tend to assume that we can solve any problem. Thus, we are prone to waste time and energy trying to fix unsolvable problems, like nothing. Instead of frantically working our way out of nothingness, we must slow down, be still, and accept nothingness as necessary to reveal and deepen our desire for and experience of God.

One of the main consequences of workaholism is that it not only impedes our opportunities to enjoy life, but it also impedes our creativity and efficiency in work. When we maximize functionality (ego), and minimize spirituality (spirit), we lose the source of our strength and actually become less effective in our work. In forgetting that God (no-thing) is the ground and source of service, we may become burnt-out, or we take drugs to keep us going for a while. Once again, we forget that uselessness is the creative source of usefulness.

In the work-trap, we become too goal-oriented and too concerned about the future. We worry about what to do, and forget that the present and its source, God, is a gift to enjoy. We forget that spiritually life is a mystery to celebrate and suffer, not primarily a series of problems to work on and solve. Being so caught up in our world of work, we miss God's presence and presents.

Indeed, as workaholics, we can easily become so busy that life passes us by. We can lose personal contact with ourselves, others, and God. When we forget that our primary focus should be on Love, life becomes increasingly absurd, and we become exhausted and disillusioned. In the busy swirl of workaholism, we must remember to pause to be useless, and be present to the now of Presence. We must remember that who and where we are, our glory lies.

Workaholism can also show its seductive face in religious activities that impede healthy spirituality. For instance, with good intentions, we can operate according to a savior complex in frantically dedicating our lives to saving people. A false assumption is that we think that our work (ego) will save people. What we do counts, but what God does counts infinitely more. Once again, we forget that we are not God.

Religious ministers can too easily become workaholics in the name of God. They become so busy in functional activities that they are too tired or lack time for prayer and other spiritual activities. In the midst of their busy life, they can easily forget their primary purpose—to help others as well as themselves to experience God. They may not walk their talk.

Workaholics are also prone to have distorted views of recreation. Vacations are a means of recuperating from work, rather than a way of vacating the ordinary to celebrate the extraordinary. As workaholics, we consider play as secondary or a reward for work rather than a necessary experience for health. We can even make play a project so that we work at playing. Life becomes a world of labor that minimizes the worlds of play, enjoyment, celebration, and Love.

We become so busy at work that we avoid being in nothingness, and therefore fail to nurture our desire for God. We need not be anxious about nothing, for in work we hold on to something. Moreover, some of us work on or grasp God as something rather than experiencing God as and in nothing.

To be sure, work is essential to healthy living. Without work, we seriously restrict our life. Indeed, work is usually necessary to achieve our goals and be successful, and without work ideas and dreams remain frustrating fictions. Furthermore, after a good days work, we feel more secure, safe, and satisfied. We feel like somebody, a good worker—not no-body. A danger, however, is that we are too tired or have no need or time for nothingness, and therefore to honor our desire for Love.

The midlife crisis of nothingness often pressures us to reevaluate our work, and if not then, usually in middle age. In middle age, most of us have gone as far as we can go in our careers. If we do not take stalk of ourselves in our middle years, we are likely to have difficulty upon retirement. Instead of listening to no-thing, we frantically search for something to do. An irony is that our avoidance of nothingness leaves us with nothing. Eventually, the nothingness of impending death engulfs us.

Most mental workers will agree that workaholism impedes healthy living, and encourage their clients to change their way of living. Although they rarely see God as an essential component of such displacement issues, they often deal with the spiritual covertly by encouraging more recreation, family time, and intimacy.

Although workaholism (as well as other displacements) are not mental disorders, they are not healthy. Thus, health providers, religious ministers, mentors, and other caretakers should help others achieve and maintain a whole and balanced life. Indeed, they can begin with themselves and be good role models.

Our therapeutic challenge is to experience a spiritual conversion—to turn away from the demonic forces of workaholism (and other displacements), and turn to the divine energies of Love. Instead of trying to fulfill our nothingness with work, we turn to Love. Instead of displacing God with work, we replace our workaholism with God, and our work becomes a manifestation of God. To do God's work may mean to do less and be more.

Rationalism

We will see that the enlightenment of rationalism may be a way of walking in darkness, for rationalism is a common displacement of God, especially with elite intellectuals, both in and out of religion. Reflect on the truth and error of what the following man, Theo, has to share.

"Since college, I stopped believing in God. A couple of philosophy and psychology professors proved to me conclusively that there were no rational reasons to believe in God. We studied scholars, like Nietzsche, Sartre, Marx, Feuerbach, and Freud who showed how God is a fiction, an illusion, a mental machination, or simply as unnecessary. They explained how we manufacture a God to ameliorate our anxieties and fears of issues like mortality, vulnerability, meaninglessness, and death.

"Since then, I have read contemporary authors, like Dawkins, Harris, and Hutchins. They have not only confirmed but also strengthened my conviction that God is an unnecessary mental construction. To use cognitive psychology, God is a false belief. To support my argument, God is rarely if ever seen as essential to mental health.

"Many authors repeatedly point out the Bible's many contradictions as well as stories that defy common sense. Moreover, they document the incredible amount of violence done in the name of religion, ministers who sexually abused children as well as religious leaders who enabled pedophiles. Need I go on?

"In regards to the God question, a main theme is that there is no rational reason for the necessity of a God. If God is not necessary, why construct one? Do you really believe in a loving father who will judge you justly and mercifully? Does a divine person really help you in times of need? Do you subscribe to an omnipotent, omniscient, omnipresent being who watches over everyone and everything? Do you buy an ultimate judge who determines whether you go to heaven or hell? Is there really a Creator who will tell you what the right thing to do is?

"Sure, you can give scholastic syllogisms about first cause or other such logical reasoning, intelligent design and watchmaker paradigms, and so forth to prove the existence of God. Actually, such arguments do not prove anything except your concept of what you think exists. There is no scientific evidence of God. Moreover, scientific arguments can give just as many or more plausible reasons for the existence of life, and do not call for a God. The same is true for biblical explanations and stories. For example, science can explain most if not all so-called miracles.

"When you bring up the issues of suffering and victims of violence, religious people will give you some bull like it is a mystery, punishment for sins, a consequence of original sin, or a result of free will. Tell that to parents who have just had their only child raped and murdered, or who have a severely disabled child. Tell that to the loved ones of the 9/11 victims. Tell that to the relatives of the millions of innocent civilians killed in wars. How could an all loving and omnipotent God allow such atrocities to occur.

"In short, I think that we have evolved to be rational animals that can make good and bad choices. We have basic drives, like the will to pleasure and power, which we must control, or dire consequences will occur. If religion helps people to control their basic instincts, it is fine with me. If the illusion of God helps you to be a decent person, that too is fine with me. However, I can be a decent and good citizen, who if you will, is virtuous, without believing in a God."

Theo is an atheist who rationally argues that God is unnecessary and does not exist. He would say that there is no rational proof of God and that one can live a virtuous life without God. A theist might counter that there is no conclusive proof that there is no God. Moreover, he might say that the atheist lacks a faith experience of God.

Such debates and disagreements will probably continue and are good because they keep the issue of God alive. Theists and atheists can be odd dance partners. A much worse scenario is not to dance, that is, to forget or take God for granted. Then, we act as if we are dead for God. As long as we wrestle with the issue of God, God is alive and relevant.

Theo makes sense and asks challenging questions. His criticisms of religion and its leaders are mostly accurate as far as they go. His critique of conceptions of God affirms the truth of trying to limit the unlimited. Moreover, his questions about absurd and unjust suffering and violence deserve concrete responses.

One could say that Theo is a disciple of rationalism. As an atheist, he uses his rational (ego) functions to conclude that a God (spirit) is unnecessary. As far as he goes, one could argue that he is mostly correct. From our perspective, his error lies in what he does not address. Theo does not go far enough in that he fails to incorporate the factors of our spiritual dimension. He errs not so much in what he says, but more so in what he fails to say. In short, a rationalist excludes spiritual dynamics, and reduces life to rational explanations.

When rationality is our exclusive avenue to truth, it becomes rationalism. Like Theo, we use our rational functions (ego), especially in their positivistic forms, as our primary way to make sense of life. We falsely assume that our cognitive powers will enable us to explain or escape our desire for Love, particularly in nothingness. We reframe no-thing (spiritual) into some-thing (rational). A logical segue is to conceive God as an unnecessary and potentially harmful concept.

Rationalists are the consummate rational animals. Hyperrationality, clear and distinct ideas, and theoretical and analytical approaches are key symptoms. They try to force experience into their ideologies and dogmas, rather than using them in service of people's experience. Their main assumptions are that rationality (ego) is the ultimate source of truth and that thinking is the only way to deal with nothingness and God (spirit).

Ironically, in their attempts to know the truth, they fail to experience the Truth.

(In contrast, as emotivists, we act the opposite: We absolutize the truth of feelings, emotion, and body language in general. Instead of the cognitive, the affective is primary so that sharing and being congruent with feelings are paramount. Our common guideline is that if it feels right, it is right. We are apt to construe holy experiences as intense emotionality.)

Thus, as rationalists we try to account for spiritual experience only with rational means in contrast to spiritual means. Our mistake is to reduce spiritual dynamics to those of the body and ego. For example, we can reduce spiritual experiences to emotionality or intense affectivity (body) or to mental machinations (ego).

We might explain god as a projection of or a wish for a perfect parent especially when we are suffering from severe stress. We may construe god as a belief that gives us purpose as well as an illusion that protects and helps us. We may see religious leaders as seeking power to control people and to accumulate wealth. From our (ego) point of view, religious beliefs are wastes of time and energy and can be unhealthy. Rationality is sufficient to make sense of and to cope with life.

Certainly, we can reflect rationally on the factors that describe spiritual and God experiences, as we have done in this book. Rationality, however, in itself is inadequate to comprehend holy experiences. We err when we reduce holy dynamics (like mystery, sacredness, imminent transcendence, nothingness, etc.) to mere rational explanations, and exclude spiritual ones. Moreover, any concept or explanation of God, including our own, falls very short of and limits experiences of God.

It is important to note that most rationalists as well as workaholics and individualists are not atheists. Although most atheists are rationalists, most rationalists are not atheists. For example, many mental health workers believe in God, but most are rationalists in their profession insofar as they do not include God as essential to health.

Even (and some would say especially) as religious persons, we can follow scripts of rationalism. In doing so, we live out of our theoretical minds rather our experiential hearts. We make ourselves and others fit and follow our religious concepts. We answer any questions, and explain life's mysteries. We know what is true and right not only for ourselves but also for others. Our (left or right) ideologies get in the way of love. We can strip life of its Love in our sincere attempts to be certain of the truth.

We can also take a rationalistic approach in spiritual formation and direction. For instance, subscribing to psychologism, we can overemphasize the importance of cognitive restructuring, affective sharing, and self-fulfillment. We can invest an enormous amount of time and energy in the pursuit of self-fulfillment at the expense of controlling or forgetting God. With good intentions, we can get in God's way. We forget and fail to bow in awe to the Truth of all truths.

Some learned intellectuals believe that they can eventually explain and account for any phenomenon, and that which is beyond rationality is secondary and perhaps irrelevant. Like our atheist friend, some subscribe to scientism where they reduce all phenomena to scientific understanding. That which does not fit within the scientific model is irrelevant or secondary.

Others may reduce everything to psychological understanding. These advocates of psychologism may look down on spiritual experiences, and construe them as misguided illusions, false beliefs, or rationalizations held by the ignorant or insecure. They dismiss or rationalize nothingness and God, or they see nothingness as a disorder and treat it with therapy and medication.

Some rationalists act on the premise that perception is reality. In such extreme cognitive psychology, the individual determines what is appropriate. Thus, what I perceive to be true is true for me, and not necessarily for you. I imply that there are few if any absolute truths. Clearly, such subjectivism can lead to moral relativism, and some would say to eventual anarchy.

Conversely, other rationalists think and act quite the opposite. Instead of subjectively seeing everything as relative, they hold to objective absolutes. They assume that there are absolute truths and that your experience must conform to them regardless of your intentions. They know what is right and wrong, and they will tell you what is right. Thus, the ideologies of both extreme subjectivism and objectivism are on opposite ends of the same rationalistic continuum.

As rationalists, we risk forcing life to fit a rational model to the exclusion of transrational understanding. This can occur in both reductionist atheisms and theisms. We make ourselves the center and ultimate power of the universe. We displace faith with reason, our spirit with ego, God with ourselves. When we displace, forget, rationalize, or rigidly conceptualize God, we fail to respond to and nourish our desire to be with God. Consequently, we can become displaced and lost persons.

To be sure, rationality is an essential source of and way to truth. Faith without reason can lead to superstition, authoritarianism, or unreasonable and violent behavior. Faith needs reason to grow and be healthy. An abdication of reason leads to insanity and even violence. An abdication of faith also leads to madness, albeit normal.

In our health paradigm, rationality and spirituality, reason and faith, ego and spirit should function in harmony and benefit each other. For instance, we can use our minds to challenge and deepen our faith. We can think of ways to construe God that foster rather than impede our spiritual experiences of God. We can use our minds (ego) to find time and space (body) to increase the likelihood of God (spirit) experiences.

Sexaholism

"Since high school and especially college, I think I tried to have sex with any available woman. Admittedly, it was fun to sow my wild oats, and many women seemed to be willing to help us plant our seeds and to enjoy its fruits. It seemed like all my frat brothers were doing it or wanted to do it, and many of our sorority sisters were ready and willing to go along with us.

"I continued to live this so-called free life. It was easy, for there is a culture of mass media and venues that foster recreational sex. However, with some ambivalence, I gave up this lifestyle when I met the woman whom I eventually married. It is not that I stopped lusting after women; I still savor a female body. I stopped having sex with women because of marriage vows and because it was simply unwieldy in terms of time and energy.

"However, do not jump to the conclusion that I am a stellar husband and father, or the paragon of purity. Although I am not sexually involved with other women, I am in to cybersex. I spend an awful lot of time on line watching porn, and sometimes getting into chat rooms.

"As soon as my wife is out of the house, I give the kids something to do on their own, and I practically run to the computer. Sometimes in the middle of the night, I'll get out of bed to watch porn. Even at work, I'll get on a porn line when I get a safe chance, but I know that this is risky.

"I have to admit that I no longer have the old college, carefree swagger. Now I'm starting to feel guilty and even embarrassed. It is not something I brag about or would recommend. I admit I would not like it if my wife were into porn. I know that it is wrong and not healthy; otherwise, I would recommend it. For me, it is a sin. Although I am faithful, in another way I am being unfaithful. For instance, when my wife and I make love, images of other women come to my mind. This is not good.

"Nevertheless, I look forward to weekends, for this is when I usually get more time for porn. I make up excuses for my time on the computer, such as doing research or something for work. Moreover, I want to go on business trips because I have more time and accessibility for porn. Sure, masturbation often accompanies my porn explorations. Indeed, neither is this good for my relationship with my wife.

"Still, practically everyone thinks we are the model family, and in some ways we are. We are successful in our professional careers, are active in community affairs, are friendly with our neighbors, and are members of church committees. People would be shocked if they knew of my private life. Yes, I feel like a hypocrite.

"I do not think that I am a sex addict, but maybe I am one. I know that I cannot abstain for very long. The urge to look waxes and wanes, but eventually it stalks me and demands satisfaction. Sometimes, I just do it to get it out of my system, but sooner than later it comes back as strong as ever. Moreover, I have noticed that I look at women with eyes of lust, undress them, and imagine having sex with them. Again, this is not good. How do I get out of this quicksand of lust?"

If this good man is not a sex addict, he is very close to being one. Most mental health providers would say that he is in serious trouble, and that he will continue to accrue consequences that impede healthy living. For instance, his porn behavior impedes his relationship with his wife, takes away time and energy with his family, reinforces a lustful attitude, and engenders shame and its unworthiness. Unless he makes some radical changes, life will probably get worse, and certainly not better.

For many reasons, cybersex is the fastest growing untoward behavior. Such sex is easily available, can be free, is virtually inexhaustible, gives the illusion of safety and anonymity, and offers immediate gratification as well as an escape from whatever. It offers the false promise of true intimacy, but it is a lie. Pornography can never adequately respond to our desires for love.

Another common motive is to ameliorate non-genital feelings, like boredom, anxiety, depression, and various forms of stress as well as experiencing excitement, pleasure, and the illusion of well-being. In regards to our thesis, it can also be an escape from the discomfort of nothingness, while giving temporary fulfillment and an illusion of wholeness.

When we engage in any type of sexual behavior to avoid nothingness and its incumbent feelings, we seriously harm ourselves. The most serious fault is to numb our desire for God, or to displace our desire for Love with sex. Like any displacement, sex is an inadequate response to our desire for abiding Love. Thus, after we engage in sexaholic behavior, we invariably feel empty, disillusioned, and displaced.

Sex, particularly in its genital form, can be a very seductive and pleasurable way to escape from nothingness, and therefore to avoid or numb our desire for God. Whether it is with another person or with oneself, sex can temporarily fulfill but never expel nothingness. Quickly, nothingness returns and demands a response of Love.

Think of adolescents. In many ways, our culture and its mass media enable them to escape nothingness, like its restless boredom, irritating questions, and evolving identity by engaging in sexuality. Some social scientists and educators practically expect them to have sex. Sex offers easy and reliable satisfactions as well as a sanctioned respite from the difficult and unsettling sense of becoming mature. It is often easier, albeit not better, for us to have sex than to engage our search for meaning.

At any age, we can ameliorate our anxiety, loneliness, and desire for love with sex. One could argue that it is a national/world pastime. Moreover, we can hold on to something or somebody rather than being in nothingness. For instance, a mid-life adult may regress to youth and engage in promiscuous sexuality as an escape from nothingness. Sex offers the illusion of having no care in the world and of being young again, when there was time for everything and not nothing. Sex seems so much better than nothing.

Unlike adolescents who use sex to satisfy new and intense genital drives, adults are more likely to have sex to escape from idiosyncratic and existential depression, boredom, anxiety. The immediate gratification of sex enables us to avoid listening to our uncomfortable feelings. The fallacy is to assume that sex or any process (eating, gambling) or substance (alcohol, other drugs) is an adequate response to nothingness, and therefore to God. Simply stated, sex cannot satisfy our desires for Love.

Those of us who avoid nothingness and displace God with our ego functions can be especially susceptible to using sex as a periodic displacement. Rationalists for instance, may find the immediacy of sex a welcome experience, for they can come out of their theoretical (ego) worlds into an experiential (body) world. They can retreat from an abstract world of complex mediation to a concrete world of simple immediacy.

Likewise, workaholics may welcome sex as one of the few times they can take time out from work simply to play and be, while avoiding nothingness. Disciples of individualism can feel some semblance of being intimate with rather than distant from someone. Perfectionists can pursue imperfect pleasure while finding some respite from their perfectionism.

Would it not be helpful if health providers would tune in to and respond to such dynamics? Rather than taking only a physical and psychological approach, they could include spiritual factors as well. Indeed, to take only a spiritual approach (pray more, etc.) could be just as detrimental to one's health as physical and psychological reductionisms.

Although health providers often offer medical and psychosocial help, they rarely suggest spirituality and God in their health plan. We have argued that the paucity of spirituality and God in academic and clinical health venues is detrimental to health. Ideally, we should offer and integrate all three—medical/physical, psychological/social, and spiritual/God—approaches to health.

Power is also part of the sexual experience—the arrogant power of control, the invigorating power of ecstasy, the quiet power of fulfillment and completion, the strength in being able to let go of oneself, and the potential power of procreation are all present. Such power may give us the illusion that we are more powerful than we really are instead of being radically and ultimately powerless. Moreover, when we divorce sexual power from committed love, we try to be our own Higher Power and become narcissistic. Once again, there is little room for God.

Nevertheless, we can also experience a certain kind of ecstasy and transcendence in sexuality that points to the spiritual. Like in all displacements, including unhealthy sex, there is a hint of the spiritual. From a therapeutic viewpoint, it behooves us to recognize the hidden Spirit in sex, and strive to come to an overt and fuller experience of Love.

Stated another way, any displacement involves a covert and lingering spiritual Presence. Especially in sex, there is an adumbrated presence of God. Our mistake (or sin as defined as a separation from God) is that we use sex to avoid or displace Love rather than to celebrate Love's presence. From this perspective, when we engage in casual sex, we are also seeking God. In particular, pastoral counselors would benefit others if they evoked the hidden Spirit in their penitents' sins.

What makes such sex less than healthy and holy is that we fail to nurture the spiritual in sexuality with committed love. Only a permanent commitment of love can foster the spirituality of sexuality because only being in Love is an adequate response to the Spirit of sex. Clinically, we must meet our spiritual drives with spiritual responses; otherwise, sexuality becomes fragmented or less than whole or healthy. Without healthy love, sex can become a displacement of God.

In short, a displacement of Love with sex can be a meaningful and pleasurable experience, but it does not foster wholistic growth. Without committed love, our physical and psychosocial dimensions operate while we repress, minimize, or forget our spiritual self. Thus, sex becomes a substitute for Love and therefore of God. In such sex, we are less than we can truly be.

To be sure, there are many motives for unhealthy behaviors. Sexaholism as well as any displacements and addictions also have psychological and physical components. For instance, brain chemistry can play a powerful role. Psychological factors, such as sexual fixation, trauma, and general immaturity, are significant. Moreover, never underestimate the force of habit in any behavior, good or bad.

Sex (or any) addictions and sex (or any) displacements never work. There are no exceptions. They never succeed in finding what they really need because they ask sex to be Love/God. They get fleeting glimpses and a temporary feel for the enduring unity, serenity, and freedom that only Love offers. To recover, sex addicts must avoid lust, accept their powerlessness, and surrender to a Higher Power. They must follow this Truth (Love).

In short, sex without Love is not healthy because it is the inverse of sexual fulfillment in Love. Sex as a displacement becomes exclusive as contrasted to the inclusive fulfillment in loving sex. Sex without Love is isolating and self-centered, not communally orientated.

In time, nothingness, or the presence of God in absence, demands Love. The older we become, the less we can rely on sex, and Love beckons us. As we grow older, the Spirit of sex and life calls us more clearly and strongly to listen and respond to and in Love. In this sense, the elderly can be the best lovers.

Lovism

Listen to Angela who is a good and admirable woman. "Call me what you want. Some people would label me as a secular humanist. Secular sounds too harsh, for I believe in and practice a spiritual life. Perhaps, spiritual humanist fits me better.

"Others might call me a reverent agnostic, for I do seriously question the existence of God, and I am a spiritual person. Moreover, I do not like the arrogant, condescending, and rationalistic attitudes of many atheists. If I am an atheist, I am one who is open to being wrong and who respects those who believe in God.

"My mom and dad are good, practicing Catholics, and they raised me to be a good Catholic as well. My entire education was Catholic, and I am grateful for the fine education and character formation that the teachers gave me. In college, I started to question my religious teaching and even the existence of God. A venerable teacher encouraged me to question as long as I sought the truth. His advice stuck with me, and I continue to be a truth seeker.

"I cannot prove that God does not exist, or can you prove that God does exist. Both you and I can argue our positions, and we can point out the limits in each other's arguments. I hope we can avoid demeaning each other, and accept and respect each other's differences. After all, both of us are trying to make the best sense of life. Let me briefly explain my position.

"For me, the spiritual life is paramount. I try to live a virtuous life, and consider love to be the cardinal virtue. So far, I think we agree. My call is to be compassionate, patient, forgiving, grateful, loving, and so forth. This truth liberates me from my illusions of happiness without unhappiness, and sets me free for a good and meaningful life. Such truth is what I seek and try to promote.

"I do not see any necessity for a God. There is too much evidence against a transcendent, merciful, and loving God who intervenes for you or me. It does not make sense to me that there is a personal God, a transcendent Father or Mother, who watches over and takes care of me, answers my prayers, and will judge me after death. If you construe God as your ultimate concern, you could say that for me God is the love of truth, namely the truth of living a virtuous life.

"As a licensed counselor, I see no need to include God in my therapy practice. Of course, if a client wants to talk about God or religion, I will listen and process. However, I would not introduce God or religion into our conversation. I do not think that such matters are within the purview of psychotherapy.

"In short, I think I can live a good, virtuous, and meaningful life without believing in a God, particularly God as a transcendent person. Truth is what matters for me, and the truth is to live a life of love and its accompanying virtues. Personally, what matters most to me is to love my husband, children, parents, and other loved ones as well as I can.

"Nevertheless, I am sending our children to a Catholic school so that they receive religious instruction and formation. You might ask why I am doing this if I question the existence of God. Well, I think religion gives them a solid moral framework, good character formation, and the teachings of a God-centered life. When they are adults or sooner, they can question what they have been taught. Like my spiritual mentor, I think it is good to question basic beliefs in order to grow. If they were not taught religion, there would be little to question, and consequently little growth.

"I will remain open to the question of God. Now, for many reasons, I do not understand the necessity of a transcendent God. I still go to church with my husband and children, for there is a great deal of truth in religion. Maybe someday I will come to worship a personal transcendent God. For now, I will be open to how life unfolds. If you wish, call me a spiritual agnostic."

One could argue that many religious people are not as spiritual or even religious as Angela is. She is open to the possibility of a God, and she respects those who believe in God. She is giving her children a religious education because she wants them to have character formation and religious knowledge to discern and make up their own minds about the truth. However, for herself, she sees no good reason to posit a God who is a transcendent person.

From our perspective, insofar as this woman focuses on love as the paramount truth in life, she implies the source of love, God. She rejects God as a transcendent person, but does not reflect on God as an imminent presence. She sees God as someone outside herself, and not one who dwells within her. Our view has been that God is not only beyond us, but is also the most intimate part of us. For her, the love and truth are most important. For me, the greatest truth is uncreated, cocreating Love who is beyond and within us.

Since love is our paramount dynamic of being holy and healthy, love can be a particularly subtle and seductive displacement of God. Such love, or "lovism," means that we displace our desire for God with an exclusive desire for people. Unlike Angela who is open to God, we try to exclude God, who is the source and model of our love.

For some of us, "God is love," means that when we love each other, our love equals God. We construe God as symbolic of perfect human love. We see ourselves as the ultimate form of life, and become secular humanists that have no need for God. Being self-sufficient and omnipotent (ego), we save ourselves from nothingness (powerlessness), and thereby miss the power of God (spirit).

We may handle the nothingness of death by considering life after death as the heritage that we leave on earth primarily through good works. In a sense, this is our notion of heaven; we live forever through our acts. Although our beliefs contain truth, they nevertheless exclude faith in a divine reality who/that dwells in our lives on earth. Furthermore, our rationalizations of death enable us to avoid nothingness, or our desire for more than exclusively human love.

We might construe God as a symbol of perfection so that a person is God when he achieves his nirvana-like state of self-actualization. Again, there is truth in such a Jungian approach. God calls us to be God-like, and the Christian way is to emulate Jesus Christ, or the incarnated God. From this perspective, God made us to be gods, or like Christ.

Other advocates of lovism may understand God as a symbol of universal truth or cosmic consciousness. Similar to our spiritual agnostic counselor, these philosophers (lovers of wisdom) seek Truth as their ultimate concern. Love is a way to arrive at and more importantly to experience the ultimate Truth, perhaps the Being of beings. Instead of seeing love as the ultimate Truth, they see love as a way to the Truth.

In short, our proposal has been that Love is the Truth and wellspring of wholeness and holiness. In Love, we promote the well-being and goodness of community—self, others, and God. We discover that the meaningful order of Love is the only adequate answer to the meaningless chaos of nothingness. In and through nothingness and Love we find the ground for a meaningful and actualizing life. In Love, life makes ultimate sense. Moreover, I contend that this is part of personal health.

Numerous studies have supported love as the core of mental health. No other experiences are more important than the interpersonal experiences of love. We have showed how our love for one another comes from and implies God who dwells within, among, and beyond us. Human love and divine love are both immanent and transcendent, and are inextricably related. One without the other causes unnecessary problems, and is less than the Truth—and, less than healthy.

Thus, the exclusion of one love violates or at least impedes the other. Exclusive love of people falls short as a substitute for the love of God—and, the exclusive love of God falls short as a substitute for the love of people. Humanism without God and God without humanism are inadequate ways to live.

Although love is our most important endeavor, it can have serious pitfalls, such as falling into the extremes of empathy or narcissism. As empathic lovers, albeit with good intentions, we focus on others at our own expense. We falsely assume that our love will "make" others happy, and we are willing to do almost anything "to make" them happy, for then we will be "happy." In short, our wellbeing depends on how others think, feel, and act. When others feel good, we feel good.

Problems especially escalate when we need a sick or bad person to change in order to feel healthy and good ourselves. When we enter this prison of codependent love, we abdicate our control as well as empower someone who is unreliable or dangerous, or both. Moreover, our focus on and futile efforts to change others results in neglect of ourselves. We sacrifice ourselves and forget to love ourselves.

As narcissistic lovers, our love centers on ourselves at the expense of others. We act as if we are more important than others. Love means that people should be in service of us, or at least not get in the way of satisfying our needs. Thus, we are apt to use others to satisfy our needs. Instead of abdicating our power, we try to control others. Our love centers too much on self, and not enough on us. In the extreme, we could care less about others. My focus is on me, not you. I love myself, and look out for number one—me.

For instance, although your narcissistic spouse loves you, he (or she) will often manipulate you to satisfy himself. When push comes to shove, he will satisfy his needs before yours or your children's needs. He will put himself before you and whoever else. His world is more important than your shared world. Indeed, if you are an emphatic lover, you are a target for a narcissistic lover. Your toxic dance of love will be intensely frustrating. You will try to change him, and he will use you.

When we subscribe to such scripts of lovism, we can easily forget God. Once again, we escape our radical powerlessness and its desire for a Higher Power. We live the illusion that we are more powerful (can change others) and more important than we are. Rather than surrendering to God, we become gods without God.

Another displacement is to avoid people while loving God. We try to experience God only in solitude, while withdrawing from people. As avoidant lovers, we do not have to be concerned about the nitty-gritty and risk of human relationships. Perhaps, we are afraid of rejection, or we feel unworthy of another's love. We feel relatively safe, secure, and worthy only with God. We forget that God does not exist for us without us.

Eventually, however, we will experience the painful consequence of our avoidance of intimacy with others. Our health as well as our intimacy with God will suffer. In short, since we are essentially related to God and others, our avoidance of one will affect the other.

From a 12-step perspective of health, we must admit our powerlessness (ego), that is, we must accept that we cannot control, change, or cure anyone, or we should not make ourselves more important than others. Rather, in order to cope effectively, we must surrender to a Higher Power (Spirit), or to a God of our understanding. On our own, we have less power than need be, and our life becomes less manageable. To become free and empowered, we must turn our will and life over to the Power of Love.

If we continue to practice a one-sided love (emphatic, narcissistic, avoidant), we will usually come to a crisis in our middle or elderly years. Nothingness eventually demands that we find a balanced way of being in Love. As codependent, empathic lovers, we must learn to love ourselves as well as we love others. If narcissistic, we must learn to love others without hidden agendas. If in isolation, we can act on our need to connect with others as well as we do with ourselves and God. Eventually, our imbalance will seek balance in love with self-God-others.

Religionism

Religion and its people should and often does help us experience God and live a good life. However, we can also use religion to control others, to gain power and wealth, or to justify violence. Religion can help us live a life of Love or, religion can be a displacement of Love. Listen to this zealous Christian.

"It baffles me why people fail to follow the way of the Lord. You only have to read the Bible to know what to do and be right. There may be some shades of gray, but most of life can be seen in terms of black and white. Moral relativism drives me nuts. Some people can justify almost anything. They act as if there are no moral absolutes.

"Look, I know there are plenty of ways to go astray. I have been there and done that. I have lived a life of debauchery. I was running with booze, drugs, women, or whatever it took to get high, and ran away from the Lord. Thank God, I hit bottom and had my conversion. I gave my life to Jesus, and became an active member of my church. Finally, I have purpose, direction, and peace in my life. I feel sorry for those who have not surrendered to the Lord and are saved.

"There is no good reason to be lost, to live a decadent life, or to follow the scripts of a Godless society. Unfortunately, many of my past friends still party as a way of life. I pity them. I tell them where to find the truth that will set them free. I tell them that they can find what is right and wrong by following the church's teachings, reading the right Bible, researching the right religious websites, and listening to the right church leaders. I tell them what the ways of God are, and what are the ways of the devil. The truth is there for the asking. May God have mercy on them.

"Every day I pray for them and others who live in darkness. I try to give them the light, the life, and the truth. I point out their errors, and give them resources to find the truth. There should be no uncertainty, for there are sources to dispel any doubt. You can be sure that there is a God who will answer your prayers. Of course, God's ways are not always our ways. Without faith, nothing makes sense.

"Of course, like anything important, finding your savior is not easy. You must study the right teaching, listen to the right pastor, and be with the right people. Reading scripture, frequent prayer, participate in religious services, take part in group discussions, serve on church committees, do good works, spread the good news, evangelize, and support your church are not easy. It is even more difficult to admit your sins, make amends, surrender to the Lord, and follow his teachings. Trust me, you will eventually find that it becomes easier and better.

"I pray for sinners, and that includes me. I know that I do not save myself, but only the Lord, Jesus can save me. Believe me; he can save you, too. Listen to what has set me free, or who saved my life. There is no need to be lost in darkness, for there is light to guide you. That light is Jesus Christ. The wages of sin are damnation, but if you follow the right way, you can gain eternal bliss."

This man subscribes to his form of Christianity. For some, this committed Christian is admirable, and he makes good and helpful sense. They wish they had his certainty and confidence. His critics might say that he conveys a pious arrogance that is more likely to repulse rather than attract people. He not only knows what is right and wrong for himself but also for others.

Religion can be the most subtle and dangerous displacement of God, for we do it in the name of God. As disciples of "religionism," we try to displace God with religion. We may preach and even follow religious rules and exercises without living much of a spiritual life. Instead of our ego being in service of our spirit, our ego is dominant at our spirit's expense. Our religious ideology is more important than the practice of Love.

Like the man in our vignette, we can develop a safe and powerful way of living, for it seems that we always know the right way. We sincerely think, plan, and decide our religious life so that there is little room for spiritual ambiguity and mystery. There is no doubt about our faith, and there is not much place for nothing. We are certain of what is right and wrong. When we lack the love and humility of divine dependency, we are proudly control and become our own redeemers. One could argue that theistic and atheistic critics rightly reject such a religion and its god.

A more subtle and benevolent type of religionism can take the form of perfectionism. As holy perfectionists, we try to follow the letter of the law, behaving exactly right. According to our black or white code, there is no room for ambiguity or ambivalence, and certainly not for imperfection. Our folly is that we think we have all the exact answers for how and why we should behave. We try to make our life conform to our unrealistic and rigid theories, beliefs, and standards. Often with good intentions, we displace God/Love (spirit) with our draconian truth (ego).

Reflect on Terry's plight of perfectionism. "No matter what I do, I am never good enough. I try to do God's will—to love unconditionally, accept and understand, give without any expectations of return, be positive and affirmative, give what I want to receive, etc. etc. Still, things do not change, at least for the better. In fact, I feel worse. It seems the more I try to do my very best, the worse life gets.

"Then I make matters worse in that I criticize myself. I reason that if only I was more loving and understanding, my life and marriage would get better. If I were perfect, how could he demean and hurt me. How could anyone reject a perfect person? Does not love cure all? I know that this is crazy thinking, but this is how I often feel.

"My best friend told me that my biggest imperfection is trying to be perfect. I have to admit that she may be right, but what is wrong with being perfect? Admittedly, I have to be careful with my kids so that I do not impose my standards on them. I know what it is like to get all A's and one B, and be reprimanded for the B.

"I know in my mind, at least part of it, that much of life is gray. However, when things are gray, I get anxious and try to make them white or black. You might guess that people dislike my well-intentioned judgments. It is not easy to be perfect, to have the right answers, and to have perfect love that casts out all fear and uncertainty.

"Didn't the Son of God command us to be perfect? Isn't perfection our goal? Wasn't Jesus perfect, and we are supposed to be like him? God would not ask us to do the impossible. I don't always feel this way, for part of me knows that I am out of bounds, and sometimes I just forget about it. Even then, I know that my demons of perfectionism are lurking in the shadows of my mind, waiting to devour me. Will I ever have any peace? My lot in life seems so dismal."

Most counselors would say that Terry is a good woman who is on an unhealthy track. Indeed, her subtle control is not arrogant like that of an extreme religious zealot. Her friend is right in that her most serious imperfection is her perfectionism. Moreover, Terry knows that her will-to-perfection is wrong, for she does not want to impose it on her children. Terry would do better to practice a spirituality of imperfection.

The etymology of perfection gives us a therapeutic hint to another meaning of perfection. Coming from the Latin *per* (through) and *facere* (to make), perfection literally means, "to make it through" life in our best, imperfect way. In this sense, perfection incorporates imperfection, and our perfection rests on being imperfectly one with God, self, and others.

However, religious perfectionists, like Terry, find it very difficult to accept and respond to imperfections and limits as opportunities for growth. They falsely assume that errors are not ways to the truth, and mistakes are not ways to learn. They only feel good about themselves when they are perfect; only 100 percent is good enough. They feel so uneasy with a "smudged slate" that they will do almost anything to make it a "clean slate."

As perfectionists, life must go according to our vision of what should be. Like Terry, we try to live according to a tyranny of shoulds—a rigid system of what one should and should not do. When we behave and even feel contrary to this ideal self, we feel anxious and guilty. We find it very difficult to embrace our real self that is limited, fallen, broken, and sinful.

Clearly, there is little room for nothingness in the house of perfection. Nothingness exposes our limited and imperfect self. It affirms our powerlessness, dependency, and incompleteness. Nothingness proclaims that we are not in control (ego), that we are not perfect, that we will never finish our symphony, that we are not God.

We can see that perfectionism, even in the name of God, is a terrible burden to carry. As time goes on, the heavy weight of perfectionism wears us down and depletes us. If not before, nothingness in the elderly years shatters our illusion of perfectionism as well as the certainty of religionism. We find ourselves weary and yearning for peaceful rest. No longer are we so sure; in fact, we are dreadfully unsure, which can be our saving grace.

Clergy with good intentions can practice religious perfectionism. Such religious leaders know the exact way to heaven, and may fail to honor ways that differ from theirs. Unless you do this or that, you will not make it. They squeeze life into their religious dictates. They aim to convert people to their religion rather than to God. For them, life is in service of religion (ego) rather than religion being in service of life (spirit). Such a pastor is poison to a person like Terry.

Consider the issue of zero tolerance in regards to certain behaviors. Currently, there is often not a spectrum of wrong behavior, but rather all behaviors, particularly sexual, have the same dire consequences. For instance, a person who has a collection of pictures of naked children gets the same consequences as one who engages in sexual behavior with minors. Or the twenty-eight-year-old cleric who pats a person's backside may get the same punishment as the serial sodomite. Too often, expediency (ego) trump mercy and justice (spirit). Religious leaders can make bad judgments, often due to fear and ignorance, when their ego displaces their Spirit.

Our critique neither implies a relativism that places all values and behaviors on a horizontal plane, nor an effort to minimize the value and necessity of truth. To the contrary, there is a vertical hierarchy of values. For example, the right to life and a good education are more important than other rights.

Moreover, there are many objective, absolute truths that are related to and in service of subjects. For instance, if we want to be healthy, we must satisfy our basic needs (body), function effectively, (ego), and love (spirit). One could also argue that God is an absolute reality, for without God, we would not exist.

Unfortunately, some religious leaders succumb to the demons of religionism. They forget that the magisterium is in service of pastoral care, that the right way is related to the wrong way, that knowledge should help rather than hinder, that rules and rubrics should serve people, not vice versa.

They forget that they are servants and facilitators rather than lords and rulers. They forget to embrace with love rather than preach. They forget to show love (spirit) rather than being right (ego). They forget that they are God's creatures (not creators) who cocreate the truth. They forget to smell like the sheep whom they portend to shepherd.

Indeed, all of us are prone to forget. However, when religious leaders use their power (ego) of religion to manipulate people (spirit), the harm (sin) is greater. Too many people talk (religion) the walk (spirituality), and fail to walk the talk. (It is understandable that increasingly more people leave religion and still believe in God.)

The power of religiosity can seduce us. Like our sincere zealot, we may think that we can tell other people exactly what to do to be holy and how to get to heaven. We may revert to ego motives of domination instead of spiritual motives of appeal. Instead of humbly accepting our nothingness, we become proud and cerebral in assuming that we know God's will not only for ourselves but also for others.

Instead of forming and inviting others into a community of Love, we force them into our limited religious framework. Instead of listening to and learning from their questions, we have ready-made answers for them. Instead of being humble sojourners, we lead them to the certainty of religion at the expense of spiritual growth. Instead of welcoming them to Love, we try to convert them to our religion.

As we grow older, many of us discover that our childhood religion needs to develop in order to form an adult spirituality. We find ourselves as adults with a religion that is barely beyond the cognitive and spiritual functions of early adolescence. For some people, this simple approach is adequate to live a good and holy life. For others, it is woefully inadequate, and too often they feel frustrated when they confront purveyors of religion with critical and probing questions.

For instance, when they engage religion and its ministers with questions about the existence of God, heaven, or other basic beliefs, the meaning of absurd suffering and injustice, the hypocrisy and cruelty of ministers, experiences of nothingness, desolation, or loss of faith, they often feel disappointed or disillusioned with the responses, or simply not helped. Or they may feel they are condescendingly given child or adolescent responses to adult questions.

Too often seekers of spiritual truth are given rote, abstract theologies that impede their spiritual experiences. Responses like have more faith, it is a mystery, a theology degree is necessary to understand, or referral to a catechism are often inadequate and insulting. In response, many of us simply withdraw from or give up on organized religion.

An alternative to dropping out is to challenge and help our religion and its leaders, and thereby ourselves. Instead of being dependent on religious leaders, we can be cocreators of religion. Instead of looking up to ministers of religion, we can look at them straight in their eyes. With them, we can develop a religion that nurtures and fosters an adult spiritual relationship with self, God, and others.

Clearly, we should not subscribe to a religion to avoid nothingness, for then we retard our spiritual growth. Moreover, we risk becoming caricatures of holy persons. We can come across as cerebral know-it-alls rather than struggling sojourners. Although we go through the proper motions, people feel uneasy with us, and avoid our religion. However, when we face and share our nothingness and its valley of death, our spirituality and its religion invite others to explore themselves.

In developing a mature religious vision, we re-member. Remember that God is no thing, and is found in all things. Remember that no-thing is the basis of our healthy dis-ease that engenders holiness and health. Remember, crumbling in nothingness can be the prelude to health in all things.

Indeed, health providers, or anyone, should not proselytize and impose their religion on their clients. On the other hand, why do counselors avoid helping clients form their spiritual vision of life or whatever makes ultimate sense to them? What prevents counselors from journeying with clients through nothingness, helping them learn from their displacements, and finding a Higher Power or God of their understanding? Is not pursuing the source, meaning, and destiny of life essential to health?

Conclusion

We have seen that displacements of God are often well intentioned and make, albeit not the best, sense. In short, they impede our health (waste time and energy, fail to empower, impede freedom and serenity, lack enduring meaning, etc.). When we persist in displacing God, we eventually alienate ourselves from God, others, and self, and consequently become displaced people.

Indeed, displacements offer magnetic rewards, like power (ego) and pleasure (body) as well as giving temporary repose, vitality, and fulfillment. Moreover, as disciples of displacements, we can enter into collusion with others that enable us to delude one another in regards to the efficacy and health of our displacements.

The fact is that displacements do not work insofar as they fail to foster a healthy and holy life. Pleasure (body) and power (ego) cannot adequately fulfill our desires for Love (spirit). Thinking, feeling, and behaviors without Love simply fall short of giving enduring meaning and purpose to life.

In short, God displacements can seduce us with the illusion of fulfillment. We must remember that any-thing falls short of no-thing, that no-thing evokes our spiritual desires, and that ultimately only people in and with Love, not displacements, can adequately respond to our nothingness.

Our experiences of Love, not displacements or concepts of God, or anything else, save us from our nothingness, and this redeeming feature is love for and from community—God, others, and self. We can have a doctoral degree in theology or write a PhD dissertation on love, and be far from experiencing God. Conversely, we can have little formal education and be intimate with God. Formation and experience always trump information and theory.

Remember, God dwells within us and pervades our being together. The Truth is that being in Love is the paramount sustaining source of, reason for, and destiny of our being. Love is our hope of finding permanent meaning in life, and with faith and reason, we come to Love.

8

HEALTHINESS AND HOLINESS

W̲E HAVE PRESENTED AND used a model of personality and health that differs from most other theories, primarily because it includes the spiritual as its paramount dynamic. In this last chapter, I will respond to questions such as: What is healthiness? What is holiness? Are they the same? If not, how do they differ? What is unhealthiness? What is normality? What are their interrelationships? What is the relevance of God to these and similar questions?

Less than Healthy Persons

When we are less than healthy, we are relatively fixated and closed rather than dynamic and open. For instance, if we are neurotic, we develop and repeat processes that repress, deny, and distort experiences. Consequently, our life becomes too anxious and difficult. Wasting considerable time and energy in fruitless thinking and behavior, we feel stuck and weary.

Whether the causes are psychological or organic, or both, we suffer too much pain in trying to function normally. For instance, we may experience clinical depression and anxiety, psychosomatic illnesses, obsessiveness and compulsiveness, low self-esteem, debilitating guilt, and to the extreme, bipolar mood swings, delusions, and hallucinations. Our existence becomes a heavy burden to bear, more hell than heaven.

A subtle fallacy is to assume that if we avoid such unhealthiness, then we are healthy. This assumption is incorrect, for a mere prevention of unhealthiness or psychopathology does not constitute healthiness. As we have seen, healthiness means to live a wholistic life. Indeed, our prevention of unhealthiness is part of being healthy, but healthiness not only includes but also goes beyond mere prevention and normality.

From our perspective, many of us are neither healthy nor unhealthy in that we lead normal lives of adequacy. We manage to satisfy our needs (body), cope efficiently (ego), and prevent psychopathology (normality). Indeed, this is good and necessary. A question, however, is do we realize ourselves and relate to ourselves, others, and God more than adequately?

My contention is that too many of us forget to live with and in an orientation of Love—the hallmark of a healthy and holy person. Although we maintain ourselves and may manage to achieve satisfaction and success (body and ego processes), our spiritual life is far less than it realistically can and should be.

When we are merely normal, we live contented lives; however, we invest ourselves too much of energy in ego or body processes and forget or minimize our spiritual life. For example, like the successful workaholic, our lifestyle is normal and perhaps admired. Nevertheless, we are unwilling, unable, or forget to choose the abnormal—the spiritual, or to live a life that includes and goes beyond normal, everyday living.

Some of us are immature because we have had few opportunities and little encouragement to lead lives other than adequate ones. We are unable to go beyond sheer normality (the physical and psychosocial) to foster the spiritual. However, if given the opportunity and encouragement, we may aspire to be spiritually mature.

Furthermore, cultural and environmental forces often promote less than healthy living. For instance, when our culture reinforces pleasure and power over love, having over being, individuality over community, information over formation, expediency over justice, as well as the general restriction of spiritual experiences, we sanction and promote mere normality. In this way, we forget the spiritual and displace its origin and destiny: uncreated and cocreating Love. To wit, when we displace God, we become merely normal, less than whole.

When we fail to grow through nothingness, minimize the spiritual, and displace God, we are less than healthy, or we are mad. We are not mad in the sense of the psychotic person who is abnormally mad, or the neurotic person who functions with excessive anxiety. We are normally mad when we fail to foster and integrate spiritual experiences as the core of our lives. In short, the way most people live does not necessarily mean it is the better way. Thus, we can and should question our normal way of living.

If we live a life of mere adequacy and contentment, we preclude or at least impede availability for and promotion of spiritual living. To do just enough, to hold on, and to satisfy the minimum demands of life are forms of normal madness. If we desire to live the way of healthiness, we must be willing and able to be somewhat out of the majority formation and consequently abnormal. Indeed, we must be courageous.

Healthy Persons

What does it mean to be healthy? What do we have to do or be in order to be healthy? In light of our way at looking at life, healthiness is imperfectly perfecting relationships with self, others, God, and the world without impediments of psychopathology and spiritual displacement. This means that to be healthy, we sustain and foster an ongoing actualization and harmony of our physical (body), psychosocial (ego), and spiritual (spirit) selves.

We have seen that we can never achieve complete actualization because we imperfectly grow in perfection. We are pilgrim people—people always in process, emergent selves. Thus, we are never completely healthy, happy, good, serene, or in love. We are always growing in healthiness, happiness, serenity, goodness, and love. If life is worth living well, it is worth living imperfectly.

As imperfectly healthy people, we continually want to accept, listen to, and integrate the knowledge of our body. We appreciate that feelings, emotions, and body language are important sources of truth. We are in tune with our own "expressions" and are sensitive to the expressions of others.

Sexuality is also important to us. We take pride in being a man or a woman. We avoid both repressing our sexuality and using sex as a displacement of God, but rather value affection and sex as essential ways of relating to self, God, and others. We are incarnated/sexual spirits who strive to grow older together in Love.

Healthy persons also function in their ego mode. Rather than being preoccupied with other things beside our job, we are free to focus on our work. To that end, we learn how to implement our ideas and values so that they become real and effective.

When we have a strong ego, we can communicate logically, explicitly, and publicly as well as integrate feelings, thoughts, and experiences. We can reflect on life with discernment. Our executive functions also enable us to take charge and to detach from what may impede effective coping. Healthy individuals have a grasp on life, manage well, and use their minds to achieve a good life.

Rather than repressing or minimizing one system for another, we behave in ways that are appropriate to our situations. If ego interaction is called for, we function rationally and do not love explicitly. If play is appropriate, we avoid task-oriented work, and behave playfully. Most mental health providers address these and similar body and ego issues.

Differing from most models of health, we have seen how the spiritual dimension is the core of a healthy person. An essential part of being healthy means that we become intimate with ourselves, others, and God in and through our nothingness as well as other experiences. Instead of displacing God, God permeates our lives. The ground of and reason for our existence is being one with God, self, and others. Unfortunately, health providers seldom if ever pursue or foster these spiritual issues.

As we grow through life's deserts and promised lands, we become holy people. Although we value and promote our physical and psycho-social capabilities, our spiritual experiences and values are paramount. Virtues, such as love, hope, faith, compassion, understanding, freedom, enthusiasm, forgiveness, contrition, serenity, and gratitude, permeate our lives.

Major traits of holy and healthy people are serenity and goodness. Since we strive to live in harmony with others and ourselves, we grow in serenity in both happy and unhappy times. Our connection with our inner community of Love enables us to maintain and nurture our interior serenity and freedom regardless of what happens.

We do not need (though we may want) any person or situation to change to maintain our balance. In short, when we reside in Love, we keep our inner harmony as well as manage more effectively. We change what we can (ourselves within limits), and accept with serenity what we cannot change (others, though we make an impact). With God and others, we can wisely discern what and who we can and cannot change.

A good life means that we behave in ways that engender oneness, or to unite people, self, and God. We intend and try to do what we can to live harmoniously in Love. To that end, we practice seeing, revering, and fostering the Presence in self and others where we are one. We avoid looking at ourselves as primarily individuals (ego) who use others for individual gain. Rather, we strive to be reasonable and faithful people who foster the communal good.

Healthy people do not submit or unconsciously fall into the formation of the mad majority. Rather, we freely opt to live in the normal world as well as out of it. Thus, we are both normal and abnormal. We are normal insofar as we can satisfy our basic needs, manage effectively, and live according to most of societal standards. We are also abnormal in that we actively live a God-centered life, promote the spiritual life, and accept and cope with the consequences of such an abnormal life.

Indeed, as healthy people we are normal in that we realize that we live in and manage well in the everyday world. We know that normalcy is a necessary dimension of reality and healthiness. At the same time, we are abnormal in that we choose to develop spiritually and to implement our spiritual values in our everyday lives. We are "in" (*en*) the culture and "against" (*contra*) the culture. We "en-counter" the culture. Let us consider another type of normal/abnormal person—the holy person.

Holy Persons

To be holy, we must live according to the values and invitations of Love—our Divine Spirit. Love of self, God, and others is our paramount motivation and ultimate concern, and our holy orientation permeates all our behavior. Our body and ego behaviors disclose God, and our spiritual experiences proclaim God. Ideally, every action is in some ways in service of Love, or of God. We strive to see, hear, respond to, and manifest the presence of God always and everywhere.

Since holy people center their life on God, their experiences incorporate the qualities and dynamics of spirituality. As holy people, we see ourselves and others interrelated with one other and with our Source and Destiny. Consequently, we do not judge people primarily according to their functions, talents, or possessions, but we see people for who and what they are and can be—people from and of Love. Our love, faith, and hope help us to manifest, evoke, and respond to life's unifying Source and Force, to God, residing in all of us.

Living in the presence of God, we humbly and courageously pro-claim God. We do not proselytize or constantly verbalize our vision, but neither are we embarrassed to speak of God. We accept people as they are, and when appropriate, we show how God may relate to their concerns. Rather than preaching to people, we respond to the God who dwells in them. We see others as well as ourselves as sanctuaries of God.

Nevertheless, holy people are not ashamed to talk of the very reality they stand for. When a situation calls for explicit discourse on God, we have the courage to speak of God. In a sense, we never stop speaking of God in implicit terms insofar as our behavior is a radiation of Love. As a holy person once said, always profess God, and when necessary, use words.

The radical sign of holy people is Love; that is, they manifest God. If we are holy, we take time and space to love God in solitude and with others. We use our (ego) mind to structure our lives (body) to nourish our hearts (spirit). We are careful to give both Martha and Mary their due time and space. Rather than forgetting the sacred and focusing on the profane, we celebrate the profane in and through sacred love.

We have seen that holy experiences also include existential indebt-edness and guilt. To be holy involves being aware of our indebtedness to others, and consequently we live a life of gratitude. Moreover, our exis-tential guilt motivates us to become better, and our desire for God keeps us seeking glimpses of God. Indeed, we accept that we will never be fully satisfied until we rest in God.

To that end, we are vigilant in taking time and space to worship in solitude and with others. Since consistent worship is countercultural, we dare to be abnormal in standing up for God. We strive to be full of grace, or of God's love. Hopefully, people sense a sacred Presence who unites us.

Ironically, our holiness enables us to be aware of our demons. We openly affirm that our humanity includes the constant possibility of be-ing bad. By recognizing and saying no to our evil inclinations, we grow stronger in goodness and further away from evil. In this way, we can use evil to help us be better as well as to understand and help others with their dark side.

As we have seen, we grow in and out of our nothingness to a pro-gressively deeper appreciation of life. In nothingness, we experience our powerlessness that points to a Greater Power (Love) that is part of and beyond us. In nothingness, we desire Being, Truth, and most importantly: Love, and we avoid displacing God with substitute objects and activities.

We realize that we are not on earth primarily to be happy, but rather to live a good life that includes both happiness and unhappiness. Indeed, our life includes unhappiness, absurdity, and evil, and we confront them with acceptance, meaning, and the good. Our human condition means that our lives are fraught with ups and downs, twists and turns. How and why we ride this roller coaster highly influences the kind of life we live.

Paradoxically, our weakness, unrest, and mortality can challenge and enable us to be strong, secure, and alive. When we accept our humanity as being a mixture of ambivalent polar opposites, we will find the courage to change what we can, and the wisdom to accept what we cannot control, change, or cure. Being in Love, we live freely and serenely.

Healthy and Holy People

Our ideal is to be healthy and holy persons who live in Love for and from self, God, and people. We accept and grow from our nothingness as well as actualize our spiritual lives. Rather than displacing God, we journey through our nothingness to find our place in love with and for self, God, and others. Nevertheless, although healthy and holy people share many similarities, there are differences between them.

For instance, we can be healthy without direct worship of God. We have not yet come to love God explicitly, but rather love God implicitly in our relationships with others. For example, we may be a spiritual agnostic or atheist. Because of our openness and love, we may come to a confrontation with God—to accept or reject God. If we accept and follow God, we become overtly holy and often religious.

We have indicated that too many of us opt neither for nor against God, but we try to lead marginal lives with God. We consider God as one experience among many—not an experience of paramount and sacred import. We seek God especially in times of need and stress, and tend to forget or displace God in times of plenty. We maintain a normal and less than healthy (mad) relationship with God.

We have seen that it is normal, though not healthy, to displace God. Rather than investing our spiritual energy in Love, we displace it in other activities and objects. Instead of being dedicated to God, we become addicted to counterfeits of God. Nevertheless, as we have explained, a displacement of God is an affirmation of God's hidden (displaced) presence. Our challenge is to convert: To turn away from displacements and toward God. As professional and lay (parents, siblings, friends, et al.) health providers, we can manifest and evoke the hidden desire and presence of Love.

Holiness, however, is no guarantee for healthiness. We can be holy but unhealthy. Many holy people are far from being perfect models of mental health, yet they are good and holy people. Holy people may be unable to be open to or integrate certain significant experiences because of past traumas, fixations, negative learning, poor self-esteem, repressions, fear, distrust, learning disabilities, organic impairments, etc.

For example, some holy persons are obsessive and compulsive. Although they experience God, intrusive thoughts and relentless urges plague them. They are good people who are burdened with an anxiety disorder. Other holy persons may repress their anger or sexuality, or both. They do not willfully reject their experiences, but various factors restrict their freedom to change. Indeed, their challenge is to become healthy as well as holy. Some achieve this goal, and many do not. Fortunately, it is possible to be a "sick saint."

Rather than rejecting and fighting our unhealthiness, holiness can help us to accept, manage, and even grow from our pain. Instead of identifying with or being consumed by our unhealthiness, we realize that our lives are infinitely more than our psychological problems. Indeed, our pain rarely disappears, but it can dissipate when we see in light of eternity.

Nevertheless, holiness is not a magical panacea for unhealthiness. Although psychopathology does not preclude holy experiences, we should strive to be healthy. Nor is holiness synonymous with healthiness. A catchy phrase—"holiness is wholeness"—can sound good, but be wrong. Or, the phrase, "divinization is humanization," is true, but it runs the risk of placing the reality of God totally in human hands. In short, holiness promotes wholeness, as does wholeness promote holiness.

When we are holy and healthy, we are open to and function appropriately in all our spheres. Our constant and pervasive concern is love for and from self, others, and God. Out of nothingness and through Love, we discover and become ourselves, and we bring Love to the world and the world to Love. We have the freedom and courage to be out of normal formation and the commitment to celebrate and suffer our abnormal concerns. Through our life of Love, we become holy and hopefully whole.

BIBLIOGRAPHY

Abata, Russell M. *Helps for the Scrupulous*. Ligouri, MO: Ligouri, 1976.

Achor, Shawn. *The Happiness Advantage*. New York: Crown, 2010.

Adler, Alfred. *The Individual Psychology of Alfred Adler*. Edited by H. Ansbacher and R. Ansbacher. New York: Basic, 1956.

Ai, Amy L., et al. "Spiritual Struggle Related to Plasma Interleukin-6 Prior to Cardiac Surgery." *Psychology of Religion and Spirituality* 1 (2009) 112–28.

Ajaya, Swami. *Yoga Psychology*. Honesdale, PA: Himalayan International Institute of Yoga Science and Philosophy, 1976.

Alcoholics Anonymous. New York: Alcoholics Anonymous World Services, 1976.

Allen, John L. *A People of Hope*. New York: Image, 2012.

Allport, Gordon W. *The Individual and His Religion*. New York: Macmillan, 1950.

Armstrong, Karen. *A History of God*. New York: Knopf, 1993.

Aslan, Reza. *Zealot: The Life and Times of Jesus of Nazareth*. New York: Random House, 2013.

Augustine. *The Confessions*. Garden City: Doubleday, 1960.

Azar, Beth. "A Reason to Believe." *Monitor on Psychology* 41 (2010) 52–56.

Barron, Robert. *The Strangest Way*. New York: Orbis, 2002.

Barth, Karl. *God Here and Now*. Translated by Paul M. van Buren. New York: Harper & Row, 1964.

Bartz, Jeremy D. "Theistic Existential Psychotherapy." *Psychology of Religion and Spirituality* 1 (2009) 69–80.

Benson, Herbert. *The Relaxation Response*. New York: Harper, 1987.

Berdyaev, Nicolas. *The Divine and the Human*. London: Bles, 1949.

Berger, Peter L. *The Power of Now*. Novato, CA: New World Library, 1999.

———. *The Sacred Canopy*. New York: Doubleday, 1967.

Bertocci, Peter A. *Religion as Creative Insecurity*. New York: American Book-Stratford, 1958.

Binswanger, Ludwig. *Being in the World*. Translated and critical introduction by Jacob Neddlemen. New York: Basic, 1963.

Bolen, Jean Shinoda. *Close to the Bone: Life-Threatening Illness and the Search for Meaning*. New York: Scribner, 1996.

Bradshaw, John. *Homecoming*. New York: Hill, 1973.

Brother Lawrence. *The Practice of the Presence of God*. Springdale, PA: Whitaker, 1982.

Brown, Norman O. *Life against Death*. London: Routledge, 1959.

Buber, Martin. *I and Thou*. Translated by Ronald Gregor Smith. 2nd ed. New York: Scribner, 1958.

Cameron, Peter John. *The Classics of Spirituality*. New York: Alba House, 1996.

Carrier, Herve. *The Sociology of Religious Belonging*. New York: Herder & Herder, 1965.

Catoir, John T. *World Religions: Beliefs behind Today's Headlines*. New York: Alba House, 2004.

Chambers, John, et al. "Critical Cultural Awareness." *American Psychologist* 69 (2014) 645–55.

Chopra, Deepak. *The Seven Spiritual Laws of Success*. San Rafael, CA: New World Library, 1994.

Ciarrochi, Joseph. *The Doubting Disease*. New York: Paulist, 1995.

Collins, Vincent C. *Acceptance*. St. Meinard, IN: Abbey, 1979.

Comte-Sponville, Andre. *The Little Book of Atheist Spirituality*. Translated by Nancy Huston. New York: Viking, 2006.

Coomaraswany, Ananda K. *Hinduism and Buddhism*. New York: Wisdom Library, 1960.

Coward, Harold, ed. *Life after Death in World Religions*. New York: Crossroad, 1996.

Craig, William Lane, and Walter Sinnot-Armstrong. *God? A Debate between a Christian and an Atheist*. Oxford: Oxford University Press, 2004.

Csikszentmihaly, Mihly. *Flow: The Psychology of Optimal Experience*. New York: Harper Perennial, 1999.

Cummings, Charles. *Eco-Spirituality toward a Reverent Life*. New York: Paulist, 1991.

———. *The Mystery of the Ordinary*. New York: Herder & Herder, 1984.

———. *Spirituality and the Desert Experience*. Denville, NJ: Dimension, 1978.

Cummings, Nicholas, et al., eds. *Psychology's War on Religion*. Phoenix: Zeig, Tucker & Theisen, 2009.

Danielou, Jean. *From Glory to Glory: Texts from Gregory of Nyssa's Mystical Writings*. New York: St. Vladimir's Seminary Press, 1979.

———. *Introduction to the Great Religions*. Notre Dame: Fides, 1964.

Dawkins, Richard. *The God Delusion*. New York: Houghton Mifflin, 2006.

De Lubac, Henri. *The Discovery of God*. New York: Kennedy, 1960.

De Mello, Anthony. *Awareness*. New York: Doubleday, 1990.

DeThomasis, Louis. *Fly in the Face of Tradition: Listening to the Live Experience of the Faithful*. Chicago: ACTA, 2012.

Dewart, Leslie. *The Future of Belief*. New York: Herder & Herder, 1966.

Doerff, Frances. *The Art of Passing Over*. New York: Paulist, 1988.

Dondeyne, Albert. *Contemporary European Thought and Christian Faith*. Translated by Ernen McMullin and John Burnheim. Pittsburgh: Duquesne University Press, 1958.

Downey, Michael. *Understanding Christian Spirituality*. New York: Paulist, 1997.

Dumm, Demetrius. *Flowers in the Desert*. New York: Paulist, 1987.

Duquoc, Christian, ed. *Opportunities for Belief and Behavior*. New York: Paulist, 1967.

Durkheim, Emile. *The Elementary Forms of the Religious Life*. Translated by Joseph Ward Swain. Glencoe, IL: Free Press, 1947.

Eberstadt, Mary. *How the West Really Lost God*. New York: Templeton, 2013.

Eckhart, Meister. *Teacher and Preacher*. Edited by Bernard McGinn. New York: Paulist, 1986.

Eliade, M. *The Sacred and the Profane*. New York: Harper Torch, 1959.

Emmons, Robert A. *The Psychology of Ultimate Concerns*. New York: Guilford, 1999.

Erikson, Erik H. *Identity: Youth and Crisis*. New York: Norton, 1968.

Evely, Louis. *Suffering*. New York: Herder & Herder, 1967.

Farber, M. *The Foundation of Phenomenology*. Cambridge: Harvard University Press, 1943.

Ferguson, Kitty. *The Fire in the Equations: Science, Religion, and the Search for God*. Grand Rapids: Eerdmans, 1994.

Feuerbach, Ludwig. *The Essence of Christianity*. Translated by George Eliot. New York: Harper, 1957.

Fleming, David A., ed. *The Fire and the Cloud: An Anthology of Catholic Spirituality*. New York: Paulist, 1978.

Fowler, James W. *Stages of Faith: The Psychology of Human Development and the Quest for Meaning*. San Francisco: Harper & Row, 1981.

Frankl, Viktor E. *The Doctor and the Soul: An Introduction to Logotherapy*. New York: Knopf, 1955.

Freud, Sigmund. *Civilization and Its Discontents*. Edited and translated by James Strachey. New York: Norton, 1962.

———. *The Future of an Illusion*. New York: Anchor, 1964.

———. *Moses and Monotheism*. New York: Knopf, 1939.

———. *Totem and Taboo*. Translated by James Strachey. New York: Norton, 1952.

Froese, Paul, and Christopher Bader. *America's Four Gods: What We Know about God and What That Says about Us*. New York: Oxford University Press, 2010.

Fromm, Erich. *Psychoanalysis and Religion*. New Haven: Yale University Press, 1950.

Gilligan, Carol. *In a Different Voice*. Cambridge: Harvard University Press, 1982.

Gladwell, Malcolm. *Outliers: The Story of Success*. New York: Little, Brown, 2008.

Goldbrunner, Josef. *Holiness in Wholeness and Other Essays*. Indiana: University of Notre Dame Press, 1964.

Goodenough, Erwin R. *Psychology of Religious Experiences*. New York: Basic, 1965.

Gorsuch, Richard L. *Integrating Psychology and Religion*. Westport, CT: Praeger, 2002.

Gould, Roger. *Transformations: Growth and Change in Adult Life*. New York: Simon & Schuster, 1979.

Grandin, Temple. *The Autistic Brain: Thinking across the Spectrum*. New York: Houghton Mifflin Harcourt, 2013.

Groeschel, Benedict. *Spiritual Passages*. New York: Crossroads, 1983.

Greeley, Andrew M. *When Life Hurts: Healing Themes from the Gospels*. Chicago: Moore, 1988.

Haase, Albert. *Coming Home to Your True Self: Leaving the Emptiness of False Attractions*. Downers Grove: InterVarsity, 2008.

———. *This Sacred Moment: Becoming Holy Right Where You Are*. Downers Grove: InterVarsity, 2010.

Hageman, Louise. *In the Midst of Winter*. Denville, NJ: Dimension, 1975.

Hamma, Robert M. *Along Your Desert Journey*. New York: Paulist, 1996.

Hammarskjold, Dag. *Markings*. Translated by Leif Sjoberg and W. H. Auden. New York: Knopf, 1964.

Harris, Sam. *Letter to a Christian Nation*. New York: Knopf, 2006.

Heidegger, Martin. *Being and Time*. Translated by John Macquarrie and Edward Robinson. New York: Harper, 1962.

———. *An Introduction to Metaphysics*. Translated by Ralph Maheim. New Haven: Yale University Press, 1959.

Helldorfer, Martin. *The Work Trap: Solving the Riddle of Work and Leisure*. Winona, MN: St. Mary's, 1981.

Heschel, Abraham J. *Who Is Man?* Stanford: Stanford University Press, 1965.

Hesse, Herman. *Siddhartha*. Translated by Hilda Rosner. New York: New Directions, 1951.

Hillman, James. *Blue Fire*. New York: Harper Perennial, 1989.

———. *The Soul's Code*. New York: Random House, 1996.

Hitchens, Christopher. *God Is Not Great: How Religions Poison Everything*. New York: Twelve, 2007.

———. *Mortality*. New York: Twelve, 2012.

Hocking, William Ernest. *The Meaning of God in Human Experience*. New Haven: Yale University Press, 1912.

Homans, Peter. *The Dialogue between Theology and Psychology*. Vol. 3. Chicago: University of Chicago Press, 1968.

Hood, Ralph W., et al. *The Psychology of Religion*. New York: Guilford, 2009.

Horney, Karen. *Collected Works*. New York: Norton, 1963.

Hurnard, Hannah. *Hinds' Feet on High Places*. Wheaton, IL: Living, 1987.

James, William. *The Varieties of Religious Experience*. New York: Mentor, 1958.

Jaspers, Karl, and Rudolph Bultmann. *Myth and Christianity*. New York: Noonday, 1958.

John of the Cross. *The Collected Works of St. John of the Cross*. Translated by Kieran Kavanaugh and Otilio Rodriguez. Washington, DC: Institute of Carmelite Studies, 1973.

Johnston, William. *The Inner Eye of Love*. New York: Harper & Row, 1978.

———. *Mystical Theology: The Science of Love*. New York: HarperCollins, 1995.

Jones, Alan. *Journey into Christ*. New York: Seabury, 1990.

Jones, Christopher. *Scott: A Meditation on Suffering and Helplessness*. Springfield, IL: Templegate, 1978.

Jung, C. G. *Modern Man in Search of a Soul*. Translated by C. F. Bayes. New York: Harvest, 1955.

———. *Psychology and Religion: West and East*. Translated by R. F. C. Hull. New York: Pantheon, 1958.

———. *The Undiscovered Self*. Translated by R. F. C. Hull. New York: New American Library, 1959.

Jurji, Edward J. *The Phenomenology of Religion*. New York: Westminster, 1963.

Kapoor, Raj. *Mend the Mind, Mind the Body, Meet the Soul*. Fort Bragg, CA: Lost Coast, 1998.

Kapuchinski, Stan. *Say Goodbye to Your PDI (Personality Disordered Individual)*. Deerfield Beach, FL: Health Communications, 2007.

Keen, Sam. *Fire in the Belly: On Being a Man*. New York: Bantam, 1991.

Keys, Corey L. M., and Jonathan Haidt. *Flourishing Positive Psychology and the Life Well-Lived*. Washington, DC: American Psychological Association, 2003.

Kierkegaard, Soren. *Works of Love*. New York: Harper & Row, 1962.

Koenig, H. G. *Is Religion Good for Your Health*. Binghamton, New York: 1997.

Kohlberg, Lawrence. "Education, Moral Development, and Faith." *Journal of Moral Education* 4 (1974) 5–16.

———. *The Psychology of Moral Development: The Nature and Validity of Moral Stages.* San Francisco: Harper & Row, 1984.

Kraft, William F. *Achieving Promises: A Spiritual Guide to the Transitions of Life.* Philadelphia: Westminster, 1981.

———. *The Normal Alcoholic.* New York: Alba House, 1999.

———. *Sexuality and Spirituality: Pursuing Integration.* Eugene, OR: Wipf & Stock, 2005.

———. *The Ways of the Desert.* New York: Haworth, 2000.

———. *When Someone You Love Drinks Too Much.* Ann Arbor, MI: Servant, 2002.

———. *When You Love a Functional Alcoholic.* New York: Paulist, 2011.

Kreeft, Peter. *Making Sense Out of Suffering.* Ann Arbor, MI: Servant, 1986.

Kubler-Ross, Elisabeth. *Death: The Final Stage of Growth.* New York: MacMillan, 1975.

Kung, Hans, ed. *The Unknown God?* New York: Sheed & Ward, 1966.

Kurtz, Ernest. *The Spirituality of Imperfection: Storytelling and the Journey to Wholeness.* New York: Bantam, 1992.

Lambert, Nathaniel M., et al. "Can Prayer Increase Gratitude?" *Psychology of Religion and Spirituality* 1 (2009) 139–49.

Lamott, Anne. *Help, Thanks, Wow.* New York: Riverheart, 2012.

Langford, Peter E. *Approaches to the Development of Moral Reasoning.* Hillsdale, NJ: Erlbaum, 1995.

Lawler, Phillip. *The Faithful Departed.* Jackson, TN: Encounter, 2011.

Lepp, Ignace. *Atheism in Our Time.* New York: Macmillan, 1963.

Levinson, Daniel J. *The Seasons of a Man's Life.* New York: Knopf, 1978.

Lewis, C. S. *Mere Christianity.* San Francisco: HarperCollins, 2001.

———. *The Four Loves.* New York: Harcourt, 1988.

———. *The Joyful Christian.* New York: Simon & Schuster, 1996.

———. *Beyond Personality.* New York: Macmillan, 1945.

Lindbergh, Anne Morrow. *Gift from the Sea.* New York: Doubleday, 1991.

Loncaric, Terry. *Discovering the Holy Power of Laughter.* St. Meinard, IN: Abbey, 2004.

Luckmann, Thomas. *The Invisible Religion.* New York: Macmillan, 1967.

Luhrmann, T. M. *When God Talks Back: Understanding the American Evangelical Relationship.* New York: Knopf, 2012.

Luijpen, William A. *Existential Phenomenology.* Translated by Henry J. Koren. Pittsburgh: Duquesne UniversityPress,1960.

———. *Phenomenology and Atheism.* Pittsburgh: Duquesne University Press, 1964.

Maloney, George. *God's Community of Love: Living in the Indwelling Trinity.* Hyde Park, NY: New City, 1995.

———. *God's Exploding Love.* New York: Alba House, 1967.

———. *On the Road to Perfection: Christian Humility In Modern Society.* Hyde Park, NY: New City, 1995.

Marcel, Gabriel. *Being and Having.* London: Deare, 1949.

———. *The Mystery of Being.* 2 vols. Translated by Rene Hague. Chicago: Regnary, 1950.

———. *Problematic Man.* New York: Herder & Herder, 1967.

Martin, James. *The Jesuit Guide to (Almost) Everything: A Spirituality for Real Life.* New York: HarperOne, 2010.

————. "More Than a Feeling." *US Catholic*, July 2010, 37–38.

Maslow, A. H. *Motivation and Personality*. New York: Harper, 1954.

————. *Religion, Values, and Peak-Experiences*. Columbus: Ohio State University Press, 1964.

————. *Toward a Psychology of Being*. New York: Van Nostrand, 1962.

May, Gerald G. *Addiction and Grace*. San Francisco: Harper & Row, 1989.

May, Rollo. *Love and Will*. New York: Dell, 1969.

McGlone, Gerard J., and Len Sperry. *The Inner Life of Priests*. Collegeville: Liturgical, 2012.

McGrath, Alister, and Joanna Collicutt McGrath. *The Dawkins Delusion? Atheist Fundamentalism and the Denial of the Divine*. Downers Grove: InterVarsity, 2007.

McNamara, William. *Mystical Passion: Spirituality for a Bored Society*. Mahwah, NJ: Paulist, 1970.

Merton, Thomas. *Contemplation in a World of Action*. New York: Doubleday, 1979.

Miller, Gerri. *Incorporating Spirituality in Counseling and Psychotherapy*. New York: Wiley, 2003.

Moore, Dom Sebastian. *God Is a New Language*. New York: Newman, 1967.

Moore, Thomas. *Care of the Soul*. New York: HarperCollins, 1992.

————. *Contemplative Prayer*. New York: Doubleday, 1971.

————. *The Life of Man with God*. New York: Image, 1962.

————. *Soul Mates*. New York: HarperCollins, 1994.

————. *The Soul's Religion: Cultivating a Profoundly Spiritual Way of Life*. New York: HarperCollins, 2002.

Moustakas, Clark. *Loneliness*. New Jersey: Prentice-Hall, 1961.

Mowrer, O. Hobart. *The Crisis in Psychiatry and Religion*. New York: Van Nostrand, 1961.

Munsey, Brenda, ed. *Moral Development, Moral Education, and Kohlberg*. Birmingham, AL: Religious Education, 1980.

Murchland, Bernard. *The Meaning of the Death of God*. New York: Vintage, 1967.

Norris, Kathleen. *The Cloister Walk*. New York: Riverhead, 1996.

Nouwen, Henri J. M. *The Inner Voice of Love: A Journey through Anguish to Freedom*. New York: Doubleday, 1996.

————. *The Wounded Healer: Ministry in Contemporary Society*. New York: Doubleday, 1972.

Novak, Michael. *Belief and Unbelief*. New York: Macmillan, 1965.

————. *The Experience of Nothingness*. New York: Harper & Row, 1970.

O'Collins, Gerald. *The Second Journey: Spiritual Awareness and the Mid-Life Crisis*. New York: Paulist, 1978.

O'Dea, Thomas F. *The Sociology of Religion*. New Jersey: Prentice Hall, 1966.

Oldman, Ari L. *The Search for God at Harvard*. New York: Ballantine, 1991.

O'Murchu, Diarmuid. *Poverty, Celibacy, and Obedience: A Radical Option for Life*. New York: Crossroad, 1999.

————. *Quantum Theology: Spiritual Implications of the New Physics*. New York: Crossroad, 1997.

O'Reilly, Bill, and Martin Duggard. *Killing Jesus: A History*. New York: Henry Holt, 2013.

Otto, Rudolf. *The Idea of the Holy*. New York: Oxford University Press, 1958.

————. *Mysticism East and West*. New York: Collier, 1960.

Padovano, Anthony T. *The Estranged God*. New York: Sheed & Ward, 1966.

Paloutzian, Raymond F., and Crytal L. Park. *Handbook of the Psychology of Religion and Spirituality*. New York: Guilford, 2005.

Pargament, K. L. *The Psychology of Religion and Coping: Theory, Research, Practice*. New York: Guilford, 1997.

Paragament, Kenneth I. *Spiritually Integrated Psychotherapy: Understanding and Addressing the Sacred*. New York: Guilford, 2007.

Parnika, Sam. *Erasing Death*. New York: HarperOne, 2013.

Paul, Margaret. *Inner Bonding: Becoming a Loving Adult to Your Inner Child*. San Francisco: Harper & Row, 1992.

Peck, Scott. *Further along the Road Less Traveled: The Legendary Journey toward Spiritual Growth*. New York: Crossroad, 1996.

Pieper, Joseph. *Leisure: The Basis of Culture*. New York: Pantheon, 1952.

———. *Only the Lover Sings: Art and Contemplation*. San Francisco, Ignatius, 1990.

Rahner, Karl. *Foundations of Christian Faith*. New York: Seabury, 1978.

———. *On the Theology of Death*. New York: Herder & Herder, 1961.

Remen, Rachel Naomi. *My Grandfather's Blessings: Stories of Strength, Refuge, and Belonging*. New York: Riverside, 2000.

Richards, Scott P., and Allen E. Bergin. *A Spiritual Strategy for Counseling and Psychotherapy*. 2nd ed. Washington, DC: American Psychological Association, 2005.

Robinson, John T. *Honest to God*. New York: Westminster, 1963.

Rogers, Louisa. *The Spirituality of Wellness*. St. Meinard, IN: Abbey, 2014.

Rolheiser, Ronald. *Forgotten among the Lilies*. New York: Doubleday, 2005.

———. *The Holy Longing*. New York: Doubleday, 1999.

Rohr, Richard. *Falling Upward*. San Francisco: Wiley, 2011.

Rossetti, Stephen J. *Why Priests Are Happy*. Notre Dame: Ave Maria, 2011.

Rudin, Josef. *Psychotherapy and Religion*. Translated by Elizabeth Reinecke and Paul C. Bailey. Notre Dame: University of Notre Dame Press, 1968.

Rumke, H. D. *The Psychology of Unbelief*. New York: Canterbury, 1962.

Salinger, J. D. *The Catcher in the Rye*. Boston: Little, Brown, 1945.

Sardello, Robert. *Facing the World with Soul*. New York: Harper Perennial, 1994.

Sartre, Jean-Paul. *Being and Nothingness*. Translated by Hazel E. Barnes. New York: Philosophical Library, 1956.

Schachtel, Ernest. *Metamorphosis*. New York: Basic, 1959.

Schachter-Shalomi, Zalman, and Ronald S. Miller. *From Age-ing to Sage-ing*. New York: Warner, 1995.

Scheler, Max. *Man's Place in Nature*. Translated by Hans Meyerhoff. New York: Noonday, 1961.

Schleiermacher, Friedrich. *The Christian Faith*. Vol. 1. New York: Harper & Row, 1963.

Sheehy, Gail. *Pathfinders*. New York: Morrow, 1981.

Simmons, Henry C. *In the Footsteps of the Mystics*. New York: Paulist, 1992.

Smith, John E. *Experience and God*. New York: Oxford University Press, 1960.

Solomon, Andrew. *Far from the Tree*. New York: Scribner, 2012.

Spiegelberg, H. *The Phenomenological Movement*. 2 vols. The Hague: Mujhoff, 1960.

Spinks, G. Stephen. *Fundamentals of Religious Belief*. London: Hodder & Stoughton, 1961.

———. *Psychology and Religion*. Boston: Beacon, 1963.

Strasser, Stephen. *Phenomenology and the Human Science*. Pittsburgh: Duquesne University Press, 1963.

Taylor, John V. *The Go-Between God*. Philadelphia: Fortress, 1973.

Teilhard de Chardin, Pierre. *The Divine Milieu*. New York: Harper & Row, 1960.

——. *The Making of the Mind*. New York: Harper & Row, 1961.

Teresa of Avila. *The Interior Castle*. Translated by Kieran Kavanaugh and Otilio Rodriguez. New York: Paulist, 1979.

Tillich, Paul. *The Courage to Be*. New Haven: Yale University Press, 1952.

——. *Dynamics of Faith*. New York: Harper Torch, 1957.

Tolle, Echart. *The Power of Now*. Novato, CA: New World Library, 1999.

Tuoti, Frank X. *Why Not Be a Mystic?* New York: Crossroad, 1995.

Tyrrell, Thomas. *Urgent Longings*. Mystic, CT: Twenty-Third, 1994.

Underhill, Evelyn. *Mysticism: A Study in the Nature and Development of Man's Spiritual Consciousness*. New York: Dutton, 1971.

——. *The Mystics of the Church*. New York: Schocken, 1964.

——. *Practical Mysticism*. New York: Dutton, 1915.

Urrea, Luis Alberto. *The Hummingbird's Daughter*. New York: Little, Brown, 2005.

Van Croonenburg, Bert. *Gateway to Reality*. Pittsburgh: Duquesne University Press, 1965.

Van Der Leeuw, G. *Religion in Essence and Manifestation*. 2 vols. New York: Harper & Row, 1963.

Van Kaam, Adrian. *Religion and Personality*. Englewood Cliffs, NJ: Prentice Hall, 1964.

——. *The Transcendent Self: The Formative Spirituality of Middle, Early and Later Years of Life*. Denville, NJ: Dimension, 1979.

Van Zeller, Dom Herbert. *The Inner Search*. New York: Sheed & Ward, 1957.

Vycinas, Vincent. *Earth and Gods*. The Hague: Mujhoff, 1961.

Wach, Joachim. *Types of Religious Experience: Christian and Non-Christian*. Chicago: University of Chicago Press, 1951.

Walsh, Roger. *Essential Spirituality: The 7 Central Practices to Awaken Heart and Mind*. New York: Wiley, 1999.

Ware, Kallistos. *The Orthodox Way*. Crestwood, NY: St. Vladimer's Seminary Press, 1995.

Warren, Rick. *The Purpose Driven Life*. Grand Rapids: Zondervan, 2002.

Watts, Allan W. *Nature, Man, and Woman*. New York: New American Library, 1960.

Webber, Meletios. *Steps of Transformation*. Ben Lomond, CA: Conciliar, 2003.

Weber, Max. *The Sociology of Religion*. Boston: Beacon, 1964.

Weigel, George. *Evangelical Catholicism: Deep Reform in the 21st Century Church*. New York: Basic, 2013.

Weigel, Gustave. *The Modern God*. New York: Macmillan, 1959.

Weil, Simone. *Waiting for God*. Translated by Emma Crawford. New York: HarperCollins, 1973.

Weiner, Eric. *Man Seeks God: My Flirtations with the Divine*. Waterville, ME: Thorndike, 2012.

Whitaker, Robert. *Anatomy of an Epidemic: Magic Bullets, Psychiatric Drugs, and the Astonishing Rise of Mental Illness in America*. New York: Crown, 2010.

White, Victor. *God and the Unconscious*. New York: World, 1952.

Whitehead, Alfred North. *His Reflections on Man and Nature*. Edited by Ruth Nanda Anshen. New York: Harper, 1961.

Whitehead, Evelyn E., and James D. Whitehead. *Christian Life Patterns: The Psychological Challenges and Religious Invitations of Adult Life*. New York: Doubleday, 1979.

Wicks, Robert J. *Bounce: Living the Resilient Life*. New York: Oxford University, Press, 2010.

———. *Riding the Dragon*. Notre Dame: Sorin, 2003.

Wojtyla, Karol. *Sign of Contradiction*. New York: Seabury, 1979.

Yancey, Philip. *Where Is God When It Hurts?* Grand Rapids: Zondervan, 1977.

Young, William P. *The Shack*. Los Angeles: Windblown, 2007.

Zuckerman, Miron, et al. "The Relation between Intelligence and Religiosity: A Meta-Analysis and Some Proposed Explanations." *Personality and Social Psychology Review* 4 (2013) 325–35.